Catalyzing the Field

Catalyzing the Field

Second-Person Approaches to Contemplative Learning and Inquiry

Edited by
Olen Gunnlaugson, Charles Scott,
Heesoon Bai, and Edward W. Sarath

Cover image by Olen Gunnlaugson

Published by State University of New York Press, Albany

© 2019 State University of New York

All rights reserved

No part of this book may be used or reproduced in any manner whatsoever without written permission. No part of this book may be stored in a retrieval system or transmitted in any form or by any means including electronic, electrostatic, magnetic tape, mechanical, photocopying, recording, or otherwise without the prior permission in writing of the publisher.

For information, contact State University of New York Press, Albany, NY
www.sunypress.edu

Library of Congress Cataloging-in-Publication Data

Names: Gunnlaugson, Olen, editor.
Title: Catalyzing the field : second-person approaches to contemplative learning and inquiry / edited by Olen Gunnlaugson, Charles Scott, Heesoon Bai, and Edward W. Sarath.
Description: Albany : State University of New York Press, [2019] | Includes bibliographical references and index.
Identifiers: LCCN 2018013574 | ISBN 9781438472836 (hardcover) | ISBN 9781438472829 (pbk.) | ISBN 9781438472843 (ebook) Subjects: LCSH: Transformative learning—Case studies. | Reflective learning—Case studies. | Contemplation—Case studies. | Intersubjectivity—Case studies. | Mindfulness (Psychology)—Case studies. | Education, Higher—Psychological aspects—Case studies. | College teaching—Psychological aspects—Case studies.
Classification: LCC LC1100 .C39 2019 | DDC 370.15/23—dc23
LC record available at https://lccn.loc.gov/2018013574

10 9 8 7 6 5 4 3 2 1

Contents

Introduction   vii
    Olen Gunnlaugson, Charles Scott, Heesoon Bai, and Edward W. Sarath

1. Mindfulness in Education: Contemplative Inquiry in a Community of Learners   1
    Kathryn Byrnes and Jessica S. Caron

2. Meditating Together, Speaking from Silence: The Theory and Practice of Interpersonal Mindfulness   27
    Nancy Waring

3. Intersubjectivity in the Holistic Teaching of the Sociology of Religion at Glendon College in Toronto   41
    Véronique Tomaszewski

4. Being with Horses as a Practice of the Self-with-Others: A Case of Getting a FEEL for Teaching   59
    Stephen J. Smith and Karen LaRochelle

5. A Disciplined Practice of Collaboratively Working on Teaching as Contemplative Professional Practice   73
    Thomas Falkenberg and Michael Link

6. Awakening to Wholeness: Aikido as an Embodied Praxis of Intersubjectivity   87
    Michael A. Gordon

7. Self, Other, and the System   107
    Ian Macnaughton

8. Walking Steps: Contemplative Wanderings with
   Humanbecoming 127
   Deborah Sally Thoun, Anne Bruce, and Coby Tschanz

9. Contemplative Learning: A Second-Person Approach to
   Physical Fitness 147
   Sally K. Severino and M. Andrew Garrison

10. Teaching Creativity and Building Community in the
    Undergraduate Classroom: Self-Awareness, Empathy, and
    Character through Relational and Contemplative Practice 161
    Sean Park

11. A Three-Tiered Monastic Approach to Intersubjective
    Dialogue for Application within Higher Education 185
    Mary Keator

12. No Mind in Community: Cultivating "Fields in Good
    Heart" in an Intellectual and Professional Praxis-Enhancing
    Commons 203
    Arden Henley

Contributors 219

Index 227

Introduction

OLEN GUNNLAUGSON, CHARLES SCOTT, HEESOON BAI, AND EDWARD W. SARATH

This book represents our third collection of essays on contemplative inquiry and learning in higher education. Our first book, *Contemplative Learning and Inquiry across Disciplines*, explored contemplative inquiry in a transdisciplinary fashion. In that volume, we aimed to contribute to the growing understanding of how contemplative inquiry and practice is now common across academic disciplines. Beginning with an overview by Arthur Zajonc, the volume contains essays that explore contemplative inquiry in philosophy, political science, economics, information technology, education, music, and other disciplines.

That collection now sits alongside a rapidly growing compendium of volumes on the subject of contemplative inquiry in education. These include: *Contemplative Practices in Higher Education: Powerful Methods to Transform Teaching and Learning*, by Daniel Barbezat and Mirabai Bush; *The Contemplative Practitioner: Meditation in Education and the Workplace*, by Jack Miller; *Meditation and the Classroom: Contemplative Pedagogy for Religious Studies*, edited by Judith Simmer-Brown and Fran Grace; *Mindful Teaching and Learning: Developing a Pedagogy of Well-Being*, edited by Karen Ragoonaden; *Contemplative Studies in Higher Education*, edited by Linda Sanders; *Contemplative Approaches to Sustainability in Higher Education: Theory and Practice*, edited by Marie Eaton, Holly Hughes, and Jean MacGregor; *Re-Envisioning Higher Education: Embodied Pathways to Wisdom and Social Transformation*, edited by Jing Lin, Rebecca Oxford, and Edward Brantmeier; *The Heart of Higher Education: A Call to Renewal*, edited by Parker Palmer, Arthur Zajonc, and Megan Scribner; *Meditation as Contemplative Inquiry: When Knowing Becomes Love*, by Arthur Zajonc; *Yoga Minds, Writing Bodies: Contemplative Writing Pedagogy*, by Christy Wenger; *Introducing Contemplative Studies*, by Louis Komjathy; *Cultivating a Culture of Learning: Contemplative Practices, Pedagogy, and Research in Education*, edited by Kathryn Byrnes, Jane Dalton, and Elizabeth Hope Dorman; *Lectio Divina as Contemplative Pedagogy: Re-appropriating Monastic Practice for the Humanities*, by Mary Keator; and *Contemplative Literature: A Comparative Sourcebook on Meditation and Contemplative Prayer*, edited by Louis Komjathy. The last one listed here is an in-depth anthology of primary texts on meditation and contemplative prayer from a wide range of religious traditions, with commentaries by international experts. Furthermore, the list of volumes on mindfulness, specifically, in higher education is equally impressive, with several volumes now in publication, which we will not list here: not enough space.

Contemplative approaches to higher education have been emerging across a wide cross-section of disciplines and fields from the work of scholar-practitioners who are pushing the boundaries of traditional theories and practices of postsecondary instruction and learning. In addition, scholar-practitioners are finding ways in which long-established contemplative theories and practices can optimally fit into or be shaped by existing academic disciplines. While contemplative practices have been foundational to wisdom traditions throughout various cultural periods, more recently these practices are being reexamined across different contexts of learning, particularly in mainstream North American institutions of higher education.

Many scholars are finding it increasingly necessary to incorporate the rigors of contemplative practice within academic contexts, discovering that contemplative process and method are well equipped to enhance, deepen, and broaden academic thought and praxis across disciplines. As the essays in that first volume make clear, contemplative practices help focus the mind; offer the dispassionately reflective capacities of mindfulness; reduce stress; create and uncover meaning, insight, and wisdom; as well as facilitate awareness of both inner and outer worlds and our fruitful engagements in them. Among the most significant contributions is that these practices help students and instructors deepen their awareness of and engagement with self, others, and the world.

We read the proliferation of contemplative approaches to studies, instruction, and learning in higher education as a poignant sign that the current life-world situation of our time is one that needs to regain a measure of dynamic balance, wisdom, and intelligence capable of embodying sustaining and sustainable alternative courses for the future. Our current academic world, characterized by increasing complexity, connectedness, and change, is increasingly asking for curricular and pedagogical approaches that effectively address these realities.

The Intersubjective Turn

Our previous, companion volume to this work, *The Intersubjective Turn: Theoretical Approaches to Contemplative Learning and Inquiry across Disciplines*, offered an overview of intersubjectivity. Because some readers may come to this volume without acquaintance with our previous volume, we feel it would be valuable to offer our overview of the intersubjective and its place in contemplative inquiry and practice. To begin with, we will quickly posit here a working definition of intersubjectivity, borrowed from Scheff (2006, p. 196): "the sharing of subjective states by two or more individuals" that enables such sharing is empathy: intersubjective experience is, to varying degrees, an empathic experience in which we consider how others are experiencing the world and attempt to see through their eyes, walk in their shoes.

Intersubjectivity is a subject of inquiry in psychology, sociology, anthropology, philosophy, and religion. Its focus, of course, is the relational aspect of our being. To give a small scholarly background to intersubjectivity: Edmund Husserl (1970, 1988) began his work in phenomenology in exploring the subjective realm of experience. But he came to see that there was, quite naturally, an inner kinship between us, specifically through our bodies; we come to see each other as experiencing beings. The interior, phenomenal world is inhabited by many subjective beings in relation to one another; there are multiple subjectivities. Thus, shared experiences give rise to intersubjective phenomena that are themselves shared. Objective realities are experienced both subjectively within ourselves and intersubjectively between ourselves. The intersubjective world is what he referred to as the *Lebenswelt*, the "life world." It is the world of immediate, felt, collective lived experience and the development of conscious or unconscious standards and conventions that may arise from these shared experiences. It is a common field in which our lives and experiences are intertwined. This world is fluid, dynamic, and indeterminate. The intersubjective realm plays an enormous role in defining ourselves and our relations to others and the world.

Martin Buber contributed significantly to the framing of the intersubjective in his extensive articulation of dialogue (as ontology: interbeing) and the *I-Thou* relationship. The *I-Thou* relationship is "spoken" or manifested with the whole being, one to another. The relationship is one of addressing and being addressed, again from and to the whole being: being to (and with) being. The *I-Thou* relationship brings the fulness of being of both *I* and *Thou* into realization: this is the heart of the intersubjective.

Buber's (1965) concept of the "interhuman," expressed in his later life, emphasizes the individual ontology—the *I* and the *Thou*—as distinct beings, and, paradoxically, at the very same time there exists the occasion for a shared ontological reality; this is the dimension of interbeing, also articulated by, among others, Thich Nhat Hanh (2000, 2005). But even in his early work, Buber (2000) insisted the *I-Thou* relationship could exist in the three spheres of nature, the human, and the spirit. The intersubjective turn is this intentional, ontological orientation to the other—human, more-than-human, or spirit—as a whole being through the simultaneous acts of our addressivity and receptivity. Buber writes, "Relation is mutual. My *Thou* affects me, as I affect it. We are moulded by our pupils and built up by our works. . . . How we are educated by children and by animals! We live our lives inscrutably included within the streaming mutual life of the universe" (p. 29). In his later essay "Elements of the Interhuman," Buber (1965) writes:

> To be aware of a man [sic] . . . means in particular to perceive his wholeness as a person determined by the spirit; it means to perceive the dynamic centre which stamps his every utterance, action, and attitude with the recognizable sign of uniqueness. . . . It is possible only when I step into an elemental relation with the other, that is, when he becomes present to me. (p. 80)

The intersubjective has also been the focus of a significant amount of recent scholarship. As Gunnlaugson (2009) has written:

> Intersubjective theory has surfaced in recent decades from diverse developments in consciousness studies, integral studies, philosophy of mind, transpersonal psychology and feminist critical theory among others. Partly in response to the problematic legacy of Cartesian rationalism that proceeds epistemically by objectifying and depersonalizing one's self and the world (Ferrer, 2001), a number of intersubjective theorists (Bai, 1999, 2004; De Quincey, 2000, 2005, Heshusius,

1994; Thompson, 2001) have made the effort to establish the validity of certain shared processes of knowing born through and inside relationship. In doing this, these contributions have provided an important epistemological rebalancing and movement towards more integrated visions of knowledge and the processes of knowing. (p. 27)

Bai, Scott, and Donald (2009) define intersubjectivity as "the capacity and ability to sense and feel everything in terms of the bond and strength of intimate relationship" (p. 324). It is a consciousness that is based in active participation with the other; it is not an objectified, dualistic, abstract sense of placing the other at a distance that cannot be bridged by meaning-making. Intersubjectivity is a "dialogical" consciousness that apprehends and communicates through language, the body, emotions, and intuition. In an earlier work, Bai (2001) characterized intersubjectivity as:

> [a] mutual sharing of thoughts, perceptions, values, in short, the content of consciousness. Subjectivity, as I define it, refers to the fact of having the "inner," psychological world of thoughts, feelings, values, and attitudes, as opposed to the "outer" world of physiological processes of the body and matter in motion. When subjectivity is shared, so that there is a transfusion of thoughts, feelings, perceptions, and desires taking place, this is intersubjectivity. We become intersubjective beings when, through sharing ourselves, we are open to each other's subjectivity and allow its transfusion across our individual differences. (p. 311)

Having extensively surveyed the contemplative inquiry and learning literature, we came to realize that contemplative studies has until more recently emphasized a predominantly first-person standpoint—a response in part to the prevalence of third-person learning approaches that typify traditional academia. Roth (2006, p. 1805) points out that first-person approaches to contemplative experience involve exploring contemplation from a subjective position within the individual learner, while third-person approaches aspire to examine contemplative experience from an objective position that is presumed to be outside of us. But within the literature to date, insufficient attention has been given to contemplative pedagogy from second-person perspectives, which involve exploring contemplative experience from an intersubjective position that is represented spatially as *between* us, in contrast to *inside* us (subjective position) or *outside* us (objective position). To our thinking and in our research, the way forward from here was clear. And while we were not yet in a position to come out and declare this with our first book, as this project came to a close, the obvious began to slowly dawn upon us.

Initial rebalancing efforts to honor first-person forms of contemplative practice within the field of contemplative education have, for different reasons, led to an omission of second-person approaches that cultivate collaborative discernment, inspire deeper shared and coemergent contemplative states of knowing, and generally move learners and educator toward a more collective focus in their learning engagements. Unlike either third-person or first-person methods, second-person approaches offer the benefits of engagement not only within our own interiority but also between participants within the greater field of awareness and ensuing conversation. The expansion and embrace of second-person methods provide a distinctive learning milieu or context in which collective wisdom and shared learning can begin to emerge from a participatory rather than individual-centered ethos within groups, teams, and the classroom as a whole; this is what Wilber (2006) refers to as "the nexus of a we" (p. 153). Furthermore, within the contemplative realm, the intersubjective can extend out into the more-than-human realms.

In no way denying the necessity for first- and third-person contemplative approaches or practices, the move to opening our interconnections within second-person approaches represents a filling out of the learning culture that is always already present in each classroom, though to varying extents either ignored or sidelined in favor of more traditional methods that are centralized in the individual learner.

Second-person approaches to contemplative education draw from various fields, including intersubjective theory, where we find the notion of the *intersubjective field*, which forms between any two or more persons where there are always at least three points of view: mine, yours, and ours together (Orange, 1995; Sarath, 2013). Support for this work has surfaced within and more broadly across the fields of leadership development, dialogue education, consciousness studies, psychotherapy, creative arts, and collective intelligence, among others (see the introduction to *The Intersubjective Turn: Theoretical Approaches to Contemplative Learning and Inquiry across Disciplines* for references to relevant works in these various fields).

In his proposal for a new field of contemplative studies, Roth (2006) advocates integrating critical third-person and first-person approaches to contemplative study. Yet despite these important developments, peer-reviewed books of current scholar-practitioners' accounts of second-person contemplative approaches to learning across higher education settings have not yet been ventured. As our first book project closed, after further conversation, we saw this omission as a clear occasion and call for our two volumes on the intersubjective dimensions of contemplative inquiry and learning in higher education. Whereas, in our first book, we advocated making the turn to contemplative inquiry and learning, we have come to realize that it is time to extend this turn in the direction of a second-person scholarship of intersubjective theories and practices.

Since that moment dawned on us, and through the development of this two-volume project, we have grown to appreciate the promise of how second-person contemplative approaches to learning and teaching will contribute significantly to the field of higher education at large. In a larger educational sense, there is the promise of an expansion and shift to a more relational sense of being as well. We feel a growing need for continued engagement with the current landscape of contemplative education, pedagogy, and curriculum, only this time from the perspectives of leading second-person contemplative researchers and practitioners. Building from this epiphany, and in embarking upon and finally completing this project, our conviction that the promise of second-person contemplative approaches can play a significant role in helping us create deeper, more meaningful, and sustainable relationships with others and with the various ecologies that surround us has grown not only in each of our reflections but in our practices and lives as scholar-practitioners.

Having explored theoretical frameworks and approaches to contemplative inquiry in *The Intersubjective Turn*, we now offer this volume that applies theory to practice in the realm of the intersubjective.

Theory and Practice

Since the Ancient Greeks, the dynamic interplay, often fraught with tensions, between theory (*theoria*) and practice (*praxis*), has been a source of considerable reflection and debate. To wit, Aristotle held the view that the desirable lifestyle for human beings was largely in service of the intellect or *theoria*. The contemplative arts were generally understood by Aristotle (1999) as an activity that served as an end in itself and in many respects was cut off from a more active engagement in the polis. On the other hand, Plato's concept of *theoria* (in the *Republic*) is deeply interwoven with one's way of being in the world; in his allegory of the cave, the individual who leaves the cave subsequently returns to it, adjusting the eyes to the relative darkness and working in and with that reality. Theory becomes grounded in interpersonal practice. Pierre Hadot (2002) reminds us of the central role that contemplative practices played in the evolution of the systems of logic and rational thought, typically presumed to be largely intellectual endeavors, that are ascribed to the same tradition of ancient thinkers. While there is "no denying the extraordinary ability of the ancient philosophers to develop theoretical reflection on the most subtle problems of the theory of knowledge, logic, or physics," he writes, it is also important to recognize the engagement in contemplative disciplines that were "intended to effect a modification and transformation in the subject who practiced them" (p. 6). Nightingale (2004) adds that "by linking philosophical theorizing to an institution that was at once social, political, and religious, the fourth-century [BCE] thinkers identified theoretical philosophy as a specific kind of cultural practice," adding that this move grounded *theoria* in social and political realities (p. 4).

While we subscribe to the approach conveyed in the accounts of Plato, Hadot, and Nightingale, we also share the concern, consistent with the bulk of educational criticism, that the prioritization of theory over practice still takes place as a pillar of the Western model of education, from grade school to graduate school. In other words, applied forms of experiential knowledge, particularly at the individual level when based in or informed by other ways of knowing—somatically, phenomenologically, emotionally, spiritually, among others—have become entirely secondary or marginalized altogether. Committed to countering this pattern, we begin this book by restating the theme that weaves through each of our three volumes—that of the fundamental importance of practice in institutions of higher learning. Moreover, that practice is not simply intellectual; it embodies, as previously stated, rigors that are somatic, phenomenological, emotional, and spiritual.

We build from the insight of curriculum scholar Ted Aoki's (2005) conceptualization of *praxis* as "the total person—head, heart, and lifestyle, all as one—given to an ethical life within a political context." From this vantage point, theory and practice are "seen to be in a dialectical unity" (p. 116). As Carr and Kemmis (1986) observe, *praxis* "remakes the conditions of informed action and constantly reviews action and the knowledge which informs it" (p. 33). The pairing of theory and practice through reflexivity is central to an ethical practice of contemplative learning and inquiry.

There is also the matter of context. From feminist, Indigenous, postmodern, poststructural, postcolonial, and sociocultural perspectives, contemplative practice is contextually situated: historically, economically, politically, socially, environmentally, and spiritually. We need to attend to multiple dimensions of context in our practice.

Practice in the Intersubjective Realms of Contemplative Inquiry

And if few educational aims are more important than the bridging of theory and practice, then the emergent field of second-person contemplative education holds as an arena where opportunities to fulfill this aim are particularly promising. Even a cursory look at the range of second-person experience underscores this point: The cohering silence of group meditation, Bohmian dialogue where participants connect to their deeper stream of shared meaning, the collective reading and interpretation of sacred texts across traditions, the spontaneous and creative exchange of improvised music, dance, or theater ensembles—these are but a few of a growing number of examples of formats that harness the deeper transformative capacities of second-person contemplative practice that can be implemented in higher education classrooms. Having, in our previous volumes, established theoretical terrain to substantiate inroads to support this kind of work, we are delighted now to present a rich and diverse series of applied case studies that ground this conceptual understanding in various pedagogical scenarios.

This present book devoted to practice in the intersubjective dimension of contemplative learning is created not only in recognition of the usual theory/practice divide and the latter's usual marginalization but also, more importantly, to reinforce the generative notion that intentional forms of practice create and guide consciousness. Contemplative practice opens us to the inner subtle regions of consciousness, of which everyday mind ordinarily lacks awareness or to which it lacks access and receptivity. In other words, contemplative practice brings forth contemplative consciousness. And intersubjective contemplative practice generates shared beingness, what Thich Nhat Hahn (2000, 2005) refers to as "interbeing" or contingent or dependent arising. Interbeing in second-person contemplative practice creates what Nakagawa (2000) calls a "pedagogy of communion." He elaborates that it "concerns the communal modes of relationships that take place in the deeper formative dimensions of reality. In communal relationships, all beings are interconnected, unified, and interpenetrate one another without obstruction" (p. 50). Intersubjectivity involves an openness to being in contact with another at these deeper levels: by and with another person, a group of people, a text or idea, an animal, plant, mineral, or the entire cosmos. Intersubjectivity informs and makes claims on our individual subjectivity.

Let us repeat: mindful practice generates consciousness and hence brings us into contact with the interior dimensions of subjectivity, which, when it becomes shared, is a central dynamism of the contemplative turn in higher education. As longer-term practitioners inevitably come to appreciate, the necessity for sustaining regular, committed practice is clear, whether this realization comes from the teachings of the various wisdom traditions that have housed many of the contemplative approaches explored within this volume or from the latest research in neuroscience.

As editors of this three-volume series, we are particularly excited about the intersubjective turn in contemplative learning. We note that the principal context of our growth and development is through modes of learning and engagement that take place in the intersubjective dimension—in the relational field with others. Learning via contemplative inquiry and practice is no exception. The core value of the intersubjective domain of human learning is most noticed when there has been a rupture to it; all of us can recall instances when college students, faculty, or staff have suffered due to breakdowns in communication or understanding. From this and other, more personal, evidence, we should conclude that intersubjectivity is an absolutely essential psychic nutrient for human growth and learning. By the same token, as contemplative-oriented educators, we will need to know how to work with and apply intersubjective principles and ways of being in our pedagogical practice, in the service of stimulating and facilitating learning and growth in people with whom we work and teach. Such recognition in our view opens a wide horizon of deep, complex, and life-changing learning for contemplative educators and their students to engage.

Given that relationships with other human beings and the "more-than-human" dimensions of life are indispensable to the deeper sense and significance of life, any educational modalities or practices that draw directly from the contemplative quality of our intersubjective relationships are increasingly valuable. Because intersubjectivity lies at the very heart of relationship, the various forms and expressions of second-person contemplative pedagogy represent important attempts toward the ongoing exploration, development, and realization of our collective humanity in the classroom.

Because the editorial team of this contemplative learning and inquiry trilogy are dedicated long-term theorists/practitioners (contemplative and pedagogical), the occasion to edit these volumes has been an inspiring opportunity for us to join our authors in attempting to integrate these realms into various expressions of research and praxis. We give a brief outline of each chapter included in this volume as follows.

The Chapters

The one element that binds this collection of essays is *relationships in teaching and learning*. More specifically, the commonality is the inner, shared experiences of the participants—the intersubjective experience—engaged in contemplative practices designed around the intersubjective. We see the authors focus on the development of a respectful, gentle ethos; on mindful dialogue; on shared equanimity and respectful, critical inquiry and reflection; on "inter-corporeal mindfulness" and interactive flow; on teaching as a contemplative practice through mindfulness and self-study, and how first-person experience enhances second-person development; on a practice of Aikido that demands an intersubjective, second-person model of engagement; on the work of facilitating intersubjectivity through mindfulness, energetics, and somatic awareness; on the interpersonal dynamics of nursing students and faculty where the focus is critical inquiry and "humanbecoming," on the use of the contemplative and expressive arts in developing creativity and community, and finally on developing a spirit of contemplative, collective *communitas* among staff and faculty at a university.

As we will point out, there are many layers and manifestations of the intersubjective in these contemplative milieus. But in the midst of this diversity there is the unifying thread of the contemplative experience of the intersubjective itself, the shared life worlds, the essence of relationality. These layers and manifestations offer us a new and perhaps enticing way of possibly reconceptualizing contemplation itself.

Kathryn Byrnes and Jessica S. Caron launch this expedition with their chapter, "Mindfulness in Education: Contemplative Inquiry in a Community of Learners," which provides an account of how the contemplative features of respect, gentleness, intimacy, participation, and vulnerability can be invited into and supported in the learning ethos of an upper-level undergraduate education course, Mindfulness in Education. Rather than viewing teachers and students as disembodied beings by focusing solely on their intellectual and rational systems, the class explores how, within a community of learners, contemplative inquiry's emphasis on wholeness moves education toward a view of teachers and students as beings with not only minds, but also hearts and bodies.

Nancy Waring, in her essay "Meditating Together, Speaking from Silence: The Theory and Practice of Interpersonal Mindfulness," offers the reader a window into a graduate-level course on the theory and practice of insight dialogue, an interpersonal meditation practice developed by Western insight meditation teacher Gregory Kramer. In light of insight dialogue, the essay explores resonant theories of dialogue articulated by David Bohm (1917–1992), Paulo Freire (1927–1991), and Siddhartha Gotama (ca. 563–483 BC), known today as the Buddha. Each of these thinkers is committed to the enhancement of human understanding and compassion through dialogue, in the service of a kinder, gentler, more egalitarian world. The essay is intended to contribute to the dialogue on the intersubjective turn in contemplative education, and to suggest the value of the insight dialogue course under consideration as a model of intersubjective contemplative pedagogy.

Véronique Tomaszewski's chapter, "Intersubjectivity in the Holistic Teaching of the Sociology of Religion at Glendon College in Toronto," presents the case of an experiential, participative, and intersubjective pedagogy. Allowing for memorable intersubjective moments of comparison, rejection, and questioning encourages students to honestly connect to their beliefs, yet also to develop the critical thinker in them who mindfully uncovers the kind of sociologists they are. As Tomaszewski's and her students' testimonies reveal, "intersubjectivity" plays a performative role in the making and the shaping of a sociology-class consciousness built on equanimity. Intersubjectivity also creates the conditions and the environment conducive to a nondual, intellectual, and experiential relationship inside the classroom.

Stephen J. Smith and Karen LaRochelle continue the exploration with their essay, "Being with Horses as a Practice of the Self-with-Others: A Case of Getting a FEEL for Teaching." They explain how specific practices and programs of "facilitated equine-enhanced learning" (FEEL), while mostly attributing their personal and professional development successes to the mirroring of human consciousness in equine behavior, achieve pedagogical ends when mimetic resonances become animated by an intercorporeal mindfulness, which is to say, by a motional interbeing, relational attunement, and interactive flow. In this way, the intercorporeal dynamics of being with horses transposes readily, as an *intersubjective contemplative practice*, to the pedagogical practices of classroom life.

Thomas Falkenberg and Michael Link, in "A Disciplined Practice of Collaboratively Working on Teaching as Contemplative Professional Practice," explore teaching as contemplative professional practice, drawing on two traditions of human development that give particular attention to the importance of inquiring into and working with one's experiences of inner life for human and professional development. One is the mindfulness tradition of Buddhist psychology and philosophy and its modern Western adoption in consciousness studies, the second is the self-study tradition of teacher development that puts teachers' awareness and noticing at the center of teacher development. The considerable extent to which first-person experience enhances second-person development is highlighted in this work.

Michael A. Gordon, in "Awakening to Wholeness: Aikido as an Embodied Praxis of Intersubjectivity," reflects on how cultivating one's "mind and body coordination" through this defensive art develops embodied Non-dissension. He frames his investigation of intersubjectivity as a double-bind paradox: how can dualistic consciousness of subject-object dichotomy apply itself to resolving human conflicts while inherently operating from a position of the very dualism that creates such conflict in the first place? Through a series of vignettes and explication, the author replies with an account of Aikido as a contemplative way of being and living—based on a view of the cosmos as interdependent relationality—that demands an intersubjective, second-person model of engagement.

In "Self, Other, and the System," Ian Macnaughton explores phenomenologically how to bring individuals into the realm of intersubjectivity. This work of facilitating intersubjectivity in individuals is not only about the art of personal reflection, nor solely about practicing how to listen to their personal way of being in their life and work. It is also in knowing how to sit with others, and be in attunement, presence, resonance, feeling states, and somatic experiences with a group, with a larger sense of human-to-human interpersonal intersubjectivity, and with the even larger expanse of our interbeingness. He presents a diverse methodological range, including the following: mindfulness and other contemplative practices, energetic practices, and a number of other practices.

Deborah Sally Thoun, Anne Bruce, and Coby Tschanz provide a chapter titled "Walking Steps: Contemplative Wanderings with Humanbecoming," which explores personal experiences of teaching-learning for nursing students and faculty that cultivate intersubjective awareness, presence, and bearing witness to human being. They highlight an example of a nursing inquiry course and the synergistic resonances found among and between contemplative pedagogical approaches, course content, and the deeply connected philosophical ground of each, adding personal reflections and student accounts.

Sally K. Severino and M. Andrew Garrison's chapter, "Contemplative Learning: A Second-Person Approach to Physical Fitness," takes the inquiry into the realm of embodiment and approaches second-person intersubjective learning through the lens of a course on being physically fit. They present the neuroscientific groundwork on intersubjectivity that underpins second-person learning followed by a case study that demonstrates how second-person contemplative learning facilitates the cocreating of a new being image in the realm of physical fitness. Yet another layer of the intersubjective domain emerges through their account and analysis of their work.

Sean Park, in "Teaching Creativity and Building Community in the Undergraduate Classroom: Self-Awareness, Empathy, and Character through Relational and Contemplative Practice," describes the use of relational contemplative practices and expressive arts in a first-year undergraduate course in interdisciplinary expressive arts. Descriptions of how mindfulness meditation, interpersonal mindfulness practice, group dialogue, and Japanese *ensō* painting are offered to students serves to illustrate how they render the classroom as a contemplative, creative, and collaborative community—one rooted in a rich sense of belonging and acceptance.

In her essay "A Three-Tiered Monastic Approach to Intersubjective Dialogue for Application within Higher Education," Mary Keator provides an excellent example of how a contemplative approach perfected in one of the wisdom traditions, *lectio divina*, can be applied in a purely secular context in higher education. She offers rich, practical examples from her own teaching in the humanities of how she has accomplished incorporating "sacred reading" into her classes. Beginning with a quick review of contemplative traditions in the West and the Christian monastic origins of *lectio divina*, she then lays out the principles of *lectio divina* and how they mesh with contemporary principles of contemplative inquiry, particularly as an intersubjective contemplative practice. She pays particular attention to the dialogical elements of *lectio*, exploring listening to self, to others, and class dialogues. All the while she provides specific examples, illustrating how she has used *lectio divina* in exploring texts as varied as *Antigone*, the story of Jesus and the woman from Samaria in the Gospel of John, the *Dhammapada*, *Gilgamesh*, and the *Katha Upanishad*. She provides comments from her students as well, demonstrating how relevant and meaningful the texts became. As one student wrote: "Both of these [texts] spoke to me. They made me reevaluate my life. What was my purpose for living?" Who could not wish for a similar outcome?

Finally, in "No Mind in Community: Cultivating 'Fields in Good Heart' in an Intellectual and Professional Praxis-Enhancing Commons," Arden Henley connects the "no mind" of contemplative practice to the realm of community through the metaphor of *the commons*. The nondenominational cultivation of contemplative states of mind by members of a community quite naturally leads to warmth, inclusiveness, and, at its best, *communitas* in community settings. Contemplative states of mind are expressed in and evoke specific social practices and an egalitarian ethos that can be likened to a commons. Henley's chapter provides specific examples of the effects of contemplative practice on the evolution of graduate programs at City University of Seattle in Canada.

On the whole, this third book of the series continues to advance our explorations into the first-, second-, and third-person varieties of contemplative inquiry begun in our first volume. In support of advancing scholarship that draws upon these three perspectives of contemplative inquiry, by focusing more in-depth with applied second-person approaches, this book continues to fill out this larger project, what our colleague David Forbes (2016) has referred to as a more integral view of the field. In our previous introduction, we suggested that a contemporary educational imperative is to establish the "inextricable link between individual consciousness and the cosmic wholeness" and "to refine understanding and approaches to this wholeness through all three lenses." We believe the essays contained herein illuminate the role of intersubjective contemplative practice toward these ends.

The collection also serves in clearly demonstrating how theory can be reflectively and creatively put into practice. Our intended audience for this collection are educators, counselors, those in medical services, social workers, and others who not only wish to deepen their theoretical understandings of the intersubjective dimensions of contemplative practice and inquiry but also wish to encounter living examples of it. We think the variety of examples here serves that need. The diversity of examples serves to widen the audience to whom this volume might appeal; the connecting thread is the sphere of interbeing: the manifestation of the intersubjective turn in contemplation.

Our hope is that this final volume of essays will inspire educators with practical possibilities in undertaking the challenge Mirabai Bush lays before us of continuing to build relationships and communities from a more engaged contemplative mindset and heart. As our authors demonstrate, practices that may have roots within the various world religious or wisdom traditions can still be creatively adapted to serve in secular contexts to the extent that spirituality encompasses the religious and the secular dimensions of our lives. In this respect, Second-Person Contemplative Inquiry serves an important and unique role in bringing us into a richer contact with these deeper shared dimensions of our lives. As the underlying motivations, meaning, and shared purpose of our lives and institutions depend to an increasing extent on our ability to constructively access and build together from this place in our learning and inquiries, it is our sincere hope that this third book will inspire practitioners and scholars to continue making advances with the Second-Person project of Contemplative Learning and Inquiry.

The editors would like to acknowledge the authors, not only for their scholarship, but also for their patience and good-natured cheer in working with us. We also would like to acknowledge and are grateful for the considerable expertise and attentiveness of senior acquisitions editor Christopher Ahn, senior production editor Diane Ganeles, promotions manager Kate R. Seburyamo, and copy editor Dana Foote. It is truly a pleasure to work with such an outstanding team.

References

Aoki, T. T. (2005). *Curriculum in a new key: The collected works of Ted T. Aoki.* New York: Routledge.
Aristotle. (1999). *Nicomachean ethics.* Kitchener, Canada: Batoche Books.
Bai, H. (1999). Decentering the ego-self and releasing of the care-consciousness. *Paideusis, 12*(2), 5–18.
Bai, H. (2001). Cultivating democratic citizenship: Towards intersubjectivity. In W. Hare & J. P. Portelli (Eds.), *Philosophy of education: Introductory readings* (3rd ed., pp. 307–319). Calgary, Alberta: Detselig/Brush Education.
Bai, H. (2004). The three I's for ethics as an everyday activity: Integration, intrinsic valuing, and intersubjectivity. *Canadian Journal of Environmental Education, 9,* 51–64.

Bai, H., Scott, C., & Donald, B. (2009). Contemplative pedagogy and revitalization of teacher education. *Alberta Journal of Educational Research*, 55(3), 319–334.

Buber, M. (1965). *The knowledge of man: A philosophy of the interhuman* (R. Smith & M. Friedman, Trans.). New York: Harper & Row.

Buber, M. (2000). *I and Thou* (R. Smith, Trans.). New York: Scribner.

Carr, W., & Kemmis, S. (1986). *Becoming critical: Education, knowledge and action research*. London: Routledge Falmer.

de Quincey, C. (2000). Intersubjectivity: Exploring consciousness from the second person perspective. *Journal of Transpersonal Psychology*, 32(2), 135–155.

de Quincey, C. (2005). *Radical knowing: Understanding consciousness through relationship*. South Paris, ME: Park Street Press.

Ferrer, J. (2001). *Revisioning transpersonal theory*. Albany: State University of New York Press.

Forbes, D. (2016). Modes of mindfulness: Prophetic critique and integral emergence. *Mindfulness*, 7(6), 1256–1270.

Gunnlaugson, O. (2009). Establishing second-person forms of contemplative education: An inquiry into four conceptions of intersubjectivity. *Integral Review*, 5(1), 25–50.

Hadot, P. (2002). *What is ancient philosophy?* Cambridge: Harvard University Press.

Hanh, T. N. (2000). *The path of emancipation*. Berkeley: Parallax Press.

Hanh, T. N. (2005). *Interbeing: Fourteen guidelines for engaged Buddhism* (2nd ed.). Berkeley: Parallax Press.

Heshusius, L. (1994). Freeing ourselves from objectivity: Managing subjectivity or turning toward a participatory mode of consciousness. *Educational Researcher*, 23(3), 15–22.

Husserl, E. (1970). *The crisis of European sciences and transcendental phenomenology* (D. Carr, Trans.). Evanston: Northwestern University Press.

Husserl, E. (1988). *Cartesian meditations* (D. Cairns, Trans.). Dordrecht: Kluwer.

Nakagawa, Y. (2000). *Education for awakening an Eastern approach to holistic education*. Charlotte, VT: Foundation for Educational Renewal.

Nightingale, A. W. (2004). *Spectacles of truth in classical Greek philosophy: Theoria in its cultural context*. Cambridge: Cambridge University Press.

Orange, D. (1995). *Emotional understanding: Studies in psychoanalytic epistemology*. New York: Guilford Press.

Roth, H. D. (2006). Contemplative studies: Prospects for a new field. *Teachers College Record*, 108(9), 1787–1815.

Sarath, E. W. (2013). *Improvisation, creativity, and consciousness: Jazz as integral template for music, education, and society*. Albany: State University of New York Press.

Scheff, T. J. (2006). *Goffman unbound! A new paradigm for social science*. Boulder, CO: Paradigm Publishers.

Thompson, E. (2001). Empathy and consciousness. *Journal of Consciousness Studies*, 8(5–7), 1–32.
Wilber, K. (2006). *Integral spirituality: A startling new role for religion in the modern and postmodern world.* Boston: Shambhala.

1

Mindfulness in Education

Contemplative Inquiry in a Community of Learners

KATHRYN BYRNES AND JESSICA S. CARON

> Knowledge is an event, not an object. Contemplative knowing, likewise, is personal and experiential. Therefore, in order to communicate it fully we must find a way to lead others to the same experience. They too must come to "see" what we have come to know.
>
> —Arthur Zajonc, *Meditation as Contemplative Inquiry*

Contemplative inquiry requires a commitment to cultivating a relationship with and an understanding of oneself, as well as interdependent relationships and understandings of others and the world. It is a journey of cognition, of "coming to know" (Rose, 2013, p. 32). In Zajonc's (2009) terms, knowing becomes both personal and experiential through the integration of first-, second-, and third-person ways of knowing (Roth, 2006). The social field created by contemplative inquiry impacts self-awareness and mindful awareness through the features of contemplative inquiry as described by Zajonc (respect, gentleness, intimacy, participation, and vulnerability, transformation, and insight).[1] These seven features are guiding principles for contemplative inquiry that can be enacted in unique ways by educators and students depending on the context and the content of academic study.

We, a teacher educator and a former student of education and now teacher, experienced how the contemplative features of respect, gentleness, intimacy, participation, and vulnerability can be invited into and supported in the learning ethos of an upper-level undergraduate education course, Mindfulness in Education (MIE). The course has been successfully completed by seventy-five students in four cohorts between 2010 and 2014. A unique aspect of this course in design and implementation was the community of learners created. A course necessarily consists of a group of individuals. The movement toward a community of learners requires a shift from viewing learning as transmission or acquisition to viewing learning as a "process of transformation of participation" as described in detail by Rogoff (1994). The sociocultural view of learning, developed by theorists such as Vygotsky and Dewey, was a response to predominant behavioral theories and practices in the first half of the 20th century. In a transmission model of education, educators are the experts and students learn by encoding and retaining information. In an acquisition model, students are the experts as they explore paths of learning, often without any guidance to situate the information in a larger context. In a community of learners model, students and educators collaborate through learning activities that situate the information within a larger context. The relationship between a community of learning model and contemplative inquiry will be examined in this chapter.

The design of the MIE course invited students to study mindfulness models in education and develop first-person experience with mindfulness practices. Class sessions began with a 20-minute lab focused on a different mindfulness practice each week, such as breath awareness meditation, yoga, mindful speaking, or emotional awareness. After transitioning from a first-person perspective in the yoga/meditation room, the class integrated second-person philosophical and scientific seminar-style dialogue on course readings, videos, or audios, such as Gibbs and Gibbs's (2013) *The Mindful Way to Study: Dancing with Your Books* and Richard J. Davidson's (2012) "Contemplative Neuroscience." By engaging directly with the scholarly texts, references, and practical techniques, students appraised the value of various contemplative practices for their own lives and learning.

Tools of mindfulness allow teacher educators to facilitate students' authenticity as future teachers while encouraging students to reflect on their anticipated vocation. Mindfulness "means paying attention in a particular way; on purpose, in the present moment, and non-judgmentally" (Kabat-Zinn, 2003, p. 145). Mindfulness is a quality of attention guided by an intention to be in direct experience with the present moment, reserving evaluation for the future. Mindfulness is one contemplative practice and was studied and investigated in the MIE course as a secular concept. Contemplative knowing utilizes mindfulness in its process of sustained attention, open awareness, and inquiry into the inner workings of the mind and the nature of reality. By enhancing mindful qualities of teacher candidates, they can begin to understand how contemplative inquiry benefits their own learning as well as the learning experiences of their future students.

In a community of learners model, all participants actively engage in structuring individual and collective learning opportunities. By authentically participating and engaging with the material through contemplative inquiry, students in the MIE course engaged the material through intersubjective, collective methods. Students designed course agreements to guide dialogue, experimented with a 21-day mindfulness practice, shared short educational autobiographies, recited poetry, and researched and cotaught about a mindfulness model of education; these activities cultivated the features of contemplative inquiry though the model of a collaborative learning community.

One cohort, which included 17 undergraduate students ranging from sophomores to seniors at a small liberal arts college in New England, will be the focus of this chapter. This was the second cohort, out of four, to participate in the MIE course. The course occurred over 16 weeks from January through May with a two-week spring break in March. The course met twice a week with a mandatory lab from 8:00 to 8:30 a.m., followed by the course meeting from 8:30 to 10:00 a.m.

The MIE class served as an elective education course for education minors. All students fulfilled at least two prerequisite education courses (Contemporary American Education and Educating All Students) prior to enrolling in MIE. Thus, all students demonstrated their commitment to studying current practices and culture within the American education system and entered the course with foundational knowledge and experiences in K–12 schools. However, there was a diversity of majors (English, Government & Legal Studies, History, Psychology) represented within the cohort. The coauthor of this chapter, Jessica, is reflecting on her experience as a student in the course. She was a junior English major and had just returned to campus after a semester studying abroad in France.

This chapter will illustrate, through a case study of one particular course iteration, how the features of respect, gentleness, intimacy, participation, and vulnerability created opportunities for transformation, insight, and meaningful contemplative inquiry, for both individual students and the community as a whole. These particular features of contemplative inquiry and a community of learners model can be applied in unique ways in other higher education courses. We offer here one instantiation of these principles.

Respect

> . . . the integrity of the other, to stand guard over its nature, over its solitude, whether the other is a poem, a novel, a phenomenon of nature, or the person sitting before us. We need to allow it to speak its truth without our projection or correction.
>
> —Arthur Zajonc, "Cognitive-Affective Connections in Teaching and Learning"

Respect is crucial for positive, meaningful relationships in a learning community. Designing class agreements is one pedagogical tool that can delineate the expectations for respect and offer guidelines for conduct. Clear, explicit expectations allow all students to operate from a similar framework and remove uncertainty concerning the structure of interactions. In small groups of three to four, students generated principles of respectful communication. We listed all of the ideas on a board in the classroom and a class website. With the list of suggestions, I adapted, modified, and edited the proposed ideas into short, simple, concise statements, which summarized our intentions for the learning community. The revised list was distributed at the next class session, and after some discussion it was either further revised and/or approved by consensus. The following are agreements devised by this cohort:

- Seek to understand before you seek to be understood.
- Be responsible for the energy you bring to the space.
- Challenge yourself to transform.

The collective creation of the agreements reinforced a collective responsibility to uphold the agreements. Jessica reflects on the impact of this collective agreement process on her experience as a learner in the class as follows.

"Seek to understand before you seek to be understood." Listen, take a step back, and pay attention to what you can learn from others. This was my definition of our first class agreement, but every student's interpretation differed slightly. The differentiations in personal definitions were a sign of internalization, of a new way of knowing acquired from the class. The agreements became a way of knowing that translated into a way of living. By having students create a list of behavioral attributes they wished to follow through the agreements, students were more likely to embody them. Throughout the class, my peers consistently referred to the agreements, helping us stay focused on important qualities in a classroom such as demonstrating respect.

The agreements also had to be modeled by the professor; Professor Byrnes modeled respect for each member of the community by modifying the traditional power roles of the professor-student relationship. For the first time in my educational history, I felt as if my peers' and my ideas were as valuable as the professor's input. The combination of Professor Byrnes's model leadership and the students' genuine care for each other created the class ethos. By learning to listen to one another and be in tune with ourselves, we learned to mold a new fashion of living and learning.

The involvement of students in this process, as opposed to a list of predetermined expectations generated by the professor, invited and supported a respectful learning environment. Students experienced how their ideas and experiences were valued and how each person was a contributing member of the community. During a midcourse evaluation, one student offered the following observation:

> I think the classroom atmosphere is one of the most important parts of this class. There's such a wide range of knowledge and experience with mindfulness, but everyone is respectful and open to new ideas. Considering I came to the class with very little experience with mindfulness practices, I've found the material really accessible, which I did not necessarily expect. (March 2012)

I often prefaced the agreements activity with the acknowledgment that the students collectively possessed more experience and intelligence than I did as a single individual. Their respect for each other, as learners and human beings, was both a skill and a way of practicing mindfulness.

Gentleness

> Don't just do something, sit there.
>
> —Sylvia Boorstein, *Don't Just Do Something, Sit There*

Zajonc (2006) references Goethe's gentle empiricism as a second stage of contemplative inquiry. Students often have experience with a less-than-gentle approach to learning and are challenged to employ a gentle empiricism toward their study of MIE. Some students believe that learning is about achievement and achievement happens only when they do more and more. The process of contemplative inquiry requires humility, curiosity, openness, and acceptance, not purely strident effort. The preceding quote resonates with many students who struggled to just "sit there," who lacked compassion toward themselves when not "doing" more to achieve. To face and potentially overcome habitual learning patterns, students practiced gentleness with themselves, with each other, and with ideas throughout the course.

Gentleness was often most profoundly experienced as students experimented with a 21-day mindfulness practice. Each student chose a formal or informal practice to engage in every day for a minimum of 10 minutes for 21 days. Practices ranged from drinking a cup of tea, writing a gratitude journal, practicing yoga, and meditating on the breath to walking in nature. Students created a short log each day of their practice, noting the length of their practice, and provided three words to describe the experience as well as bullet points and/or pictures explaining any insights, observations, or questions that arose. At the conclusion of the experience, students wrote a one-page reflection addressing overall challenges and outcomes of the experiment. Jessica explains her analysis of the 21-day mindfulness experiment for herself and her classmates as follows.

Being gentle with oneself, a simple concept but a challenging ideal when you have been raised in a culture of achievement. The 21-day practice forced my peers and me to recognize that the purpose of the assignment was self-growth. To do well, you could not merely put in more time and work, visit the professor during office hours in search of the "right" answer, or mindlessly follow instructions. You had to face and develop your genuine emotions and responses. This approach to learning was surprisingly rare in a college culture that expected students to cram as much information into their heads as possible.

Initially, I started with a 21-day sitting meditation; however, I quickly realized the experience was torturous rather than enjoyable. Each day I would mentally berate myself for being unable to listen to Jon Kabat-Zinn's soothing voice and felt like I was failing the assignment. I kept asking myself—why? Why could I not meditate? Why did my mind not settle down after daily, focused attempts? I remember during one class session, a peer mentioned how much meditation had helped him learn to quiet his mind, and I remember this comment exponentially increasing frustration with myself. I shared these feelings with a peer. I told her that every time I tried to sit and meditate my thoughts spun out of control, my heart raced, and I felt like crying. I asked her why? Why didn't it work for me? What was wrong with me? I will never forget her response: "Jess, practices come and go. Someday, meditation may work for you. People change. For now, go with what works and don't try to fit yourself into a mold that isn't you." With this feedback, I decided that the classroom exploration of meditation during our labs was enough for me at that time and decided to switch my practice to a recently developed passion for writing. I began to journal every day for half an hour. This transition helped me process the class, my life, and my experience with meditation; it was exactly the type of practice I needed at that time.

The discipline required for students to do the same thing every day for three weeks and the gentleness needed to support the inevitable challenge of the experience were significant. While some students struggled with both the discipline as well as the practice of gentleness, others faced one as a bigger challenge than the other. A key aspect of this assignment was the dialogue in small groups and as a whole class about the challenges and opportunities for learning. Students and I gained insight and wisdom from our experience with the 21-day practice and by learning from each other. While the assignment was personalized, the collective engagement in the experience provided opportunities to learn from and with each other. Students practiced engaging with respect and gentleness as they discussed their challenges and insights creating the conditions for intimacy, the next stage of contemplative inquiry.

Students were often surprised by the difficulty of this assignment and how quickly they became critical of themselves in this process. One student wrote:

> In the past, I've appreciated the idea of being gentle with oneself and accepting "mistakes" in mindfulness practice and in life simply for the sake of being kind to oneself. But I've never realized so acutely why that gentleness makes sense in mindfulness practice: because the mistakes themselves truly don't matter as long as the intention is there. (April 2012)

As this student noted, repetitive daily practice gave students the time and space to realize the deeper purpose of practice: personal recognition of the importance of gentleness, a gentleness that allows one to notice the infinitesimal nature of mistakes. Jessica's capacity to experience gentleness in her courses including MIE was supported by the study of a growth mindset earlier in the course.

Dweck's (2006) concept of growth versus fixed mindsets encouraged further exploration around the concept of failure and revealed that the way I interpreted my personal experience with the 21-day practice could indeed change. In a growth mindset, one accepts and embraces change and challenge, while in a fixed mindset success and failure is seen as black and white. Dweck (2006) noted, "Mindsets are just beliefs. They're powerful beliefs, but they're just something in your mind, and you can change your mind" (p. 16). Supplementing hands-on concepts and conversations with readings such as Dweck's *Mindset* enhanced what I like to call personal "self-revelations" and allowed an intimacy with concepts at a depth that made me come alive in ways I had never before experienced in the traditional classroom setting.

Intimacy

> I define connection as the energy that exists between people when they feel seen, heard, and valued; when they can give and receive without judgment; and when they derive sustenance and strength from the relationship.
>
> —Brené Brown, *The Gifts of Imperfection*

Love or intimacy is rarely discussed or expressed in the hallowed halls of academia. There seems to be a fear that if we approach teaching and learning through an epistemology of love and intersubjectivity, we will lose the rigor and critical thinking we value and expect from ourselves and our students. Palmer and Zajonc (2010) clearly express the contemporary need for and the potential impact of an integrated education through an epistemology of love. Contemplation requires us to connect with each other, with the material being studied and with ourselves. By making sense of our own lives and by attempting to see clearly our own minds and behaviors, we create space for growth and a transition from *me* to *we*.

Students reflected on their lives through an "Educational Autobiography" assignment. Each person prepared a creative five-minute presentation sharing a brief snapshot of meaningful educational experiences and their impacts. Some students addressed themes such as family, music, sports, or creativity, while others highlighted a pivotal or turning point event. Over the first five to six weeks of the course students individually reflected and analyzed their own educational journey and discovered how their journeys were both unique and similar in surprising ways. The connections formed during this early assignment facilitated students' willingness to "feel seen, heard, and valued," as Brown (2010, p. 19) notes, while honing their capacity to see, hear, and value each other. One student expressed his appreciation for the assignment by acknowledging:

> I really value how comfortable I feel in this class. This is the class where I feel most eager to contribute in small discussions. I really appreciate the autobiographies we did at the beginning as well, because it has allowed me to see past the exterior of people and get to know them in a way I wouldn't otherwise have known. I feel a connection to everyone in our class, even if I haven't actually talked with them yet. When you share intimate parts of your life, you put a lot of trust in the people you share it with. (March 2012)

The intimacy cultivated through this assignment allowed students to take more risks and become more vulnerable as learners. They saw "past the exterior of people" and often described how well they came to know their classmates, acknowledging that they sometimes knew them in deeper ways than people they considered good friends. In the following, Jessica expresses how intimacy in MIE was rare during her college career and the impact it had on the social field created within the cohort.

At College X, stumbling across student discussions about academics in the dining hall is not unusual. In many casual conversations, peers who were drowning in lab reports, papers, and exams struggled to understand the purpose of our MIE class and often deemed the 21-day practice and educational autobiography assignment as fluff or nonacademic. They viewed the work in our class as a lighter, easier course load in comparison to the more rigorous traditional courses. Even at a liberal arts school, I was shocked by how much fear and closed-mindedness there was toward self-exploration and personal intimacy with academia.

I never realized how much developing lasting connections with peers could enhance your learning. The intimacy developed through sharing educational autobiographies connected students, serving as a means for connecting this class to other components of life, and bridged the objective distance between self and subject that students often face. For some classmates, education had been a linear path from elementary school to college, for others education was defined through a specific event or series of events such as traveling or sports, and for others education was defined through familial and place-based connections. By sharing and reflecting on meaningful past learning experiences, an invisible social field was created within the class. We cultivated genuine appreciation for one another and a curiosity to learn what each person had to offer our learning community.

A crucial aspect to the intimacy is the choice to share what is real and authentic and also appropriate for the audience. The danger of intimacy in a learning environment is that it has the potential to detract or limit rather than enhance the learning potential of the community. For example, a student could choose to share about a traumatic event from their educational history in a manner that further traumatizes others. Making choices about what to share was informed by guidelines included in the syllabus, which is described in the next section on vulnerability. Becoming vulnerable is one component of cultivating intimacy in a community of learners.

Vulnerability

> When we were children, we used to think that when we were grown-up we would no longer be vulnerable. But to grow up is to accept vulnerability. . . . To be alive is to be vulnerable.
>
> —Madeleine L'Engle, *Walking on Water*

Vulnerability, as Madeleine L'Engle observes, is part of being human, part of being alive. In an academic environment, vulnerability includes questioning preconceived ideas, sharing assumptions, being open to alternative perspectives, and exploring habits and patterns of mind that could be limiting. In the course syllabus I include a caveat adapted from a syllabus from a 2002 Mindfulness class, written by C. T. Tart, titled, "Further Clarification: What This Course Is and Isn't":

> This is a course that is both intellectual and experiential. . . . The intellectual aspects of the course contribute to the experiential and vice versa. The experiential exercises I will suggest to you and ask you to report on involve learning to pay clearer and sustained attention to your ongoing experience in a purposeful way, in order to increase your understanding of yourself and of the world. It is a first-person method of inquiry. I ask you to consider and honor the following standards of personal responsibility: Be aware of the context in which you are experiencing your own growth, both personal and intellectual. Please respect your own and others' capacities and limitations. Please respect your own privacy, your peers' privacy, and the overall purpose of the class. (pp. 5–6)

Vulnerability is about embracing wholeness, sharing who we are as human beings and learning from our experiences and challenges as well as through the experiences of those around us. Sometimes that means sharing what we don't know and what challenges us in appropriate, context-specific ways. We discuss and practice the standards of personal responsibility highlighted in the syllabus throughout the course.

In this second iteration of the Mindfulness class, I added a poetry recitation assignment. The goals for the assignment were to deepen our connections to each other, reflect on the process of mindful learning and our developing understanding of mindfulness, and cultivate skills of mindful speaking and listening. Students chose or wrote a poem demonstrating mindfulness for them. They memorized and recited the poem twice, once where everyone just listened and once where each person had a copy of the poem. The process of memorizing a poem connected students to the material and to the ideas in deeper ways than just reading a poem aloud. The repetition, the time spent learning and practicing, changed each person's understanding and meaning he or she ascribed to that poem. One student reflected:

> Trying to memorize it prompted me to rethink the emotions and memories that it evokes. Although I have not completely figured it out and could not concisely articulate why this poem is so well engraved in my mind and resonating in my heart, I got to think of it and share it to the class. As I shared, the sentiments shared in the poem—the sheer depression, fear, and stress that is gracefully said, rationalized, and accepted—are

frequently the feelings I experience as well. In this sense, poetry recitation helped me get a tiny little glimpse into the nature of myself that is so hard to grasp. (March 2012)

Students were invited to be in front of the class sharing something personally meaningful to them. The art of public speaking, of mindful speaking, required the discipline to memorize and spend significant time with a piece of writing, and the presence of mind to be in the present moment and share those words in a meaningful way for the audience. Students could choose a poem of any length and were encouraged to challenge themselves with both the content and the length of the poem. Poems ranged from those by Dr. Seuss to Mary Oliver. The assignment often evoked fear and anxiety in many students, challenged their comfort zone, and made them vulnerable in a classroom setting. Jessica describes her experience of vulnerability as follows.

We were asked to choose a poem and recite it to the class without looking at the text. The only stipulation: the poem had to relate to mindfulness in some form. Initially, there was much discomfort around the assignment: some were thrown off by its open-ended nature, some feared the task of memorization, and others feared the task of public speaking. In order to successfully complete the assignment, all of us had to learn to sit with the vulnerability of the task ahead.

Personally, I had to overcome the fear of failure. I had to embrace my nervousness of making a mistake and letting the class, professor, and myself down. I have always had difficulty memorizing text and was extremely uneasy at the thought of reciting a poem in front of the class. Only by being open to failure could I grow. After the strong connections built with my peers throughout the semester, it was easier to take that risk. The community helped me embrace my weakness and muster enough confidence to try despite the uncertainty of success. Rising to this challenge helped me realize that poetry recitation is not so scary. As a casual poetry writer, sharing a poem allowed me to reanalyze, reinterpret, and emotionally reconnect with the work in new ways and reaffirmed my passion for poetry while paving another possibility for spoken word in the future.

The community of learners supported many individual students to take risks intellectually and creatively by embracing their wholeness as learners. As Jessica has expressed in previous sections, learning with a growth mindset encourages taking risks and being challenged rather than taking an easier, known path. Jessica's experience with poetry and poetry recitation in the past influenced, but did not limit, her choices for the poetry recitation assignment. She used her confidence and support of her classmates to be open to failure.

Participation

> We move and feel with the natural phenomenon, text, painting, or person before us; living out of ourselves and into the other. Respectfully and delicately, in meditation we join with the other, while maintaining full awareness and clarity of mind. In other words, contemplative inquiry is experientially centered in the other, not in ourselves. Our usual preoccupations, fears, and cravings work against authentic participation.
>
> —Arthur Zajonc, "Cognitive-Affective Connections in Teaching and Learning"

Respect, gentleness, vulnerability, and intimacy allow students to participate in their learning process with their whole selves, integrating inner and outer characteristics. Participation engages all of our senses and emotional and mental faculties in the service of "joining with the other, while maintaining full awareness and clarity of mind." Participation in a community of learners model is active, collaborative, and connects to a larger context beyond one's individual story. Through the learning activities in the MIE class, students experimented with tools to enhance mindfulness in their work as students and in their lives. Their participation increased over the course of the semester from sharing a five-minute educational autobiography and poetry recitation to coteaching a full 90-minute class session. Students' experience was carefully scaffolded, as they transformed from being students to teachers of mindful education. Students gained experience and capacities as mindful learners before experimenting with mindful teaching.

For the teaching experiment, students indicated preferences from a list of mindfulness models/programs in Pre-K–12 education such as Montessori, MindUP, or Mind-Body Awareness Project. I organized groups of three to four people, and each group had one month to visit a school, interview a student and a teacher experienced with the model, and plan a 90-minute lesson on the chosen model for their MIE classmates. The lesson needed to both tell and show what the model does and feels like for students and teachers. The teaching experiment/class facilitation built on the knowledge students developed about mindfulness in the first half of the semester and gave them an opportunity to apply their skills of attention, emotion regulation, and compassion as facilitators and with their peers as students. As a group, students met with me twice before the facilitation to discuss their research and lesson plan, and once more following the facilitation to debrief the experience. Throughout the teaching experiment, students practiced maintaining their enhanced awareness and clarity of mind, acquired through personal mindfulness practice, while teaching the class about a mindfulness model of education. Through a demonstration with a Möbius strip, Jessica explains how participation in the teaching experiment assignment connected internal and external learning.

During the beginning of MIE, Professor Byrnes introduced us to the Möbius strip. It looks like an infinity circle or a figure eight on its side. As we twisted a strip of paper to create a physical representation, we saw and traced with our finger how the outer circle becomes the inner circle. With a simple twist, outer and inner become one. You cannot have internal learning without external experimentation and vice versa.

The combination of individualized, experimental mindful practices (such as meditation and yoga) with external discussions and reflections linked our internal and external learning. Rather than passively taking in information about different contemplative education models, we researched through site visits, interviews, and individual research for the class facilitation projects. Pairing external research with the challenge of creating an engaging, informative presentation for the class invited us to utilize the outer knowledge acquired through inquiry and transform it into a new, internalized form, ensuring both our own individual awareness expansion and the expanded wisdom of our peers.

It is foundational that an upper-level education class require students to demonstrate their understanding of the course content through a pedagogical experiment teaching their classmates. Many students were surprised how difficult it was to apply skills practiced within the confines of our class or lab to the experience of teaching. They became the main agents who facilitated learning in the classroom, which was an empowering and revealing experience. Students struggled to design engaging lessons that included a mindfulness practice central to the model, present information about the model articulately, and complete the teaching experiment within the 90-minute class time. They considered how to use both time and space appropriately and effectively for their classmates.

While facilitating the class, students needed to know the plan they designed and also be able to adapt the plan to meet the needs of the class. In one example, a facilitation group briefly checked in with each other while the class was doing another learning activity and changed the next activity to increase the level of energy in the room. By observing student behavior and facial expressions, they were able to meet the needs they saw expressed. Many beginning teachers are so focused on themselves and their lesson plan, making it difficult to pay attention to students' learning needs while retaining sufficient confidence to revise the original lesson plan. This is a skill more often demonstrated by experienced teachers. Students' ability to participate at this level of teaching and learning was enhanced because of the qualities of respect, gentleness, intimacy, and vulnerability of the community of learners.

Outcomes of Contemplative Inquiry: Insight and Transformation

> We shall not cease from exploration, and the end of all our exploring will be to arrive where we started, and know the place for the first time.
>
> —T. S. Eliot, "Little Gidding"

Zajonc describes the next stages of contemplative inquiry as insight and transformation. We view these stages as the outcomes of the previous five stages. Insight is a lens of direct perception on one's mental, physical, and emotional habits, challenges, and patterns in relationships. Transformation involves "re-forming" mental processes, behaviors, and emotional responses based on insight from seeing how one's mind works, how others' minds work, and the capacity to directly perceive the outside world. As Goethe explained, "Every object well contemplated opens an organ of perception in us" (qtd. in Zajonc, 2009, p. 179). Insight is the "object well contemplated" and transformation is the new "organ of perception."

Students in MIE expressed a shift in how they identified, understood, and worked with emotions as one means of demonstrating insight. Students often expressed a positive shift in their view of other classes during the semester they were in the mindfulness class. They perceived their habits, challenges, and often their relationships with a new lens as well. In the following subsection one student's design journal expressed her insight into the practice of meditation and emotional awareness. The next subsection on transformation depicts how openness to ambiguity transformed one student's approach to his required math class. Insight has the potential to lead to transformation and the next two subsections will speak to this phenomenon.

Insight

Emotional awareness was one of the key insights students demonstrated during their semester of studying MIE. The following two journal entries by Evelyn,[2] each several weeks apart, address her initial perception concerning the impact of meditation and her experience of practicing meditation. She also explored how denying destructive emotions or grasping constructive emotions limited her direct experience in the world.

> Journal 1: Meditation to me has always seemed like a beneficial practice for other people, but any time I ever thought of incorporating it into my daily life, I assumed that it wouldn't work. . . . I am beginning to understand the importance of taking a moment out of each day to focus on paying attention to my breath. . . . The first couple chapters of Gunaratana's book *Mindfulness in Plain English* made me aware of how heavy of a load we all are carrying, and how I do constantly feel unsatisfied. I can't decide if the author was exaggerating a little bit about how humans are never "touching life" (without meditation), but I feel convinced by this argument. . . . I am intrigued about all of the evidence that there is of the positive effects of meditation on peoples' mental and physical health. I believe this to be true, however I am skeptical if I will actually feel a real difference in myself after this semester is over. I am excited to see what happens, and about all of the other mindfulness techniques that could be available to me.
>
> Journal 2: I have been surprised by what happens when I allow my negative emotions to enter my mind, instead of pushing them away. I imagined that doing this while meditat-

ing would just cause me to become stressed out, and lose all focus, but instead, I have been able to focus on the emotion for a moment, and then let it go. It now makes sense to me why so many meditation experts seem to be advocating for this "openness." It is like I only have the ability to get over certain feelings once I have truly faced them in this "mindful" context. . . . I also noticed how when I brought up happy emotions, I was resistant to letting them go. I think that I definitely identify with my positive emotions, and I used to think that this helped me be a happy person. I think most people would say that they want to feel connected to their happy emotions, but I know this is not the idea behind mindful practices. I am eager to contemplate this further. I have trouble seeing the negative side effects from identifying with emotions of joy.

Viewing her emotions simply as emotion rather than identifying herself as "a happy person" was a process Evelyn continued to work on throughout the semester. She recognized how she could let go of a negative emotion and she learned to see how she might be able to let go of positive emotions in the future. She realized how she was able to take a new perspective with friends or family members but didn't think about taking a new perspective for herself. Evelyn's insights about her habits of mind and her emotional awareness influenced her life as a student and as a human being. Jessica shares how her learning experiences during MIE created new insights about "doing school."

College X is an elite institution, and in order to maintain the "success" afforded by top grades, I initially put all my energy into specific, targeted tasks that felt extremely disconnected. However, after taking this class, I felt less driven by the traditional model of success. The way I saw education completely changed; I focused on internalizing class material rather than "doing school" and consequently altered the way I approach all subjects. I often found myself journaling outside of class about concepts that truly captivated me. I made time for the elements of academics that interested me most; I spent less time on graded components, such as papers and exams, and more time talking to professors during office hours and studying and analyzing the readings independently, on my own time. I learned how to get what I needed for my own personal development rather than focusing purely on molding my work to fit the professor's ideals. Furthermore, changing my personal philosophy strengthened my ability to make interdisciplinary connections. For example, in my French Literature class, I saw how the concept of translating raw emotions in Baudelaire's 17th-century poetry connected directly to my desire to translate emotions into the figures I drew in Drawing class, a challenging task but one that many have faced over many generations and across many disciplines.

Transformation

Transformation means to change one's current form and describes both a process and an outcome. Transformation occurs as a person begins to view him- or herself, others, or the world with a new lens or new perspective. "Transformation is a movement toward increasing wholeness that simultaneously pushes toward diversity and uniqueness—become more uniquely who we are, and toward unity—recognizing how much we have in common with the universe (and perhaps even the recognition that we are the universe)" (Hart, 2000, p. 26). Wholeness involves welcoming and connecting all aspects of being a human. An orientation toward wholeness accepts the good and the bad; we cannot have one without the other. One student was taking a basic mathematics class concurrently with the mindfulness class. He observed a significant transformation in his initial negative attitude when he saw that math could be approached mindfully.

> I think that being in this class has already started to positively impact my learning in one other course: Math 50. I usually don't like math classes and I haven't taken one since my junior year of high school. . . . I have MIE the morning of my math class, so on my way there I was thinking about how I could approach math in a different way and try to change my automatic associations with math so that I could better enjoy it. Mindfulness is a practice and while I tried, I still couldn't let myself see the good in Math 50. The following class period of Math 50 came after we talked (in Mindfulness) about how using ambiguity in math classes can cultivate mindfulness and critical thinking skills. I loved the idea when we talked about it in class. When I got to Math 50, my Prof. had written "becoming comfortable with ambiguity" on the

board and told us about how this class was not going to be about memorizing formulas, being told exactly how to do something, not applying our knowledge, and then forgetting it (everything I dislike about typical math classes). He proceeded to tell us that we would be thinking critically and figuring out ways to find solutions. He said most of us would hate this and rather just be told the one correct method to solve questions, but I was really happy. MIE class had given me the vocabulary to better understand what bothered me so much about math (the expectation that we engage mindlessly and leave without applicable skills). I was able to identify Math 50 as a class that valued mindfulness. My attitude about the class changed dramatically . . .

The synchronicity of studying ambiguity in the MIE class and the Math 50 class catapulted his new mindset to learning math. He was able to recognize the emotional barriers he was putting up to learning math, see how past experiences had led him to view math as purely memorization with little meaning or application, and then change his attitude, comfort, and interest in studying math. In this case, his attitude was "re-formed" due to the insight gained about his own mindset toward the subject of math. This student faced his past failures and discomfort with the subject and was willing and able to let them go through a new, more mindful perspective. While he talked about both mindfulness and critical thinking in his reflection, his understanding of mindfulness opened the door for a transformed perspective on mathematics. He was supported in this transformation by the mathematics professor and the embracing of ambiguity in the math class.

Jessica found her awareness of everyday life transformed as she cultivated her quality of attention through MIE.

Outside of the classroom, I realized the deeper, more personal attention I spent on academics applied to all aspects of life, often in unexpected ways. One upper-level English class that studied horticultural shifts in 18th-century literature and art completely altered the scenes I saw in everyday life. When running on my usual routes, I started to noticing irony in the "natural" world. Retirement communities with floral titles such as "Evergreen Homes" or "Botany Palace" directly correlated to classroom discussions around social trends in "nature." Just like in 18th-century gardens of the wealthy, these communities with miniature ponds, manicured grass, and flower gardens, and recently planted "forests" represented a pseudo-replication of the natural world. The aesthetic scenes I passed by with a generic thought of "that's pretty" vividly shifted to poignant analysis of society's ironic attempts to capture, remake, and recreate "nature," a trend dating back to the 1700s. These new insights connected the webs of the world in new ways. I learned how to learn through MIE, more specifically I learned how to love learning in the academic context and connect it to the learning I do outside the classroom. I learned how to be truly engaged with the world around me.

Jessica's engagement as a student and learner became central to her skill as a mindful teacher.

Teachers as Learners

> It has been said that the highest learning comes in four parts: One part is learned from teachers; another part from fellow students; a third part from self-study and practice; and the final part comes mysteriously, silently, in the due course of time.
>
> —Ganga White, *Yoga Beyond Belief*

In the MIE class, students actively investigated concepts, research, and practices about mind-body awareness, meditation, emotional balance, and contemplative pedagogy. They challenged their perspectives through readings, the sharing of personal histories, and their peers' understanding of course content. They studied themselves experientially during the 21-day mindfulness practice experiment and the mindfulness labs. Their words and actions revealed an increased level of mindfulness, insight, and transformation that occurred throughout the semester.

As a result of contemplative inquiry, students often experience a transformation of, and insight into, themselves as learners, the learning process, and their emotional awareness and capacity for emotional balance. Students become active agents in their learning process. They learn how their breath can mirror the state of their minds and bodies, and how slowing down enhances their sensory perceptions. The practice allows them to study their own minds, thoughts, and emotions, as they experiment with facing ambiguity while examining contradictions and connecting critical first-person inquiry experiences with powerful second-person dialogue.

Matt Bernstein, a former student of MIE and currently a high school teacher, wrote and recited the following poem on the last day of our class in 2012, summarizing his experience with MIE throughout the semester. He expressed his journey on "the mindful path" with clarity and compassion and expressed gratitude for the community of learners who accompanied him on this path.

You expect me to meditate?
Are you kidding, this is college
I didn't come here to breathe
I came here for knowledge

I want to know how this looks when it's put in a school
I want to know what kids think about yoga with math
I don't care about my stress
I don't need the mindful path

Sitting here for twenty minutes each morning
Just sitting and wasting my precious time
Please just let us go
Come on ring the chime

Stretching's not bad
At least my body's awake
But my mind is still in the clouds
Damn, I thought this class would be a piece of cake

Too much thinking, not enough living
Sometimes you have to make a mistake
I know emotional control is important
But aren't there times when you need to just jump in the lake?

At last a much needed Spring break
The midterm was good but I'm glad to have time off
Time to relax without worrying about school
I need to get away from this mindfulness, no disrespect prof.

Back to Bowdoin and the work and the books
Let's approach mindfulness with a whole new mindset
Be positive and optimistic
I have a feeling there's a lot to this that I still don't get

Have fun with this stuff
It's really for you, Katie's not lying
I know this is hard, remember growth mindset
You just have to keep trying

Hold the phone and wait a minute
Being mindful can mean getting to dance?
Now this I'm on board with
I'm softening my negative stance

I like learning about different mindful school models
Clearly the idea that it won't work in education isn't true
Look at these examples and tell me I'm wrong
It seems that mindful education is something we really need to pursue

Seriously mindfulness is a simple as breathing
If a student stopped breathing I know you would care
So care about mindfulness
I'm serious it can be used anywhere

Coming up to the end of the semester
I can't believe it but I'm really starting to enjoy being more brainless
No more dreading mindfulness practices
Getting up for class at 8 has never been so painless

Now you want to know what I've learned
You want to know how I've been affected
With so much to choose from
Let me tell you the important things I've selected

Mindfulness is always possible
It can definitely work in a school
In an age full of stress
Why let standardized tests rule?

Students can benefit so much from awareness
They can learn more about themselves and their peers
They can grow and develop
They can learn academics and how to confront their fears

As for me, you want to know how I've been influenced
It's really pretty simple, three things come to mind
First and foremost my classmates
Never a better group will you find

They've taught me so much
About mindfulness and how to live
I don't mean to sound dramatic
But there's not enough thanks I can give

I've learned about the fixed and growth mindsets
Be willing to change and let go
It's all about impermanence, you don't have a fixed identity
There's always room to grow

Most important to me is "be here now"
Three words that are so simple yet so wise
Stay in the present
Each moment is a prize

It wasn't always easy
Not by any stretch or measure
But now I see that I learned a lot
This experience I feel I'll always treasure

Mindfulness isn't for everyone
Sometimes it's not even for me
But I can't knock its potential
It's real, that much I can see

Most important of all
I've learned to try to be happy
I've learned to care and think about others
But also to care and think about me

Matt's synthesis of his experiences in MIE acutely outlines a shift in perspective. The poem shows his initial, and continued, skepticism on contemplative education as well as his newfound respect for its transformative powers. Guiding students, such as Matt, to practice self-awareness and develop clarity about themselves as students and future teachers was the core benefit of practicing mindfulness and a contemplative way of knowing. A significant number of students in the MIE class were preparing to become educators. Preservice teachers and future educators like Matt and Jessica now have the potential to share that knowledge with future students and colleagues. Rather than viewing teachers and students as disembodied beings by focusing solely on their intellectual and rational systems, contemplative inquiry's emphasis on wholeness moves education toward a view of teachers and students as beings with not only minds, but also hearts and bodies.

Contemplative inquiry with a community of learners model moves all of us in teacher education on a path toward greater insight, transformation, and wisdom, which is needed in our current educational context to equitably and effectively educate all students. Jessica's final commentary highlights how her experience in MIE naturally integrated into her life; moreover, this course deeply impacted her teaching career and personal life as she tries to incorporate a facets-of-contemplative understanding into her own classroom each day.

Professor Byrnes and I started writing this piece the summer after I received my undergraduate degree, while our course was fresh on my mind. Fired up, enthusiastic, and ready to take on educational inequalities, I craved the challenge of putting theory to practice. Mindfulness changed my life and I wanted to cultivate a similar experience in my own English classroom. However, the madness of reality struck, and the inexplicable, overwhelming experience of being a first-year teacher threw all my ideologies out the window. Among the woes and highs—a student cussing at me, a student writing a thank-you letter to me about how I changed his perspective on poetry, and the constant struggle of managing a classroom full of diverse personalities—I stumbled across many moral dilemmas: needing to kick out a student despite understanding the personal difficulties that may have caused the behavior. I also encountered personal dilemmas: how many full weekends ought I dedicate to creating curriculum, emailing students, and correcting papers. Is it possible to do this job and have a life outside of work? The biggest struggle I faced was one of time; I always wanted to do more. My theories of creating a warm and welcoming atmosphere, of focusing on collaboration and support took the backseat to surviving the day in a high school classroom.

As I conclude my second year of teaching and take another look at this essay, I am reminded of the many steps of preparation it took to do this job. The second year, despite my doubts, is much easier. I know my school and I know what I want to teach. I know activities that do not work and how to manage classic patterns of student behavior. Reflecting back on my first year, even through the madness, I can see aspects of what I learned from Professor Byrnes's mindfulness class, both in my personal and professional life. For example, I decided to buy my own copy of the MindUP curriculum guide after I taught a lesson on it in MIE. Whenever my English students needed a 180-degree flip from their research project or grammar work, I threw in lessons about neuroscience, meditation, and the power of reflection, encouraging metacognitive discussions around the learning process. I also tried to incorporate reflective discussions on why we learned certain writing skills, grammar, or theoretical questions, a practice that my school fully supports and is, in fact, one of their major guiding principles.

Outside of the school environment, I find myself experiencing a more balanced sanity. I write every day. I make time for me, time dedicated to making me happy (coffee dates with friends, running, biking to work). Through MIE, I faced inner, deep-rooted anxieties around the learning process, and, looking back, I can see that mindfulness is how I vanquished negative learning patterns. At the end of every day, I don't dwell on my faults. I have a new sense of gentleness toward myself that didn't always exist. It now seems natural, but reflecting on this course has reminded me this was not always the case. Reflecting back on Dweck's (2006) statement, "Mindsets are just beliefs," I see how the growth mindset has become who I am and is the most powerful lesson I share with my students every day. As Zajonc observed about contemplative knowing in the opening of this chapter, "in order to communicate it fully we must find a way to lead others to the same experience. They too must come to 'see' what we have come to know." This essay took me to new depths of understanding about the purpose of MIE; I am grateful for my experiences with respect, gentleness, intimacy, participation, and vulnerability, transformation, and insight as a student in the MIE class, which is now impacting my teaching and my students' learning experiences in my classes.

Notes

1. In every iteration of these stages, the first five stages are: respect, gentleness, intimacy, participation, and vulnerability. In 2006, Zajonc outlines transformation, *Bildung*, and insight at the last three of eight stages of contemplative

inquiry. In 2009, Zajonc outlines nine characteristics of contemplative inquiry, the last four of which are transformation, organ formation, illumination, and insight. For the purposes of understanding contemplative inquiry, we view the concepts of transformation and insight as conducive and sufficient to describe the final stages and the outcomes of contemplative inquiry.

2. Student names have been changed to protect their anonymity.

References

Boorstein, S. (1996). *Don't just do something, sit there: A mindfulness retreat with Sylvia Boorstein*. San Francisco: HarperOne.

Brown, B. (2010). *The gifts of imperfection: Let go of who you think you are supposed to be and embrace who you are*. Center City: Hazelden.

Davidson, R. J. (2012). Contemplative neuroscience. Lecture. Retrieved April 2, 2016, from https://www.youtube.com/watch?v=AKKg3CDczpA

Dweck, C. (2006). *Mindset: The new psychology of success*. New York: Ballentine Books.

Eliot, T. S. (1944). "Little Gidding" in *Four Quartets*. London: Faber and Faber.

Gibbs, J., & Gibbs, R. (2013). *The mindful way to study: Dancing with your books*. San Diego: O'Connor Press.

Hart, T. (2000). From education to transformation: What mystics and sages tell us education can be. *Encounter, 13*, 14–28.

Kabat-Zinn, J. (2003). Mindfulness-based interventions in context: Past, present, and future. *Clinical Psychology: Science and Practice, 10*(2), 144–156.

L'Engle, M. (1980). *Walking on water: Reflections on faith and art*. New York: North Point Press.

Palmer, P., & Zajonc, A. (2010). *The heart of higher education*. San Francisco: Jossey-Bass.

Rogoff, B. (1994). Developing understanding of the idea of communities of learners. *Mind, Culture and Activity, 1*(4), 209–229.

Rose, M. (2013). Giving cognition a bad name. *Education Week, 32*(17), 32.

Roth, H. D. (2006). Contemplative studies: Prospects for a new field. *Teachers College Record, 108*(9), 1787–1815.

Tart, C. T. (2002). Mindfulness syllabus—for general Web viewing. Retrieved April 15, 2016, from http://blog.paradigm-sys.com/fall-2013-mindfulness-syllabus-for-web-general-viewing/

White, G. (2007). *Yoga beyond belief: Insights to awaken and deepen your practice*. Berkeley: North Atlantic Books.

Zajonc, A. (2009). *Meditation as contemplative inquiry: When knowing becomes love*. Great Barrington: Lindisfarne Press.

Zajonc, A. (2006). Cognitive-affective connections in teaching and learning: The relationship between love and knowledge. *Journal of Cognitive Affective Learning, 3*(1), 1–9.

2

Meditating Together, Speaking from Silence

The Theory and Practice of Interpersonal Mindfulness

NANCY WARING

> When someone deeply listens to you,
> it is like holding out a dented cup you've had since childhood
> with cold, fresh water.
> When it balances on the brim,
> you are understood.
> When it overflows and touches your skin,
> you are loved.
>
> —John Fox, "When Someone Deeply Listens to You"

At the heart of this chapter is an examination of a Lesley University course on the theory and practice of insight dialogue,[1] an interpersonal meditation practice developed by Western insight meditation teacher Gregory Kramer. In light of insight dialogue, the chapter explores resonant theories of dialogue articulated by David Bohm (1917–1992), Paulo Freire (1927–1991), and Siddhartha Gotama (ca. 563–483 BC), known today as the Buddha.[2] Each of these thinkers is committed to the enhancement of human understanding and compassion through dialogue, in the service of a kinder, gentler, more egalitarian world. Throughout, I use the words *intersubjective*, *interpersonal*, and *relational* interchangeably.

History of Insight Dialogue

In the mid-1990s, Kramer, then a PhD student at the California Institute of Integral Studies, conceived the idea of insight dialogue, or interpersonal mindfulness practice. In insight dialogue, meditators move from individual, silent breath-centered, or open awareness practice into deep, reflective, and connected listening and speaking in dyads, triads, or larger groups, on a given topic of contemplation.

In the interpersonal spirit of the practice, insight dialogue was articulated in a fully collaborative dissertation Kramer wrote with a fellow student. He and his coauthor had been studying the work of David Bohm, a colleague of Albert Einstein and one of the foremost quantum mechanical physicists of the 20th century. But they were not studying Bohm's groundbreaking causal interpretation of quantum physics. Rather, they were immersed in his work on a model of dialogue created out of his passionate attention to what, as he put it, "is now commonly called the problem of communication" (p. 1).

In his small gem of a book, *On Dialogue* (one of the main texts in the course), Bohm (2004) notes that the word *dialog* comes from the Greek word *logos*, meaning "the word," and *dia*, meaning "through." This derivation, he observes, suggests "a stream of meaning flowing along and through us and between us, out of which may emerge some new understanding" (p. 6).

In Bohmian Dialogue, 15 to 30 people sit in a circle and discuss a topic of mutual interest. A facilitator may be useful at the outset but usually becomes unnecessary as the group gains momentum. Bohmian Dialogue is a form of agenda-free, guideline-free, free association whose aim is nothing other than to enhance mutual understanding and allow participants to become aware of their patterns of thought.

Bohm (2004) emphasizes that dialogue is not "discussion," which derives from the same root as *percussion* and *concussion*, meaning to break things up. He likens discussion to a ping-pong game, where people are batting ideas back and forth, and the object of the game is to win or get points—a practice we excel at in the academy. In dialogue however, "Nobody is trying to win. Everybody wins if anybody wins" (p. 7).

Kramer and his coauthor, who were both practitioners of mindfulness meditation, were facilitating a Bohmian Dialogue group when they were struck by the potential of integrating the principles of Bohmian Dialogue with mindfulness meditation in order to create an interpersonal meditation practice. They then developed six formal practice guidelines:

pause, relax, open, trust emergence, listen deeply, and speak the truth. They introduced subject matter in the form of contemplations, which, depending upon the makeup of the group, might be a traditional Buddhist contemplation, such as aging, illness, or death; or a more mundane one, such as the roles we identify with, or are ascribed to us by others. As the dialogue unfolds in slow time after a period of silent meditation, participants often see that such roles are rigid and constricting. Often long-held self-concepts begin to loosen their grip. For example, students in my insight dialogue course frequently reflect that as children, they were pegged as the "smart one" or the "problem child," and that they have carried these impositions into adulthood to their detriment. When contemplating roles, work issues arise, such as performance anxiety, difficult colleagues, lack of recognition from supervisors, and the like.

Another common and illuminating contemplation is on judgment, including self-judgment. As Kramer (2007) notes in his detailed account of the practice in *Insight Dialogue: The Interpersonal Path to Freedom*, "bringing judgments into the light of meditative awareness offers us the gift of knowing . . . that they arise out of deep-seated conditioning . . . and we rest patiently in the flux of judgment" (p. 57). A mindfulness bell marks the beginning and end of each practice session, which is followed by a facilitated full group dialogue exploring what has transpired in dyads or triads.

The Guidelines

The first guideline in Kramer's (2007) work, "pause," calls forth mindfulness. It interrupts our habitual tendency to rush forward and can be likened to returning to the breath in individual meditation. "Relax" invites tranquility and acceptance, making it possible for us to let others in. "Open" elicits relational availability and spaciousness—opening the way to mutuality. We extend our awareness to others, letting go of our isolated sense of self (p. 129).

"Trust emergence" encourages flexibility and letting go, opening to whatever may emerge in the moment (p. 135), entering practice without the bias of a goal, and without trying to make anything happen (p. 139). "Listen deeply" invites receptivity and attunement. Alert to the resonance of insight dialogue with Quaker practices, Kramer offers Quaker writer Douglas Steere's delicate understanding of receptive listening as revealing "the thinness of the filament that separates [people] listening openly to one another . . ." (qtd. in Kramer, 2007, p. 160). "Speak the truth" means speaking to what is being held between the comeditators, in a fully engaged and mindful way. It is not about reflecting back, summarizing, reframing, or offering advice, or any other such communication technique. In this process of listening deeply and speaking the truth, loving-kindness naturally emerges (p. 148).

Comparing interpersonal practice with individual practice, Kramer writes,

> Interpersonal meditation reveals . . . the powerful but hidden processes by which we construct a self-image. . . . Its dynamics are similar to those of traditional personal meditation: we gradually cultivate mindfulness and tranquility; these qualities allow us to apprehend the moment to moment nature of experience; what we then realize, frees us. But because interpersonal meditation works with the moment to moment experience of interacting with another, it brings the liberating dynamic of meditation into our interpersonal lives. From there it migrates to society as a whole. (p. 4)

The Back Story: Why a Course in Interpersonal Mindfulness?

While a handful of higher education teachers have introduced Bohmian Dialogue into the classroom and been impressed by the level of group consciousness that arises (Gunnlaugson, 2014, p. 307), I am not aware of a course that conjoins Bohmian Dialogue with the practice of interpersonal mindfulness. Nor do I know of any other academic institution that offers a course in interpersonal mindfulness.

I became keen on developing such a course after profound experiences with comeditators at several of Kramer's annual 10-day training retreats at the Barre Center for Buddhist Studies in Barre, Massachusetts. I subsequently worked with insight dialogue senior teachers Janet Surrey and Florence Meyer, both of whom have trained extensively with Kramer. Surrey, a clinical psychologist well known for her work on a relational model of women's development, has in recent years incorporated insight dialogue in her clinical practice. Meyer directs the professional training program in Mindfulness-Based Stress Reduction (MBSR) at the Center for Mindfulness in Medicine, Health Care, and Society, where I completed my MBSR training under her supervision.

After having attended numerous silent retreats over 20 years, I was intrigued by the potential of interpersonal meditation to enhance interconnectedness. Not being one to jump easily into partner exercises that involve sustained eye contact, I was also a bit leery. But from the outset I found myself readily connecting with my dialogue partners and feeling embraced by their attentive and compassionate listening. Unlike on individual retreats where I sometimes want to get away from myself, I leaned into each dialogue session, eager to discover what would unfold between my partner and me.

Some of the practice sessions from my first retreat still remain vivid. I recall a contemplation on family roles in which my partner was a woman considerably older than I was. As we sat facing each other on our meditation cushions, she recounted the pain she felt as a step-grandmother, overshadowed by her beloved grandchildren's biological grandmother. I heard the stark narrative of a young woman widowed at 50, and the sole caretaker of her 10-year-old autistic daughter and bipolar teenage son. I experienced exquisite attunement of a comeditator when I spoke of my concern for my beloved then-91-year-old mother, who had recently broken her hip.

I was confident that this practice of attunement could be successfully transported into the classroom, and that a course on insight dialogue would be a good complement to Lesley's existing course on the theory and practice of mindfulness. As in that course, academic inquiry would be integrated with intensive practice. As for texts, Bohm's (2004) *On Dialogue* was an obvious choice, given his influence—unbeknownst to him—on the development of insight dialogue. Of course Kramer's (2007) book on the practice, *Insight Dialogue: The Interpersonal Path to Freedom*, was essential. I wanted us to have ample time to immerse ourselves in the texts, as we do in the practice, so selected only one more full text, *Pedagogy of the Oppressed* by Brazilian educator and social activist Paulo Freire (1972).

Freire's treatment of dialogue as an act of love, beautifully and forcefully presented in this text, resonates with Bohm and Kramer's. His theory of egalitarian dialogue as a form of pedagogy would enrich our investigation into the pedagogical process we ourselves were engaged in. His focus on the application of dialogue in the service of redressing oppression of impoverished people added a new dimension. Or, put differently, Freire would ratchet things up, leading us from Kramer and Bohm's views of the potential of dialogue to make the world more humane through agenda-free interconnectedness to dialogue as an action-oriented pedagogical and revolutionary strategy.

In addition to close reading of Kramer, Bohm, and Freire, we would investigate the Buddha's teaching on "right speech," often referred to in Western Buddhist circles as "wise speech" for ease of understanding. Including right speech was called for, given the Buddhist roots of insight dialogue and the direct application of right speech in the practice. Each class session would begin with silent meditation, followed by insight dialogue practice, and full group dialogue about the practice experience. The attunement to others cultivated by practice would set the tone for investigation of the week's readings. In other words, the academic conversation would, I hoped, unfold in the spirit of the insight dialogue guidelines: pause, relax, open, listen deeply, trust emergence, and speak the truth.

Such was the plan, which has been realized since I began teaching the course in 2007. In what follows, I attempt to offer a glimpse of the course and further consideration of ideas set forth by these thinkers. Also included is a brief reflection on an unanticipated subject of contemplation that arose in the course one year; and a departure from the subject of dialogue: I offer a touch of contemplative neuroscience, to acquaint students with the brain as an intrinsically social phenomenon.

A Bohmian View of Proprioception

The concept of proprioception is central to Bohm's theory of dialogue. Proprioception is the neurophysiological term referring to the body's ability to perceive its own movement, or more simply, bodily self-perception. If you can't close your eyes and touch your nose with your finger, your proprioception is off. (The finger-to-nose test is often used by police to check a driver's questionable sobriety.)

Explaining a breakdown of proprioception, Bohm describes a woman who had had a stroke and woke up hitting herself. Her motor nerves were working fine, but the feedback loop from her sensory nerves to her motor nerves was out of commission. She was unaware that she was touching herself and believed she was being attacked (p. 24). This is how we generally understand proprioception, or lack of it.

Bohm's contribution was to metaphorically extend the concept into the realm of thought. Bohm posited that thought itself can be proprioceptive—that is, we can be aware of our thoughts, both individually and collectively:

If everybody is giving attention then there will arise a new kind of thought between people, or even in the individual, which is proprioceptive, and which doesn't get into the kind of tangle that thought gets into ordinarily, which is not proprioceptive. *We could say that practically all of the problems of the human race are due to the fact that thought is not proprioceptive* (p. 25, emphasis mine).

Bohmian Dialogue then, was based on the idea of collective proprioception,[3] or to use another of Bohm's phrases, a "participatory consciousness" (p. 26). Such a consciousness, he wrote, had the potential to "create something new between us, something of very great significance for bringing to an end the at present insoluble problems with the individual and society" (pp. 4–5). Proprioception of thought, or self-perception of thought, is, in essence, mindfulness—a clear knowing that one is having a thought, awareness of what the thought is, attunement to it, and, at its most precise, attunement to what has given rise to the thought and to that which it, in turn, gives rise.

Continuing with this line of thinking—as we do in class—it follows that interpersonal mindfulness, practiced diligently guideline by guideline, is akin to collective proprioception. Not that we can know each other's thoughts directly, but we can follow our own and others' thought processes with refined attunement, in the service of greater understanding and interpersonal connection. Bohm's idea of collective proprioception resonates strongly with students, perhaps because of the intrinsic magic and aptness of the metaphor, and because his message is hopeful, entrusting us with a sense of mission. He clearly believes that participatory consciousness is within our reach and that we therefore have the capacity to effectively address the problems of the human race at their source.

Paulo Freire: Dialogue and the Pedagogy of Liberation

Bohm is fresh in our minds when we move on to Freire's (1972) *Pedagogy of the Oppressed*. For Freire, dialogue is "an act of creation . . . which cannot exist in the absences of profound love of the world and for men. The naming of the world, which is an act of creation and re-creation, is not possible if it is not infused with Love. Love is at the same time the foundation of dialogue and dialogue itself" (p. 77).

Dialogue, he believes, requires love, humility, faith in man, hope, and critical thinking (pp. 78–81). In his focus on pedagogy per se, Freire (1972) departs from Bohm and Kramer. His distinction between "the banking method of education"—to which he objects strongly, and the problem-posing method, for which he argues passionately—is the hallmark of his pedagogy. In the banking method, to which most of us have been subject at some point in our education, "knowledge is a gift bestowed by those who consider themselves knowledgeable upon those whom they consider to know nothing" (p. 58). The teacher is the depositor of knowledge, the students the depositories of information. This model, in which the teacher teaches and the students are taught, "negates education and knowledge as processes of inquiry" (p. 58), Freire asserts.

On the other hand, at the heart of the problem-posing method is a partnership of teacher and student. The teacher teaches, and is taught, in dialogue with students, who are both taught, and teach. The teacher is no longer merely the-one-who-teaches, but one who is himself taught in dialogue with the students, who in turn, while being taught, also teach. As Freire summarizes, "They become jointly responsible for a process in which all grow" (p. 67). In language that resonates with the "meaning making" that emerges in Bohmian Dialogue and insight dialogue, he writes, "Through dialogue, the teacher of the students, and the students of the teacher cease to exist and a new term emerges: teacher-student and student-teacher" (p. 67).

Freire's (1972) model of egalitarian pedagogy provides us with an opening to consider the project we are engaged in together in our class, as students and teacher. We recognize that in our efforts to follow the insight dialogue guidelines, both in meditation practice and academic inquiry, we are in Freire's problem-posing territory. Yet students are clear that the playing field is not entirely level. Certainly the teacher teaches and is taught, but the teacher also facilitates the dialogues, assigns the reading, and grades the papers. Is Freire's intention really to disappear the singular teacher? Is his idea practicable? We hold these questions. But at the end of the day, we are fully aligned with his idea that dialogue is a form of love, and as such, a harmonious instrument for improving the human condition.

While full consideration of the application of Freirean dialogue in liberating oppressed peoples is beyond the scope of this chapter, we do touch upon this subject. Freire makes a compelling case that if persons of privilege, such as ourselves, want to participate in the project of diminishing class inequality, we must engage in deep dialogue with the oppressed people and allow a partnership to emerge with their leaders. Otherwise, we are simply imposing ourselves, and by repeating a power-over situation, taking on the role of oppressor ourselves. We are humbled at the proposition and heartened by the possibility of Freirean dialogue to affect social change.

Right Speech:
Interpersonal Mindfulness and the Buddha

The Buddha is arguably one of the greatest advocates for mindful, compassionate, and connected speech. His concept of "right speech" or "wise speech" was so central to his belief system that it numbers among the eight factors of the noble eightfold path to liberation from suffering—the pinnacle of Buddhist teachings.[4] As Kramer notes, the "right" in right speech does not imply moral judgment. Rather, it pertains to speech that promotes harmony and leads to happiness, peace, and liberation from suffering (p. 77). Right speech is an "element of morality with special application to interpersonal practice. This element of insight is most clearly represented by the guideline 'speak the truth,' which implies kindness, mindfulness, usefulness, and other good qualities of speech" (p. 100). Right speech, according to the Buddha, is factual, true, beneficial, affectionate, agreeable, and timely. The Buddha has no time for "idle" speech—gossip or aimless chatter. He sets the bar high, and in our class, we are motivated to measure up.

Right speech implies its corollary, which might be called "right listening." And, while "interpersonal mindfulness" was not in the Buddha's lexicon, the Buddha was crystal clear about the value of relational practice. Here follows an exchange with his friend Ananda, whose questions and declarations the Buddha often uses as a teaching tool:

> "Venerable sir, this is half of the holy life, that is, good friendship, good companionship, good comradeship."
> "Not so, Ananda. Not so Ananda. This is the entire holy life, that is good friendship, good companionship, good comradeship. When a Bhikkhu has a good friend, a good companion, a good comrade, it is expected that he will develop and cultivate the noble eightfold path." (qtd. in Kramer, 2007, pp. 79–80)

Keeping the guidelines for right speech in mind supports us in our practice and also helps us to avoid lapsing into pitfalls of insight dialogue such as idle speech and what Kramer calls "superficial pleasantries," advice giving, or ordinary conversation (p. 289).

Contemplation: The Boston Marathon Bombings

By the time of the Boston Marathon bombings in April of our 2011 spring semester class, we had immersed ourselves in Bohm, Freire, and the Buddha's teachings on speech. We had had many in-class practice sessions, and students had continued dialoguing in pairs between classes. In our class several days after the bombings, we jettisoned our syllabus to contemplate this unthinkable tragedy. We began as usual with a 15-minute sitting meditation, in which I invited us to hold in our hearts and minds all of the victims of this tragedy, and all beings whom it touched in some way. The occasion called for a full group contemplation, rather than splitting up into pairs. We were already joined together in mutual shock, dismay, sadness, and confusion.

There was another level of connection—everyone knew someone who was closely involved—a runner who had heard the blasts and narrowly escaped injury. Some students had been present as spectators or knew people who had been near the finish line, where the bombs went off. I know a young policewoman, the daughter of close friends, who was summoned from her regular post in a nearby city to cover the scene in the aftermath of the bombings. She was terrified and texted her parents from the site that she loved them, as if this short message might be her last. We spoke slowly and even more softly than usual, our speech often punctuated by longer silences than usual. One woman, a fifth-grade teacher, said that her practice had helped her find a way to talk about the event with her 10-year-old students. Another woman knew Dzhokhar Tsarnaev personally. He was a high school friend of her son's and had spent a lot of time at her house. He was a sweet and friendly kid, she said. What could possibly have driven him to this heinous act?

And so it went, until our time was up. When I think of the Marathon bombings, this dialogue comes to mind, and I recall the comfort it gave us. Having by chance participated in an insight dialogue session occasioned by such a traumatic event, I see the potential for the practice as a coping strategy for people dealing with trauma in the aftermath of terrible events. Just as insight dialogue can simply emerge out of silence and evoke feelings of deep affection and connection, so it can offer consolation in the worst of times.

Notes on Mirror Neurons, Insight Dialogue, and Interpersonal Neurobiology

Near the end of the semester, I add a contemporary scientific perspective to our consideration of interpersonal mindfulness. We devote a class period to recent findings about our mirror neuron systems, which were newly discovered in the 1990s.

In *The Mindful Brain: Reflection and Attunement in the Cultivation of Well-Being*, UCLA neurobiologist and psychiatrist Daniel Siegel (2005) suggests that meditative awareness of the workings of our own mental processes poises our minds to resonate with the minds of others. In other words, individual meditation practice promotes intrapersonal attunement, which in turn promotes interpersonal attunement. Accordingly, we are neurobiologically equipped to create in our own minds a representation of others' mental states—and actually experience what another person is feeling—through the functioning of our mirror neuron systems. A basic demonstration, which Siegel often offers in workshops, is simply to lift his hand toward his face and ask the participants what comes up for them. "Nothing" is the usual answer, because the gesture is meaningless. Then he picks up a bottle of water, raises it to his mouth, and takes a hearty gulp. People inevitably report feeling thirsty. Siegel's purposeful action elicits the audience's mirror neuron response. The theory holds that the firing of mirror neurons causes us to experience what another is feeling, in this case, thirst. The same holds true for emotions—joy, sadness, and so forth. Notably, the mirror neuron system has been increasingly understood as an essential aspect of the basis for empathy.

The existence of the mirror neuron system suggests that we are hardwired for interpersonal attunement. Students are pleasantly surprised to look at intersubjectivity through an interpersonal neurobiological lens and fascinated to discover that they have these miraculous neurons that are engaged in the process of interpersonal meditation. Imagine the heightened interpersonal resonance that is accessible if we reinforce these natural neural pathways through an interpersonal meditation practice.

Final Thoughts

As Kramer writes, "A well-designed interpersonal meditation, if practiced diligently, could bring about profound transformation in individuals and groups" (p. 106). Indeed, over the semester, students become adept at practicing with the guidelines and often note that these begin to influence their individual practice and their everyday speech. One student, whose voice speaks for many, writes the following about his practice: "I feel like I am gaining an incredible amount of insight about how I listen, communicate, and am present to myself and others. These insights are helping me tremendously in becoming more focused, centered, and attuned to mindful awareness in nearly all aspects of my life" (Kaloyanides, 2012).

Surely deep listening is among the greatest academic skills. Too often, the academy—as Bohm observes about human society in general—privileges "winning" an argument over reflective and connected listening. Perhaps the most profound learning occurs when we listen with the intention of fully receiving what others have to say, committing ourselves to "trying on" their ideas, rather than preparing our counterpoints while half-listening. My hope, borne out by many students' feedback, is that those who immerse themselves in the principles and practice of insight dialogue carry their experience into their other academic pursuits, and into their inner, interpersonal, and professional dialogues.

Each time I've taught the course, I've been impressed by how enthusiastically students undertake the practice, after some initial anxiety (not unlike my own) about sitting face to face with someone they barely know and speaking their heart's truth. Their willingness to drop their guard and be vulnerable in this process shows their hunger—our universal hunger—to be received by another.

One student, an Episcopal chaplain in her 60s, offers this reflection on insight dialogue:

> Freire says that true dialogue is based on trust, love, humility, faith and hope. I find all of these qualities are developing in our dialogues far more rapidly than in most other forms of relationship. The guidelines provide a framework for trust, and I suspect we all participate in this work because of our faith and hope that real dialogue can transform us and by extension, our world. Certainly I find myself humbled by my encounters with my dialogue partners; on the face of it we all seem so

different, and when we talk we discover so much about our common humanity and feelings. I end each dialogue with a growing sense of connections and fondness, if not quite love, for my dialogue partners. (Fowler, 2012)

How different our institutions of higher learning would be if pausing, relaxing, opening, trusting emergence, listening deeply, and speaking the truth were the norm in our classrooms and in our interactions beyond. How much kinder and gentler our planet would be if we could sit together and manifest what Douglas Steere called "a readiness to respect and to stand in wonder and openness before the mysterious life and influence of the other" (p. 9).

Notes

1. The prerequisite "Mindfulness Theory, Practice and Science" for the course under consideration here is the subject of the chapter "Integrating Mindfulness Theory and Practice at Lesley University" (Waring, 2014) in *Contemplative Learning and Inquiry across Disciplines*, the precursor of this volume. Building on the certificate in mindfulness studies I developed at Lesley in 2011, I was able to design a full-scale master's degree in mindfulness studies, which launched in fall 2014.

2. Among other philosophers of dialogue, I gave some thought to Mikhail Bakhtin (1895–1975) and Martin Buber (1878–1965). Buber's ideas are especially suited to the course, and I would like to include Buber in a future iteration. I wished I could come up with a woman theorist, but none came to mind who was a good fit. The compelling performative work of Anna Deavere Smith could be an engaging addition.

3. Often quoted in meditation circles is French philosopher's Blaise Pascal's observation in his *Pensées* that all humanity's problems stem from man's inability to sit quietly in a room alone. One might say that Bohm posits that humanity's problems arise from people's inability to sit in a room together. Consider the negotiations in the Paris Peace Accords in 1973, intended to bring the Vietnam War to an end: negotiations were stalled over disagreement about the shape of the table to be used. The North Vietnamese wanted a circular table, so that all parties would seem to be of equal importance. The South Vietnamese argued for a rectangular table, to represent the two sides of the conflict. The matter was resolved with a compromise involving both round and square tables—two round tables with square tables around them.

4. We could spend a whole semester on right speech, or on the other seven factors—right view, right intention, right action, right livelihood, right effort,

right mindfulness, and right concentration, individually or collectively. Each factor warrants investigation far beyond the scope of this chapter. For a discussion of the factors of the noble eightfold path, see www.accesstoinsight.com.

References

Bohm, D. (2004). *On dialogue*. New York: Routledge.
Freire, P. (1972). *Pedagogy of the oppressed*. New York: Herder and Herder.
Fowler, A. (2012). Unpublished manuscript.
Gunnlaugson, O. (2014). Considerations for a collective leadership: A threefold contemplative curriculum for engaging the intersubjective field of learning. In O. Gunnlaugson, E. Sarath, C. Scott, and H. Bai (Eds.), *Contemplative learning and inquiry across disciplines* (pp. 305–324). Albany: State University of New York Press.
Kaloyanides, I. (2012). Unpublished manuscript.
Kramer, G. (2007). *Insight dialogue: The interpersonal path to freedom*. Boston: Shambhala.
Siegel, Daniel. (2005). *The mindful brain: Reflection and attunement in the cultivation of well-being*. New York: W. W. Norton and Company.
Steere, D. (1955). *Where the words come from*. (1955). London: Friends Home Service.
Waring, N. (2014). Integrating mindfulness theory and practice. In O. Gunnlaugson, E. Sarath, C. Scott, and H. Bai (Eds.), *Contemplative learning and inquiry across disciplines* (pp. 165–182). Albany: State University of New York Press.

3

Intersubjectivity in the Holistic Teaching of the Sociology of Religion at Glendon College in Toronto

VÉRONIQUE TOMASZEWSKI

I believe that teaching is one of the most delightful and exciting of all human activities when it is done well and that it is one of the most humiliating and tedious when it is done poorly.

—Paul Ramsden, *Learning to Teach in Higher Education*

Thanks to you, I am no longer afraid of Islam.

—Student comment in the course
Women and Religion (2014)

To know without direct experience is an illusion.

—Véronique Tomaszewski

With its intrareligious conflicts, its mystical splendors, and peace motifs, religion is approachable from a multidisciplinary perspective: for example, we can approach it to understand and analyze the mediation of religion through culture, as well as through the use of multiple forms of media by religions. Teaching such topics as "Religion and Society," "Women and Religion," "Religion, Media, Culture," "The Sociology of Religion," "Socialization and Personality," as well as "Mythes et Societé" and "Théories de la Société" in courses in French, my teaching in sociology of religion invites students to have insights into these topics by helping them to produce messages that are both relevant and meaningful to their own belief systems. I have taught my courses to about 1,500 students, who have taken courses under my guidance since the late 1990s.

In the year 2000, I replicated what I would call the "Continental European" approach that I had been trained in: read an average of about 100 pages of sociological literature a week, then come to class to discuss the ideas that you either disagree with or need clarification about. I lectured for two-thirds of the three-hour session on the readings, and then opened the discussion. In this classical pedagogy, I addressed the students en masse as "Class" and drew their collective attention to authoritative theorists to know about by reading, researching, and writing essays. Within three years, however, I came to a painful realization that students did not complete their readings, and that the majority of students were unable to summarize the main ideas, let alone discuss the authors' points. In response to the way I treated them as a collective "Class," my students behaved like a herd, remaining collectively silent, avoiding eye contact, and waiting for someone to speak. Invariably, I would take the lead to stimulate students' minds, offering a few insights that were not in my lecture, and make a joke or two, tell an anecdote about the life of the author we were reading, or relay news relating to the topic. The low attendance and lack of participation was frustrating. Students' papers varied in quality and often consisted of paraphrasing, generalizing, and using circular reasoning.

Simultaneously, epistemological questions came to the surface within my first years of teaching about how to engage students both at the macro and the micro levels of sociological inquiry. Can a Christian student deeply understand karma and Hindu tantric beliefs? How will an Ultra-Orthodox Jewish woman read about the celebration of the first menstruations of young indigenous women? Can the teacher help students to sociologically reframe their religious beliefs? How do students experience each other's beliefs and rituals? To which degree do they understand, respect, and tolerate others' faiths?

Something had to be done about my "Continental European" pedagogy, or else, I was going to lose my students: they just didn't seem that interested in what I had to offer, and what to my mind were most fascinating topics in sociology of religion. Help came from my own personal life: I was a meditator and a yoga practitioner, and I decided to integrate what I was learning from mindfulness into sociological pedagogy. Not an easy decision as the two spheres of my life were kept separate. I further decided to experiment with the intersubjective turn that's increasingly becoming part of my yoga and mindfulness studies and practice by taking this turn into my own teaching. A bold move on my part since the intersubjective turn in the field of contemplative studies and practice was still at the beginning stage. In short, I attempted to create a participatory field in my class that genuinely engages students in intersubjective ways of learning and being.

The progressive development of my own contemplative self was helping me to gradually implement an experiential, contemplative, and holistic pedagogy in my class that expanded the possibility for students to develop their sociological imagination in the area of religion. "Holistic" here means building nondual, authentic, intellectual, and intersubjective relationships inside the multicultural, multifaith, multigendered classroom. The crucial means by which such a learning environment was created are ways of mindfulness and experiential pedagogy. It is important to note, however, the result of implementing mindfulness and experiential pedagogy is not an intellectually less-demanding and less-equipped class. Indeed, the contemplative components of my pedagogy actually fortified the cognitive dimension of student learning. "Cognitive" here refers to both the conscious processes involved in acquisition and understanding of knowledge, and the formation of beliefs and attitudes, including intellectual activity, perception, and intuition. Furthermore, cognition must be associated with sensuous and aesthetic appreciation of ways of being and doing (we may call them, rituals) to be truly holistic: in holistic cognition, the body-mind-heart connections are involved.

In the following sections, I go into the details of my pedagogy as it was evolving, both in terms of my own struggle to create an intersubjective contemplative-holistic learning environment and my students' responses to my attempt. As a quick preview, I will say this much for now: students' responses (by email, in assignments, on Moodle forums, in person) brought evidence to the unique strength of intersubjectivity for its nurturing of students' learning about self and others in the world. These findings are paving the way for a shift toward a contemplative approach in sociology of religion, not just in the study of mind and culture.[1]

Struggle and Growing Conviction

Within my sociological self, a disconnection had manifested between the Cartesian supremacist view of intellectual truth (as I experienced it in the academic environment where my mind was challenged) and the holistic realizations brought about by my personal mindfulness and yoga practices. The tension from this disconnection grew in my consciousness to the point that I had to resolve it before it might break me apart. The inattentive atmosphere in class, the distracted gaze of some students, and their passive attitudes all clashed against my own level of engagement, and heightened awareness of the potentiality of the present moment progressively vanished. This work of resolving tension and restoring my pedagogic engagement took place through my careful reworking of the course materials and methods, week after week, and systematically shifting from lecturing to activities, as soon as I saw that students were losing their attention.

It became clear that what motivated me—and the students—was an authentic encounter with each other and with the authors we read and discussed, an alive and renewed quest for knowledge and understanding of themselves as much as of religion. The visits that I invited of students to my office put me in touch, beyond my students' intellectual tastes and preoccupations, with their personalities and struggles, with their embodiment as sentient beings mobilizing all their resources to learn. I felt reinvigorated in my growing conviction that my new ways of engaging with students were pedagogically genuine and sound. As synchronicity would have it, my conviction was validated by another cultural sociologist with a similar trajectory along the path of loving-kindness: bell hooks. When bell hooks came to Toronto in 2004 to talk about "Love: Connecting Self and Community," she answered positively my question about the influence of her Buddhist spirituality in her academic work. My conviction strengthened the minute that bell hooks and I looked at each other and shared the purpose of our life: to love more and better. This moment established my academic turn toward intersubjectivity.[2]

Martin Buber's philosophy of intersubjectivity with an injunction to make the secular sacred also profoundly expanded my grasp of our purpose in teaching. Indeed, each encounter with a student is the meeting of two personalities that bond in the space and time of the teaching act. This relation between student and teacher establishes reciprocity and a moral obligation of serving each other with respect and with kindness. By providing conceptual and methodological tools (e.g., forum discussions, audiovisual documents, quizzes, and group activities such as field trips and presentations), I was able to support students to learn about obscure relations of power and social problems that require improvement in experiential, dialogic, and embodied ways. "Since society is a historical object of research," I explain to my students, "you are part of the historical making of new areas of sociological inquiry, bringing preoccupations and interests from your own generation. I invite you to go inside of you, to examine your lives, to pull out what your sociological interests are in this life. Because while *we* experience something, *you are* in relation with one another and weave the very fabric of our social reality."

Giving a balance of diversely engaging assignments for each course (not just read and write quizzes, tests, and essays, and do case study analyses) encourages a plurality of modes of reasoning, formats of delivery, and constellations of knowledge within the larger frame of experiential education. Students explore different layers of meaning construction and social, religious representation according to their learning styles and preferences. The use of audiovisual material during lectures, PowerPoint or Prezi, including a video as a midterm project, allows inclusivity for students to display their auditory and visual excellence in learning while respecting different learning styles. For the kinesthetic ones (students who learn by doing and touching), field trips, in-class presentations, participation at public events, and, more recently, video presentations, offer the possibility to strive at analyzing religion as a multidimensional phenomenon (where beliefs, mediatized culture, and technology intersect). For instance, over the years, I noticed that male students tend to write less than their female colleagues on average. I would give my class options to write less and additionally or alternatively produce media works, for example, making videos. S. L. J., a student in my Religion and International Society class, detailed her evaluation of the course to include the impact of the pedagogy on her and on the class:

> Aside from addressing the main issue she is always ready to have a conversation about how anything from a newspaper article to how a new musical fusion group relates to the themes of her courses. Moreover, she is adept at integrating a combination of audio-visual presentations, student presentations, discussion, and classical lecturing into her teaching style in order to create the most effective package for immersing her classroom in the course material.

I started to use the second-person plural in class, instead of my old habit of addressing with an impersonal "Class!" to address students groups or the whole class: "This course is yours," I explain on the first day. "It is designed to empower you, to allow you to find your voice among these sociological discourses that we are going to study together. You are the course and you will give to it this year its uniqueness." Since there are many modes, the I-You moment of copresence works between students-as-tourists, between students-as-sociologists, between me-the-instructor and the-student-presenting, and between myself and other students. The 15-minute presentations often become 25 minutes of deep engagement through questions and answers with each other. For the class engagement to be authentic, there cannot be any repetitive routine or preset rules that crush creativity. S. L. J. added:

> Diversity and differences of opinion are viewed as welcome opportunities for discussion, sharing, reflection, and learning. It is this context that makes the classroom an inviting and dynamic place to be—to the extent that students were genuinely pleased to be there and would go beyond ordinary efforts to attend.

Multifaceted Contemplative-Intersubjective-Holistic Learning in Sociology

Higher order cognitive skills such as critical thinking (synthesis of ideas, reflection from one's life experience and integrity) are achieved within the contemplative approach since the intersubjective field naturally reveals the distance that exists between an individual's attitudes and the threads of feelings that weave the person's consciousness; this distance is as open and contingent in its potentiality as open space-and-time continuum. As such, the learning outcomes in my experiential courses are not just about sociological knowledge (theories and concepts) concerning religion. Much work takes place in the affective domain. Students receive and respond to others' definitions and notice, according to their sensitive listening, discrepancies between espoused beliefs and underlying messages that are communicated, and they engage in constructive challenge, open discussion, and teamwork, to work through the subtler interpersonal and intrapersonal emotional conflicts. To this linguistic context are linked self and interpersonal nonverbal awareness of one's spirituality and calibration of the latter through group process, students' presentations, and field trips. They touch upon charisma and personality, persistence, initiative, determination, leadership, and attitude. All skills are geared toward thinking outside the academic box and dogma, and inside one's contemplative space of conscious awareness. It requires the teacher's awakening to respond to the student's authentic voice that comes as an inner call to witness faith. The latter comes through writing-in-the-moment as truth about one's existence. I mirror what the student says and encourage more dialogue, as well as more inner dialogue, by giving value to the student's testimony.

How will I help them reflect deeply upon their beliefs, to be able to sociologically reframe those beliefs and strengthen their rational arguments to facilitate their experience of others' beliefs and their understanding, and to respect and tolerate others' faiths? When I design assignments and lecture contents, I consider both individual and collective parameters of my students. I want my students to be able to identify with at least one of the theories we are handling in the class. In handling the class materials, I am constantly mediating between students and sociological texts, between social issues and the real world of politics and economics; and between mediatized culture and religious beliefs (including beliefs in an afterlife). My role is to foster an effective relationship between their lived social life and written social thought for my students to experience. Getting students to conceptualize "social aesthetics" (the field of embodied social representations), for instance, is a challenge that lasts for months as students work on presentations and delve into a direct encounter with sense perception via their own cognitive mechanism. Knowing not only sociological texts but also my students well is essential to bring them closer by combining language and sociological imagination.

I introduce the contemplative practice of following the breath to students to facilitate the intense integrative work required in my course. To facilitate the multilayered transmission of knowledge, the contemplative approach offers self-reflections about not only the process of learning but also the meanings and the elements of knowledge themselves in their historicity. For example, I situate Émile Durkheim in his French, homogeneous society at the turn of the 20th century when I present his dichotomy of sacred and profane, and his social solidarity model of religious functionality. A slowing down is necessary to absorb and to reflect upon one's awareness of the process of taking in thoughts and perspectives in the here and now of Canadian society. This slowing down approach proves successful. I smiled when some of my students affectionately called the founder of sociology "Emilie."

The time necessary for contemplation expands outside the classroom into the Moodle course website forums and journals. Together, we write our common history by focusing on the present moment, which is the basis of the mindfulness practice. For instance, we suspended our scheduled coursework topic when the Paris attacks of November 13, 2015, took place. We shared news articles, online social media posts, images, and videos of different media coverage in different countries, including Al Jazeera. We posted our own reactions on our Moodle space online, sharing and commenting about our choice of a particular article and how it fits with our reading of Edward Said's *Orientalism*. In class, a heated debate between Christian and Muslim students forced some to take defensive positions, and the whole class helped deflate the tension. This distinctive moment in Religion, Media, Culture brought to the surface a relational context that needs to be explored for a deeper learning about the role of religion in our very classroom and in society. Its cultural substance was instantaneously experienced through our shared loss of innocence in Paris. All twenty-five students participated in the second-person mode I-You. I monitored to allow all voices, including the shaking ones, to be heard and felt. After arguments had been uncovered, we proceeded to ordering them, describing a hermeneutic circle: mine is a Christian perspective about fundamentalist Muslims. Yours is a moderate Muslim perspective that condemns killing innocents, not Islam. Ours is the contemplation of the connection between us as learners who do not know the Quran, but whose intelligence collectively surpasses individual understanding and whose sense of well-being needs consolidation through solidarity. As a moderator, I reflected about the group consciousness emerging back and forth in the You/yours/our modes of integration of various comments and perspectives of perceived feelings of anger, resentment, and fear. The tension lessened within two hours. We took a break and experienced calm abiding when we returned, even though I noticed difficulty in establishing eye contact between some of the most vocal students. However, we could feel some healing energy circulating among us, as the students had closed their laptops and put their phones away, breathing quietly in their well-grounded physical bodies, gratefully enjoying the life force circulating between each other.

Active strategies engage the dynamic personality of each student by allowing them to single out news of great importance, as in Religion, Media, Culture, where students' participation is graded according to the frequency of weekly comments posted on the Moodle course forum dedicated to weekly news. By responding to each other's posts, students develop a stronger sense of belonging to the class. Every student is important, even the shy ones who seldom say anything in class, or the physically disabled ones who do not come on a regular basis. Their sense of mastery, of competence, comes from media content analysis and from learning concepts. Experiencing independence in their choice of news, they are uncensored as long as there is no hate speech or depreciation of another student's faith. My students all have shown a spirit of generosity and true compassion. The same course also encourages increased communication. In the process, I add listening skills—a necessity to deflate tensions arising when we cling to words and concepts instead of opening up to experiencing the speaker's engagement.

In Religion and Society, the most multi-faith class that I teach, conflict resolution through deep listening is necessary. Once, I prevented a fight between a Muslim and a Protestant who felt threatened by the Muslim student's finger pointing and shouting in the name of his God during his presentation. Tension had increased to a level of intolerance and a few students left. I called a break. When class resumed, we sorted out differences using a restorative circle technique. I had volunteers taking turns to listen to each other's discomfort and hurt. One student took the lead to call on a few other students to express concerns. We practiced in class: hearing (breaking down the flow, recognizing intonation and clues to decode and interpret attitudes), understanding (figurative and nonfigurative), and responding (reacting, participating) from one's heart to center attention back in an integrative and holistic manner. Reconciliation preserved the integrity of the class, and we finished the term feeling more assertive and yet more open.

In my class, students conduct participant-observation to observe how gender, experience, rituals, and beliefs are reified as "social aesthetic formations," in the sense that they manifest the cognitive aspects of religious life. What my students get to see is this: that these formations are experienced through the senses (religious music, statues, calligraphies, icons, smells and tastes, etc.), and they produce feelings of awe, gratitude, and so on in the participants, which in turn become the experience of meaning that participants find in religious texts and other rituals. These experiences, as the result of early exposure to religious events, often leave lasting psychological traces important in determining levels of religiosity of cult or sect members and rates of conversion to other faiths. As a matter of fact, my students testify in class that their field trip reinforces their own faith, or their atheism, and awakens critical thinking. None are left indifferent to field trip experience, as attested by hundreds of student feedback responses.

"This course," I warn new students, "is not meant to make you question your religious beliefs. We are not here to prove that God exists or does not exist. It is designed to study theories that make you reflect upon your own beliefs so that you remain authentic. If anything, it will make you stronger in your faith, be it in a God or in scientific truth." I am profoundly motivated to facilitate in my students a deep experience of true volition through my contemplative, intersubjective methodology. My own grasp of sociological phenomena is enhanced through Eastern philosophical and contemplative means that, in my view and experience, surpass even phenomenological methods focused on "situation." Starting from the realization that students, as all sentient beings, interpret what they sense, they become, through my teaching, aware of four sources of cognition, four ways of knowing, beyond the direct one contingent upon their sense organs (e.g., seeing a statue, hearing the call to prayer, etc.). There is also a mental registration, for instance, a concurrent sense consciousness (that may say: Islam, Hinduism, love, etc.). In the same way that they are aware of their breathing when they settle in class, during their field trips, I encourage my students to become more mindful through breathing deeply when they listen and record how their mind processes what they experience. Of course, the highest level of cognition would be yogic: direct, nondual realization of the true nature of things, an inward wisdom where gaps between thoughts are experienced. But for the purpose of our course, we want ourselves to be more connected to our cognitive processes and observe if there are any prejudices toward other religions, judgments about religious symbols, and so forth, in order to identify them as such: thoughts, mental energy, and currents that can be let go of without grasping, if we choose to.

So how do my students construct and deconstruct meaning, which would give depth to their field trip experiences? My short answer is: through intersubjective-contemplative experiences. My students are encouraged, through active participation and affective involvement, to connect to their authentic self, to be true to their beliefs, and yet to develop the critical thinker in them through the exercise of comparison, rejection, and questioning, all the while mindfully engaging with each other. Back in the classroom, unique interactions allow students to situate their observations emotionally by collaboratively connecting to other group members' remarks and by cognitively constructing the narrative of the presentation, its text and its visuals, in front of the class. Scheduled for two full sessions, students' in-class presentations may overlap onto a third week, in which case other readings and commentaries integrate our online forum. The priority given to the experiential and the contemplative, at the slower pace of human effectiveness, successfully fights the fragmented, materialistic, and quantified, often rushed, approach to knowledge in the West. Later, in the office, face-to-face encounters with each student to give feedback to students on their in-class work seals the affirmative quality of the discussion.

Holistic Pedagogy Fosters Equanimity and Raises Group Self-Awareness

Every class has a group identity that inhabits the learning space in its own specific way. Group self-awareness is enhanced when the classroom is small, and students are encouraged to engage in eye contact and to move around. In large classrooms, some students sneak in and sit at the back, away from everyone else's gaze, which makes it challenging to create the kind of learning space conducive to raising self-awareness. The quality of relationships within the group is related to the quality of the learning space. Even arrangements of tables and chairs contribute to this quality. Ever mindful of how I may affect the quality of the learning space, I create a learning environment like course forums wherein students write emails and postings to share and comment with others, structuring religious meanings and their connotations in harmony with their own consciousness. Consistent with a contemplative epistemology, these exercises allow focusing on what is meaningful for the group without any expectation, such as establishing oneself as an expert. These exercises are potent in dissolving boundaries among students.

While holistic pedagogy is about facilitating mind-body-heart connections in each student within the safe container provided by the teacher, it also favors intersubjective contemplative copresencing among group members during group work that nurtures tolerance of differences and compassion toward each other. I ask my students to form groups of two to five who live near each other or are interested in focusing on the same religion. In the case of students with learning disabilities, I invite them to form a group of their own (still the maximum size is five). These students typically cannot work with others, for their own sense of group awareness is paralyzing to them, and often they are unable to present in front of the whole class. In that case, they present their research privately to me in my office.

Group self-awareness enables students to work on resilience for group members by helping each other overcome difficult situations. In this way, week after week, the class grows a sense of meaning-making.

Collaboration in class becomes a skill to bring into life, helping them to hone their sense of personal leadership. Dealing with religion heightens potential tensions between group members. For instance, when one very religious student tried to impose her unconditional views about her religion on other students, while other group members adopted a more critical view, tension mounted. Using a variety of theories also creates some friction, as students have preferences for one theorist over another. Marxist students, for instance, rarely have patience for Muslim students displaying a high level of religiosity through their clothes or speech, so they tend to target them in their choice of topic for presentation. I meet groups in my office and mediate differences by applying the same intersubjective contemplative approach that I have in class. This time, within the confines of my office space, sitting closer together, our minds, bodies, and hearts listen and feel each other more intimately. Applying leadership skills from the Social Change Model to balance individual sensitivities, I use deep listening first to welcome each student expressing difficulties at finding a balance within the group. I turn toward other group members to hear their personal account about either a relational difficulty in the group or about a way to conduct their field trip, and we go around the group in this manner. Then, as an agent of change, I allow each member to reflect upon what another student has expressed, and to offer an opinion or a solution or just a comment. This mini-session reflects the core of my teaching philosophy: intersubjectively contemplative, inclusive, yet individualized pedagogy. It reflects how students can engage themselves as leaders first by developing an awareness of self, by getting in touch with their integrity and congruity, and then by bringing that inner power out to contribute equally to the group wisdom, insights, and actions.

Beyond the classroom, I offer workshops that aim to refine the experiential approach and deepen our knowledge and understanding of college students. During the wellness week, a workshop introduces Glendon students to nonviolent communication through mindfulness-based breathing exercises including body scan. From there, they practice efficient verbal and nonverbal communication skills that encourage self-expression as well as collaboration. This hands-on approach to students' leadership brings students to the course material through mindfulness exercises. They are introduced to the "individual values" module of the Leadership Model for Social Change developed for college students by National Clearinghouse for Leadership Programs. This material, which cultivates consciousness of self, congruence and commitment, is integrated not only theoretically but also concretely by following a three-week program in class and at home. Students are encouraged to connect to their inner self and to their fundamental intelligence and innate sense of leadership.

The body and mind connection dissolves the need to convince others of the superiority or inferiority of one's beliefs. Awakening to equanimity expands the awareness of the interconnectedness and the interdependence of each other's practicing embodied sociology and gradually covering the common grounds of empirical work. In this vast array of theories lie different levels of religiosity—from the ultra-fundamentalists, to radicals and conservatives, to the ultra-liberals, to the agnostics and nonreligious. "What is the religious mind after all?" I ask students? "Can you be religious, but not spiritual? Can you be spiritual while not belonging to any religion?"

Holistic Pedagogy Increases Mindfulness of the Teacher-Student Copresence

> We may do something together. You may write to me. You may think of writing to me. And there are other ways. There are many modes of I-You.
>
> —Martin Buber, *I and Thou*

Each class begins with an awakening to one's surroundings and state of mind. I ask my students to take a few moments to settle into their seat and into the classroom, and to become aware of the environment: the small writing tablet, the white and aseptic boldness of the walls in the new building that saturates our senses, the boxing effect of an underground classroom with no windows in the basement of the building. I ask them as well to connect to their bodily sensations: that of their elbow on the small tablet, their back rounded to fit the chair, and any tension in their body, by focusing on their breath: "Are you breathing fully now?" When I sense that the class is agitated and poorly concentrated, I invite them to take a deep breath to connect their mind to their body, gently, with no judgment, welcoming and accepting sensations and thoughts and letting them go. In some circumstances, I ask students to get up and stretch their arms above their heads while breathing. At the end of a long day, I notice how crouched students are, unable to support their back up straight, distracted by their cellular phone or by classmates with whom they engage in chatting. On many occasions, students who know that I meditate ask that I conduct a short breathing meditation session. Each year, at least one student emails me or tells me in person at the end of the school year that they started meditating on their own more regularly at home and that it has made a significant difference in their life. It has lowered their level of anxiety or depression, or stress. These testimonies have confirmed that the "copresencing" (the power of *you* or the Buberian I-Thou; Buber, 1970) of interaction that happens when we all breath and experience our presence with each other in the classroom is essential to nurturing a deep learning experience and a long-lasting empowerment of the students who achieve well when they live well their experience as student and as being.

In the Women and Religion class, the premise is that women have been discriminated against, marginalized, and mistreated, or even killed, in the name of religious dogma, with the exception of traditionally matriarchal cultures such as Wicca and (Neo) Paganism, and other indigenous traditions. After opening up the socially constructed category of "women," we realize that women continue to observe religious rituals and traditions that perpetuate their own discrimination and often implicitly or openly define a creator, a god, a supernatural entity as male, masculine, and omnipotent. Understanding why women promote, renew, and pass on misogynist religious practices (some being as harsh as genital mutilation, or sati—widow sacrifice) to their daughters is the main concern of our Women and Religion course. I challenge students to answer the question: Why do women in those religious traditions accept discrimination and often physical punishment? I invite students to experience the relationship between micro and macro dimensions of religion by reenacting rituals in class, using foods, incense, candles, dance, meditation, chanting, listening to songs, and watching audiovisual material. Women and Religion is the most experiential of all classes and integrates a feminist, experiential methodology using female spiritual and religious, historical and contemporary figures and a living embodiment of beliefs through in-class experiments. Students bring family and personal objects of worship and pass them around to share their faith. In 2012, students organized a Muslim headscarves fashion show, inviting students to learn the Muslim prayer. In 2013, a student displayed esoteric art works by her Neo-Pagan sister. In 2014, students improvised a play with dialogue between Confucius, Buddha, and Lao Tzu. For a 2015 presentation on girls' genital mutilation, a group of students baked "pussy cupcakes" as they called them, with bright pink icing in the shape of labia on the top. Most students ate one without a shiver. Another presentation took place by the Don River down below the main buildings of Glendon, where we burned sage leaves and chanted an indigenous hymn to the spirit of the river. Forming a group, holding hands, and practicing deep breathing all helped us to connect and regain a sense of collective wisdom and "ontological security" (Giddens, 1991). In the deepening of the awakened moments of shared wisdom, each student's vulnerability and resilience is experienced with humility and emotion. The ongoing case of murdered and missing aboriginal women studied in our 2016 class crystalized great intensity of purpose and solidarity among students, producing over 100 posts on our forum and an ongoing follow-up in class led by aboriginal female students.

Conclusion: Possibilities of Development of an Intersubjective-Contemplative-Holistic Approach to Sociology

This essay has demonstrated that students benefit from a contemplative-holistic approach as it allows them to articulate the depth of the cognitive dimension of religion together with sociological theory. I am aware that in this chapter, only the teacher's perspective has been presented. Going forward, the next step of research I would like to conduct, for example, is a synthesis of students' analysis of Tsarnaev, the "Boston Bomber," a 19-year-old American Chechen who chose his brother's path of violent radicalization to protest against injustice. In their papers, Canadian students moved away from religious extremism, indicating the extent to which their intersubjective experience is rooted in the dissolution of the dichotomy between subject and object, between teacher and student, between theory and empirical work, and is grounded in a deep existential truth about the preciousness of being human. As such, the experiment pushed the boundaries of what "intersubjectivity" means by encouraging students to become more aware and mindful, moment by moment, of their modes of cognition and ways of relating to others, using conscious breaths.

My pedagogy inscribes itself within the larger frame of program thinking concerning an integrated curriculum and education of the whole person (body, mind, heart, and earth) that may contribute to the emancipation of students and to keeping them away from radicalization. I am conscious of my teacher role as a mediator between a student and the sociological or social empirical "text" that calls for decoding and interpretation. As a teacher, one educates with all one's heart, focusing on wisdom and compassion. I am inspired in that respect by Jack Miller, bell hooks, and Robert Hattam.[3] Teaching requires flexibility, both in terms of awakened presence to the energy in the classroom as well as in terms of timing and planning activities. For example, after the Paris massacre in November 2015, I changed the lecture topic to focus on this tragedy, as I had done in January 2015 for the *Charlie Hebdo* cartoons, and prior to these, for the question of religious symbols in Québec, and the exodus toward Syria of Canadian jihadists. We need to be open to the rhythm in our teaching. Our intuition as teachers is a hermeneutic requirement in that it requires us to remain authentic on our path to awakening. Being on this path humbles our teaching. It encourages conversations and creative shifts that help to integrate thinking with being and to transcend solely intellectual cognition. It helps us to experience impermanence and change, reconciliation and forgiveness, as core dimensions of an ethical and sociologically relevant paradigm.

The richness of the multicultural and multi-faith cohorts at York University is a blessing in many ways. Rabindranath Tagore emphasized that an atmosphere of naturalness in our relationship with one another and a spirit of hospitality are what make civilization and education possible. By expanding on the importance of our senses with our mind and intellect, students are invited to see each other as equal in the experience of interconnectedness with all elements constitutive of the class, the college, and the city (and beyond these, the world). This ethical dimension is essential to my social engagement as a teacher and as a sentient being, eager to contribute to a culture of peace, social justice, equanimity, and inclusion in my classroom that is a miniature League of Nations at Glendon. My holistic, secular approach further trained in mindfulness is now the gift of a purposeful life. But even better is how astonishing the results have been. The intersubjective nature of the individualized relationship with each and every student, as well as among students, raises the overall grade averages of these full classes.

At the praxis level, this chapter presented class situations exemplifying possibilities of human development and transformation involved in contemplative-intersubjective modes of learning and being both for students and their teacher—me. It showed that the contemplative-intersubjective approach to experiential, holistic, sociology enriches contextualization of key issues in the field of religion and sustains its micro and macro phenomena. What are the possibilities and promises of the contemplative-intersubjective approaches in higher education, hence, beyond sociology? At the ontological level, intersubjectivity is conducive to creating the vibrant quality of social and interpersonal interactions that make up cultural identity in its historical and embodied unfolding. Intersubjectivity in a class that uses a contemplative approach is about the significance of one's beliefs and practices, not just of social or political dimensions. Genuine compassion, detachment from results, and mindfulness are qualities that we need to cultivate to invite each other to open up and reveal our unique beauty. At the hermeneutic level, "intersubjectivity" is the reflexive process by which students confirm their intuitions and deeply think about themselves as social actors and witnesses. The resulting cognitive, ethical, and aesthetic process constantly mirrors students' individual sense of self and their subjective realm of meaning formation. Transforming and developing one student and one teacher at a time, the I–You paradigm is truly a core step toward a culture of inner and outer peace.

Notes

1. See how the field is sketched out in Cerulo (2002).
2. Fueled by the growth of the contemplative field in higher education across North America, my connection with mindfulness-based education trends (Mindful Schools, Naropa University, Emory Contemplative Studies at Emory University, and Jon Kabat-Zinn's MBSR program) deepened. I sat on the board of Nalanda College in Toronto with Jack Miller at OISE, who is a pioneer in meditation and experiential learning to encourage social engagement and self-understanding.
3. With Dr. Robert Hattam (from Melbourne University), we proposed that meditation practices be read as "technologies of self" (Foucault) that deconstruct a reified self, enabling the development of an altruistic mind as a basis for living an ethico-political life.

References

Buber, Martin. (1970). *I and thou*. New York: Charles Scribner's Sons.
Cerulo, K. A. (2002). *Culture in mind: Toward a sociology of culture and cognition*. New York: Routledge.
Giddens, A. (1991). *Modernity and self-identity: Self and society in the late modern age*. Stanford: Stanford University Press.

4

Being with Horses as a Practice of the Self-with-Others

A Case of Getting a FEEL for Teaching

STEPHEN J. SMITH AND KAREN LaROCHELLE

The mirror image looms large in so much of the developmental, counseling, and psychotherapeutic literatures on *being-with* horses (see Freewin & Gardiner, 2005; Hallberg, 2008). Equine-facilitated, equine-enhanced, equine-guided practices of self-care in which the horse appears as a reflection of individuated consciousness are promoted. Horse "partners" are seen as "teachers," "wise ones," and "co-counselors" whose "genuineness, unconditional positive regard and empathy" are considered to be aspects of their "innate nature" (Healing Hooves, 2015). The prescribed practices of self-care appear to be based on qualities projected onto horses that are, in turn, reflected back in images of self-affirmation. As a result, these practices, while ostensibly about healing and personal growth, may yet fall short of sustaining, caring practices of the self-with-others.

An arrested "mirror stage" (Lacan, 1968) encapsulation of the developmental, counseling, and psychotherapeutic uses of horses risks taking mimetic resonances for narrowly circumscribed individual gain (Kelly, 2014), belying a multiplicity of attunements with these and other sentient beings across species lines (Abram, 2010). The ocular imagery of self-reflection valorizes human identity and makes individual agency tellingly real at the expense of the activities of "interbeing" (Hahn, 2001, p. 111), which are not just laudable "interactions" with other beings (Gendlin, 1966), but rather, motile "correspondences" (Ingold, 2000,

p. 199; 2013, pp. 105–108) of "becoming-other" (Deleuze & Guattari, 1987). Rather than a simple mirroring of human feelings, emotions, thoughts and actions, human-horse encounters can be described as an interplay or *interbeing*, which, in the moment, dissolves the boundaries of human and horse identities.

Vietnamese Buddhist teacher Thich Nhat Hanh (2009) writes in *You Are Here*: "Look into yourself and you will see that you are not a separate entity. Your ancestors are present in you, as well as your children and grandchildren. Not only is the past here in the form of the present; the future is here, too" (p. 110). In Buddhist traditions, *interbeing* is defined as interconnectedness and interdependence, which are established by embracing selflessness (or the absence of the ego), as well as impermanence (or the ephemeral nature of all things). This interconnectedness and interdependence is captured nicely by Hanh (2009): "'Interbeing' is a much better verb than 'being,' because I am in you and you are in me" (pp. 111–112). David Abram (1996), in his earlier book *The Spell of the Sensuous*, elaborates on this interpenetrative quality of mindfulness such that the self exists "inside of, along with the other animals and the plants, the mountains and the clouds" (p. 226). Such mindfulness involves "fully seeing, hearing, feeling what meets our senses immediately, that is, unmediated, in the moment" and as an "existential vivacity" (Bai & Scott, 2009, p. 142). When we come fully to our senses, we participate in Nature, we immerse ourselves in its "existential vivacity." No longer separate from it, we are simply in it, part of the energies, materialities, and formations of Nature. We thus break down speciesist categories, hierarchies, and notions of dominance over Nature, finding an affinity with other human beings, other animal beings, in belonging together on this Earth.

There is, furthermore, a "transpecific conviviality" (Acampora, 2006, pp. 30, 93) to being with "companion species" such as horses (Haraway, 2003, 2008) whereby one finds self-care, and sometimes self-preservation, to be intrinsically tied to care of the other. The phenomenology of this extended, intersubjective care may well be cast as "kinesthetic empathy" (Shapiro, 1990) or "coenesthetic connection" (Smith, 2015b) through the cultivation of a bodily reflective consciousness. Yet here again the fuller registration of somatically felt "reciprocity" and "chiasmic" communion (Merleau-Ponty, 1968; 2003) with other-than-human lives, and horses in particular (Smith, 2011, 2014a, 2015a, 2015b), so easily becomes frozen in the mirroring of reflective human selves.

The central challenge we address in this chapter concerns the use of horses in cultivating, more than a subjectivist self-recognition, an "intersubjective contemplative practice" (Gunnlaugson, Sarath, Scott, & Bai,

2014) that, in turn, has direct applicability to the practices of teaching children, youth, and adult human beings. We turn away from anthropomorphic projections and mirrored selfhood to ask: Can the professional development aspirations of "facilitated equine-enhanced learning" (FEEL) and similar equine-guided and enhanced programs realize a somatic practice of being with other-than-human beings that is transposable in its postural, positional, gestural, expressive, and complexional dimensions to various "agogical" practices of "vital contact" (Smith, 2014b) and more specifically to pedagogical practices with children and youth and andragogical practices with adults (Smith, 1998, 2004; van Manen, 1991, 2012)? In other words, can a "pasture pedagogy" (Tom & Katz, 2013) deeply inform the practice of teaching within schools and university classrooms?

We address this question through the narrated experiences of FEEL sessions conducted for teacher educators at the authors' home institution. The sessions involved master teachers seconded to the university to deliver the preservice teacher education program. These sessions were offered over the course of the academic year as part of the professional development days for these "Faculty Associates" working with the suite of teacher education programs (see Smith, 2004; Smith & Wahl, 2010). The daylong sessions involved initial observation of horse behavior, partnered somatic exercises with one another, and guided exercises of connecting with and leading horses. The goals of the session were for participants to experience ways of relating to horses that shed light on themselves, their personal and professional relationships, and their work with student teachers. More specifically, our learning objectives were to have participants observe the postural, positional, gestural, and expressive features of horse-to-horse interaction; utilize certain of these stances and movements in trainer-guided exercises of human-to-horse communication; feel through these exercises the interplay of energy in sustaining human-*with*-horse connections; and relate these observed and felt dynamics to teaching children, youth, and adults.

The purpose of this chapter is to chart a practical path of being-with others by attending to particular moods, manners, and modes of intercorporeal connection with horses. Through attending to the narrated experiences of two workshop participants, one of whom wrote subsequently of his experience in a doctoral dissertation, and the second of whom is the coauthor of this chapter, we offer exemplification of the "vitality affects" (Stern, 2010) and "kinetic-kinesthetic-affective dynamics" (Sheets-Johnstone, 2011) of relational attunement with horses and, by extension, other animate beings. Such relational attunement dynamics and the contexts of meaning-making, whether they be pastures, playgrounds, or school classrooms, provide hints of a pedagogy that is sensed, felt, and intuited in the daily practices of living, playing, working, or simply being with others.

Joining Up

One of the most well-known horse trainers and clinicians, Monty Roberts, presents to audiences and readers a process of "join-up" that involves bringing an untrained horse to accept the leadership of a human on the ground and, in turn, in the saddle (Roberts, 1997, 2001). This practice of "join-up" is based on long and careful study of horse herd dynamics and mimicking the behavior of a lead mare in response to a horse brought into a round pen for "gentling." Variations of this process are practiced by the majority of horse trainers and clinicians, although not without some contentiousness. We need not go into the nuances of such approaches (see Smith, 2011, 2014a, 2015a, 2015b) since a task posed of the participants at a FEEL session was to find a way of joining up with horses roaming freely in a two-acre paddock and without the benefit of any ethnological wisdom. Don Nelson (2010) described his "joining up" experience in the following way.

> Even though I am not a person drawn to horses, one professional development day I signed up for a workshop involving interacting with those large strong animals. I had never wondered how a human could go out into a field and 'get' a larger, faster, stronger animal or how this 'getting' involved a joining up. I'd not ridden horses, studied them, nor felt moved to do so. Yet I felt moved to take an opportunity to see horse-guided leadership in action, and [had] been surprised to volunteer to actively participate. I'd seen the trainers release the horses into the big paddock. One was brown and the other dark greyish or something like that. I realize that by describing them as those colors I reveal how little I know about horses. The brown horse would probably be called 'chestnut' and the dark greyish might even be called 'brown' or 'bay' or 'black and tan.'
>
> I'd seen the horses set free in the big paddock and, compared to the three in the little paddock in front of me, they seemed much more to enjoy their freedom—if charging

around the place and kicking up their heels was any indication. They seemed full of energy and sunshine and the cool breeze that reminded them it was just spring, and from a distance all the racing around and energy seemed joyous and very impressive of their speed and strength. (pp. 12–13)

Don and the participants in the prior FEEL exercise had one-by-one singled out a horse amid a small herd in an adjoining paddock and practiced moving with that particular horse, directing it though clear body postures and signaling gestures. Now the participants were invited to "catch" some young horses in the very large arena. Don accepted this invitation, although not without a certain hesitation.

Their size and strength was the reason I hesitated. After the group had moved up from the small, lower paddock with its calm horses, when the trainers asked, "Anyone want to catch one of these?" I had the impression that we, a group of educational leaders, all at least inwardly took a big step back—but that may have just been me. Somewhere on the way out to the farm I had decided that I was going to use this day to make a big attempt, but the moment had arrived and I was stepping back before I stepped forward.

"You'll both be with me, right?" I asked the trainers, and now I was stepping forward. (p. 13)

Each participant in this exercise was accompanied by a trainer who provided commentary on the horses' stances, postures, ear and eye expressions as the basis of instruction on how to approach them. The trainer followed close behind Don as he used the "flagging" technique from the previous exercise to move the chestnut horse he had in his sights out of the corner of the paddock. Don then dropped his arms, softened his own posture, and began receiving the horse's movement intentions. When the chestnut mare stiffened in readiness to take off, Don retreated, creating space for the horse to relax, stretching her head to the ground. The mare no longer turned away. She moved cautiously along the fence line and Don moved with her. She stopped, and Don stopped. Slowly, surely, carefully, the space between them lessened.

Later the group outside the fence would describe this as a dance—step, step, wait—step, step, wait. It was a dance set to the music of the chestnut's curiosity, interest, and trust. Music played through its body slowly turning more and more towards me, the head turning towards and away, and eventually just its eyes on me and then shifting even the slightest bit away.

"Raise your hand, palm up. Make a noise with your hand. Wait. Do it again. Take half a step forward. Wait." And then the soft, fuzzy, muzzle of the chestnut was investigating my hand, touching and breathing softly.

I didn't know where those last instructions came from. It seemed like the trainer's quiet voice was right in the back of my head. When the horse nuzzled my hand, the tone shifted slightly and relaxed, "Now, reach up with your other hand and take the side of the halter. Take the rope and clip it on." Then, after a pause, "Now, lead her back."

And I did, my heart wonderfully full and in an amazed state that just registered that the horse was following my lead, that huge head with its deep brown eyes just at my shoulder. She would stop when I stopped and wait as the group talked, and then come back with me as, with further amazement, I led her into the barn and her stall and turned her in that little space before unclipping and saying goodbye. (Nelson, 2010, pp. 14–15)

We might say that Don "mirrored" the mare's motions. He discovered, beyond the formulaic steps of "advance and retreat," "eyes on eyes," "squaring the shoulders," and so on (Roberts, 2001, pp. 14, 37, 41–43), a feeling for the horse. Joining up with this chestnut mare became a matter of not forcing a connection but letting it come.

Finding a Connection

We turn now to Karen's experience in the prior exercise, which involved the herd of horses in the small paddock. Her experience is founded on much greater familiarity with horses as a rider and someone who remembers fondly the company of horses as a child. The following reflection contains relational insights that are aided through not necessarily prompted by this biography.

I had the privilege, on a professional development day, to interact with horses, and found their behavior and level of consciousness to be much deeper and more instructive in relation to our work with students than I had anticipated. Specifically, I studied the nuances of their communication; in particular, I was fascinated with their gestures and how they established who among them to be the "alpha" horse. I observed that their gestures were repeated when a strange human was introduced: the horses looked for the "alpha" to assert himself or herself. As I moved forward, one horse, Romeo, confronted me, and through our brief interaction, I felt connected with a common intellect and soul of Nature.

I presented myself as I do to my students when they seek gestures and signals of leadership and guidance. I gestured to Romeo to indicate my identity and to assert my role as leader. Romeo hesitated, unsure, flaring his nostrils and whinnying. I wanted to indicate direction, to guide and move him, literally and figuratively. "Move!" my body language cried out, windmilling my directional arm and taking long strides toward him. He hesitated, but then he began to move, first walking, then trotting. I continued to gesture and had him cantering and then galloping. I was then able to make him change direction, slow down, and walk. After some time had passed I felt I no longer had demands to make of him; it felt purposeless or, if it had a purpose, was too much about me and my wishes. I joined him, ran alongside him until it felt like we were coming "in sync." We started to move in unison, shoulder-to-shoulder. When I stopped, Romeo stopped too; when I went forward, bringing up my energy, Romeo moved and brought his up too, matching my gait. And when he slowed or sped up, I sped up too. I did not feel "in command"; instead, I felt mutuality—a bond or cord of connection between us. I stopped. Romeo stopped as well. Then, as we moved forward again, Romeo looked to me, turning to me. He locked my gaze, and in that instant I felt a surge of connected feeling, of respect, of knowing, and of belonging. At this moment, it was as if all the energy of getting Romeo to move, staying with him, and feeling my own precarious hold on the situation suddenly flowed into a sense of well-being and being-well with another.

This communicative experience with a horse based on indicative and mimetic gestures yielded to giving and receiving energy in a state of "interactive flow" (Lloyd & Smith, 2006). By learning to communicate with Romeo in such participatory consciousness, Karen came to feel a greater wholeness—a feeling of deeper integration with Nature—such that she no longer stood separate from it but participated in it. Through this experience, Karen came to see that she can act as a mirror rather than have the horse simply mirror her intentions. As she puts it: "I reflect others, just as they are reflected in me. As others look into me, they see themselves. As beautiful or uncomfortable as that may be, they see themselves." By relating to horses and other sentient beings in this way, the subject-object dichotomy melds together. This reciprocal conversation between beings gives us a feeling of a shared life journey—a shared destiny, a common way forward that arises from a phenomenological space of intercorporeal knowing and understanding (Acampora, 2006). The "dance" in which Romeo and Karen engaged might seem initially to be a display of dominance; yet it becomes a negotiation that leads to a deeper, somatic conversation, establishing a mutual trust and correspondence (cf. Smith, 2015b). In such proximity, and with such coresponsiveness, we enter into communion with one another. We intuit ways of *interbeing* beyond our boundaries and fears, beyond the limits even of our physical postures, positions, gestures and expressions, and the fervent attachment to egoic existence. There is push-and-pull, give-and-take. The "dance" alternates between leading and following. Respect is earned not by dominant display, or use of force, but through offering guidance by initiative, while occasionally yielding, and awaiting a similar response.

Moving Alongside

Don and Karen's experience of interspecies communication and surrendering of ego occurred with domesticated horses, breaking down the wall of separation from identifiable Nature to experience mutuality, reciprocity, resonance, and attunement. Similarly, David Abram (2010) in *Becoming Animal* tells of his adventures with animals in the wild—encounters that are very different from interacting with domestic animals, yet ones that yield a similar quality of coexistence, somatic communication, and the participatory consciousness called "interbeing." For example, startled by a mother moose, Abram reflexively responded by singing "a sustained mellifluous note, a musical call in the middle part of my range, holding its pitch and its volume for as long as I could muster" (p. 161). This sonorous reply was enough to appease the moose, who then carried on grazing with her calf. Abram had obeyed an intuition that had proven correct. He continued on his way in a feeling of calm satisfaction.

For the timbre of a human voice, singing a single sustained note carries an abundance of information for those whose ears are tuned to such clues—information about the internal state of various organs in the singer's body, and the relative tension or ease in that person, the level of aggression or peaceful intent. (p. 162)

Abram's revelatory experience with the moose was repeated in an encounter with sea lions and a humpback whale. This time Abram responded to breaching, splashing, and posturing not with a "mellifluous note" but with an exchange of guttural vocalizations. Imperiled by the sea creatures' behavior, Abram was able to convey his anxiety to them. As this exchange continued, Abram was able to transmute his emotional tone from one of hyper-defensiveness to curiosity. As he did so, he felt the effect he had on the animals "made evident, in a way I could no longer ignore, that there exists a primary language that we two-leggeds share with other species" (p. 166).

What Abram infers, then, is that in primal exigencies, our native faculties serve us best; we obey not discursive thought, and its vehicle, symbolic language, but the "kinetic-kinesthetic-affective dynamics" (Sheets-Johnstone, 2011, pp. 20, 194, 201, 224, 471, 459) of *interbeing* where the body itself speaks in tonalities, postures, gestures, and motile expressions and where a connection is realized between the inner self and outer world. The same holds true of Don and Karen, as well as other FEEL participants, who found their voices in the silences of participatory consciousness. They were and still are "engaging in a different sort of interchange" and of a kind that "includes our attunements or general engagement with otherness, which are constituted by our postures, movements, kinaesthetic qualities, spatial awarenesses, and other corporeal habits and repertoires of being" (Sharpe & Strong, 2015, p. 6).

Pedagogical Connections

We human animals have much to learn from animal "others" who, by nature, seem more in tune with their environments (von Uexküll, 2010; also Buchanan, 2008) and seemingly live each moment fully attuned to the senses, movements, currents and flows of vital, animate consciousness (Sheets-Johnstone, 2011). It would appear that only when we find a language that is informed by embodied experience, not necessarily by the use of words, and that is motivated not by discursive thought, but by feelings of reciprocity, mutuality, and identification, that we realize we are participants in Nature, not separate from it. We are reminded that our psyches are naturally, affectively attuned to our environments and the sentient beings with whom we live. As David Abram (1996) stated, "Communicative meaning is always, in its depths, affective; it remains rooted in the sensual dimension of experience, born of the body's native capacity to resonate with other bodies and with the landscape as a whole" (p. 74).

We have described key features of an *intersubjective contemplative practice* of being-with horses that fits within a professional development agenda applied to teacher education through the tropes of "joining up," "finding a connection," and "moving alongside." The join-up with a chestnut mare and the connection established with a horse called Romeo are both cases in point and reference points for consideration of wider relationships of moving alongside others in care, empathy, and compassion. These actions make manifest the motile features of reciprocity, mutuality, and identification with many different others.

The particular focus in this chapter on the dynamics of human-horse connection is an invitation for readers to engage in their own self-care and self-with-other somatic practices of teaching animation (e.g., Garbett, 2011, 2014; Tom & Katz, 2013). We maintain, with Bai and Scott (2009), that it is through "contemplative practices that manifest the arts of somatic, sensuous, relational, and contextual awareness" (p. 319) that teaching can become a more fully reflective, more mindful, *kinethically attuned* practice of the self-with-others (cf. Smith, 2006, 2013, 2014b). That reflectivity is, if the mirror analogy still applies at all, more aptly cast as the kinetic, kinesthetic, affective resonancing with another in which one becomes increasingly mindful of the other. As Karen puts it:

Since coming to work in the teacher education program, I have solidified my sense that who I am in the moment is more than enough. I carry myself in the moment of vital contact with others as a confidence and contentment in knowing the inner self in outer connectedness. Now, back in a grade six classroom, I continue to allow myself to be in the moment, not separate at all from the task and the curriculum and from the students. I step forward, comfortable in my skin, just as I found a comfort with Romeo. The reflective mirror is what my students see, their actions guided, affirmed, and sustained by what comes back to them.

Taking the lead is something I questioned with Romeo in that it need not be "bossy" but instead can be simply stepping forward and finding a place, a position, just as I do with children, to be "alongside" them. My *intersubjective contemplative practice* in the classroom manifests in a way that the children come to develop their own practices of self-care and care-for-others.

Teaching children and youth can be felt in kindred-enhancing, intersubjective, contemplative practices such as the FEEL practices taken up by Karen and Don. While the respective practices of teaching children and youth, and those of connecting with horses, carry different postural, positional, gestural, and expressive alignments, there is a relational commonality to them. Let us say that in getting a FEEL for teaching, and thus in establishing the basis for sustaining, caring practices of the self-with-others, whether they be children, youth, adults or, indeed, other kinds of animals, the mirror is really the refractive surface of otherness and the becoming of one's best self in joining up with, finding a connection with, and moving alongside many different others.

References

Abram, D. (1996). *The spell of the sensuous: Perception and language in a more-than-human world*. New York: Random House.

Abram, D. (2010). *Becoming animal: An earthly cosmology*. New York: Pantheon.

Acampora, R. A. (2006). *Corporal compassion: Animal ethics and philosophy of the body*. Pittsburgh: University of Pittsburgh Press.

Bai, H., & Scott, C. (2009). Touching the Earth with the heart of enlightened mind: The Buddhist practice of mindfulness for environmental education. *Canadian Journal of Education, 14*, 92–106.

Bai, H., Scott, C., & Donald, B. (2009). Contemplative pedagogy and revitalization of teacher education. *Alberta Journal of Educational Research, 55*(3), 319–334.

Buber, M. (1970). *I and thou*. New York: Scribner.

Buchanan, B. (2008). *Onto-ethologies: The animal environments of Uexküll, Heidegger, Merleau-Ponty, and Deleuze*. Albany: State University of New York Press.

Deleuze, G., & Guattari, F. (1987). *A thousand plateaus: Capitalism and schizophrenia* (B. Massumi, Trans.). Minneapolis: University of Minnesota Press.

Freewin, K., & Gardiner, B. (2005). New age or old sage: A review of equine assisted psychotherapy. *Australian Journal of Counselling Psychology, 6*, 13–17.

Garbett, D. (2011). Horse riding 101: The role of experience in reframing teacher education practices. *Studying Teacher Education, 7*(1), 65–75.

Garbett, D. (2014). Lessons on the hoof: Learning about teacher education through horse-riding. In A. Ovens and T. Fletcher (Eds.), *Self-study in physical education teacher education* (pp. 63–73). New York: Springer.

Gendlin, E. T. (1966). *Existentialism and experiential psychotherapy: Existential child therapy* (C. Moustakas, Ed.). New York: Basic Books.

Gunnlaugson, O., Sarath, E. W., Scott, C., & Bai, H. (2014). *Contemplative learning and inquiry across disciplines.* Albany: State University of New York Press.

Hahn, T. N. (2001). *You are here: Discovering the magic of the present moment* (S. Kohn, Trans.). Boston: Shambhala.

Hallberg, L. (2008). *Walking the way of the horse: Exploring the power of the horse-human relationship.* Bloomington: iUniverse.

Haraway, D. (2003). *The companion species manifesto: Dogs, people and significant otherness.* Chicago: Prickly Paradigm Press.

Haraway, D. (2008). *When species meet.* Minneapolis: University of Minnesota Press.

Healing Hooves. (2015). Retrieved from http://healinghooves.ca/professionals.htm

Ingold, T. (2000). *The perception of the environment: Essays on livelihood, dwelling and skill.* New York: Routledge.

Ingold, T. (2013). *Making: Anthropology, archeology, art and architecture.* New York: Routledge.

Kelly, S. (2014). Horses for courses: Exploring the limits of leadership development through equine-assisted learning. *Journal of Management Education, 3*(2), 216–233.

Lacan, J. (1968). *The language of the self.* (A. Wilden, Trans.). New York: Dell.

Lloyd, R. J., & Smith, S. J. (2006). Interactive flow and exercise pedagogy. *Quest, 58,* 222–241.

Merleau-Ponty, M. (1968). *The visible and the invisible* (A. Lingis, Trans.). Evanston: Northwestern University Press.

Merleau-Ponty, M. (2003). *Nature: Course notes from the College de France* (R. Vallier, Trans.). Evanston: Northwestern University Press.

Nelson, D. L. (2010). Reason, emotion, and awareness. Unpublished doctoral dissertation, Simon Fraser University, Burnaby, British Columbia.

Roberts, M. (1997). *The man who listens to horses.* Toronto: Alfred A. Knopf.

Roberts, M. (2001). *Horse sense for people.* Toronto: Alfred A. Knopf.

Shapiro, K. (1990). Understanding dogs through kinaesthetic empathy, social construction and history. *Anthrozoos, 3,* 184–195.

Sharpe, H., & Strong, T. (2015). *Embodied relating and transforming: Tales from equine-facilitated counselling.* Rotterdam, Netherlands: Sense.

Sheets-Johnstone, M. (2011). *The primacy of movement* (2nd expanded ed.). Amsterdam, Netherlands: John Benjamins.

Smith, S. J. (1998). *Risk and our pedagogical relation with children: On the playground and beyond.* Albany: State University of New York Press.

Smith, S. J. (2004). *The bearing of inquiry in teacher education: The SFU experience*. Burnaby, British Columbia: Simon Fraser University.
Smith, S. J. (2006). Gestures, landscape and embrace: A phenomenological analysis of elemental motions. *Indo-Pacific Journal of Phenomenology*, 6(1), 1–10. http://www.ipjp.org
Smith, S. J. (2011). Becoming horse in the duration of the moment. *Phenomenology & Practice*, 5(1), 7–26.
Smith, S. J. (2013). Caring caresses and the embodiment of good teaching. *Phenomenology & Practice*, 6(2), 65–83.
Smith, S. J. (2014a). Human-horse partnerships: The discipline of dressage. In J. Gillett & M. Gilbert, Eds.), *Sport, animals, and society* (pp. 35–51). New York: Routledge.
Smith, S. J. (2014b). A pedagogy of vital contact. *Journal of Dance and Somatic Practices*, 6(2), 233–246.
Smith, S. J. (2015a). Riding in the skin of the moment: An agogic practice. *Phenomenology & Practice*, 9(1), 41–54.
Smith, S. J. (2015b). Dancing with horses: The science and artistry of coenesthetic connection. In N. Carr (Ed.), *Domestic animals and leisure* (pp. 296–326). London: Palgrave Macmillan.
Smith, S. J., & Wahl, S. (2010). Thinking the world of teaching: Creating an SFU vision of teacher development. In E. Sandoval, R. Blum-Martinez, & I. H. Andrews (Eds.), *Challenges and possibilities in teacher education: A North American perspective (Desafios y Posibilidades en la formación de maestros: Una perspectiva de North America)* (pp. 147–168). Mexico City: University of New Mexico: Organization of American States.
Stern, D. (2010). *Forms of vitality: Exploring the dynamic experience in psychology, the arts, psychotherapy, and development*. Oxford: Oxford University Press.
Tom, E., & Katz, M-L. (2013). Pasture pedagogy: Field and classroom reflections on embodied teaching. In M-L. Katz (Ed.), *Moving ideas: Multimodality and embodied learning in communities and schools* (pp. 109–137). New York: Peter Lang.
von Uexküll, J. (2010). *A foray into the worlds of animals and humans* (J. D. O'Neil, Trans.). Minneapolis: University of Minnesota Press.
van Manen, M. (1991). *The tact of teaching: The meaning of pedagogical thoughtfulness*. Albany: State University of New York Press.
van Manen, M. (2012). The call of pedagogy as the call of contact. *Phenomenology & Practice*, 6(2), pp. 8–34.

5

A Disciplined Practice of Collaboratively Working on Teaching as Contemplative Professional Practice

THOMAS FALKENBERG AND MICHAEL LINK

For the last three years, we have been involved in a disciplined practice of working on our development as teacher educators based on the notion of teaching as contemplative professional practice (Falkenberg, 2012). This notion draws on two traditions of human development that give particular attention to the importance of inquiring into and working with one's experiences of one's inner life for human and professional development: (1) the mindfulness tradition of Buddhist psychology and philosophy (e.g., Gunaratana, 2002) and its modern Western adoption in consciousness studies (e.g., Varela, Thompson, & Rosch, 1991), and, (2), the self-study tradition of teacher development (e.g., Laughran, Hamilton, LaBoskey, & Russell, 2004), in particular that branch that puts teachers' awareness and noticing at the center of teacher development (e.g., Mason, 2002). The approach to contemplative professional practice as outlined in Falkenberg (2012) is a *first-person* form of contemplative education (see further discussion). In addition to this first-person form, we have also been meeting (in person and virtually) to discuss our inner-life experiences that we had as part of our disciplined professional practice. This, we consider, our *second-person* form of contemplative education (see further discussion below). The purpose of these meetings was to help each other make deeper sense of our first-person contemplative practice and the inner-life experiences we had as part of that practice.

In this chapter we discuss our collaborative work across our first-person experiences. These experiences are drawn from our work on our inner lives as part of our contemplative professional practice. To start, we outline the framework for that first-person professional practice. Following that, we outline our second-person contemplative practice, namely, our collaborative work across our first-person experiences. Then, we draw on data we collected from that collaborative work to identify things *we learned* about our first-person contemplative practices and our inner lives and to identify *how* our collaborative work has helped us with such learning.

A Framework for First-Person Contemplative Practice: Teaching as Contemplative Professional Practice

Our disciplined practice of working on our professional practice as teacher educators is based on a framework for first-person contemplative practice developed in Falkenberg (2012).

> I propose that teaching as contemplative professional practice has three components: an ethical component, a noticing component, and a mindfulness component. Subsequent subsections will address these components in more detail. The selection of these three components is based on the following idea about teaching as contemplative professional practice more generally: teaching as contemplative professional practice supports the teacher to live a morally better life for the benefit of those she is working with (ethical component); in order to do so, she will have to engage in ongoing work on the functioning of her inner life and professional practice (noticing component); for such work she needs to be aware of the functioning of her inner life as it is part of her professional practice (mindfulness component). The ongoing professional development makes this a contemplative *professional* practice. (p. 30)

The examples from our engagement in teaching as contemplative professional practice that we will draw upon in this chapter will focus on the third (mindfulness) component of the practice, namely, where the practice asks of us to be "in a state of non-judgmental, pre-conceptual conscious awareness of the inner-life experiences in the moment while being engaged in [our] teaching" (Falkenberg, 2012, p. 31).

Second-Person Contemplative Practice: Collaboratively Working across First-Person Experiences

Second-Person Forms of Contemplative Practice

The two traditions upon which our first-person contemplative educational practice is based (see the introduction to this chapter) consider collaboratively working across first-person experiences of one's inner life an important aspect of successful practices of human and professional development, respectively. In the mindfulness tradition this aspect is considered in the notion of "mediation" (Varela & Shear, 2002), which is "another person(s) who provides a curious intermediate position between first and second position" and who "provides hints and further training" (p. 8). In the self-study of teacher (education) practices literature, reports on collaborative self-study projects among teachers and teacher educators abound (e.g., Trumbull & Fluet, 2007).

Such collaboration provides opportunities for *second-person* forms of contemplative education (Gunnlaugson, 2009), namely, contemplative education of teachers in higher-education *through* collaborative disciplined practices of working on their professional practice as educators. The intersubjective field for such contemplative practice is the space created by the educators for their joint inquiry into their teaching as contemplative practice.

What Our Second-Person Form of Contemplative Practice Looked Like

Following our framework for teaching as contemplative professional practice, each of us has been trying to nonjudgmentally and preconceptually observe his inner life as he engages in teaching. We have been supplementing these first-person observations with second-person observations by one of us of the other's teaching. The second-person form of contemplative practice, then, was structurally framed by regularly scheduled (in person and virtual) meetings, in which we encountered each other through our reports of each of our first-person observations and the sense that each other made of one's own reports and the other person's reports. These encounters we audio-recorded and later analyzed. We will share some of this analysis in the chapter.

The practice in these encounters has been characterized by an attempt to nonjudgmentally receive the other's reports and to interpret the reported experience in light of past reports, one's own experiences and sense-making of those experiences, and the literature we read. In the conclusion to this chapter we will make the case that our practice can meaningfully be described as a second-person form of contemplative practice.

There are three domains about which we learned through this second-order contemplative practice: (1) the functioning of our inner lives as teachers, (2) the functioning of the first-person form of contemplative professional practice we engaged in, and (3) the functioning of the second-person form of contemplative practice that we engaged in. In accordance with the theme of this book, this chapter is focused on domain 3 of our learning. However, since our second-person contemplative practice consisted of our engagement with our own and each other's first-person observation reports, this chapter will by necessity also deal with domains 1 and 2 of our learning. Accordingly, in the next section we report upon *how* we have learned from our second-person form of contemplative practice (focus on the functioning of that practice) as well as on *what* we have learned through that practice (focus on the functioning of both our inner lives as teachers and the first-person form of contemplative practice we engaged in).

What and How We Learned from Our Second-Person Form of Contemplative Practice

In this section we want to draw on three excerpts from transcripts of three different exchanges (encounters) we had as part of our second-person form of contemplative practice. In our view these exchanges exemplify the second-person contemplative practice that we engaged in. We proceed as follows: We discuss each encounter in terms of two questions: (1) What did we learn about the functioning of our inner lives as teachers and about the first-person contemplative professional practice we engaged in? (2) What are the structural features of the particular second-person contemplative practice exemplified in the exchange that led to the learning?

Exchange 1

The exchange. In exchange 1, Mike reports on first-person contemplative experiences in connection with a feeling of annoyance about a student's behavior and the thought linked to that feeling:

> Yeah, annoyance . . . coupled with a thought, at what point to intervene or to say something? And this is the very first day, too. . . . There's all these thoughts rolling around in my head too that I'm aware of. . . . I'm realizing, I'm no longer listening to this person who is introducing themselves, this other person . . . because I'm feeling myself being annoyed and I'm aware of the fact that my thoughts are debating whether or not this is the right time to intervene or whether I should talk to this person privately later on, and so I'm aware of this whole other conversation going on.

In response, Thomas makes a link to his past noticing of first-person contemplative experiences:

> So . . . you were paying attention to your thoughts and you were aware of you having these thoughts but also your emotions. So, I want to get back to the emotions. I notice with myself that when certain emotions arise and I am able to be . . . at the meta-level where I notice these emotions either arising or being present that—let's call it the impact of these emotions—were lessened. I actually recently read that being described—I don't know what kind of wording the person used but I was reminded of exactly those experiences I had . . . I wasn't really being run over by these feelings or . . . dragged along with these feelings but there was a little bit of a being outside. It wasn't really this being in the middle of these emotions but also being a little bit outside, and thus . . . the impact [of the emotions] somehow was lessened. Of course it was still there or otherwise you wouldn't feel it, but it wasn't as intense or it wasn't the same kind of quality. Was that something you felt as well—with this annoyance?

Then Mike makes new sense of his own experience in terms of the qualification suggested by Thomas:

> I mean, it still had an impact on me, but . . . the degree of the impact I think was less than it was in the past, because I can think of other instances where I felt this way, and I was, as you say, dragged along with it and even acted on it in the moment. So I'm feeling annoyed, and I'm . . . almost controlled like a puppet by that annoyance into acting. Yeah.

> So, yeah, it lessened it but probably not to the same degree as it could have. While I was aware of it, I guess I was kind of separate from it, but I wasn't completely out of it.

What we learned. The exchange suggests an experiential confirmation of this insight about first-person contemplative practice: When being in a state in which part of our attention is directed at our emotions that have arisen, the "impact" of those emotions is lessened in terms of suffering through those emotions.

The structure of the second-person contemplative practice. Looking at the structure of the exchange, it may be described as follows: A tells of a certain type of inner experience; this reminds B of an experience of a similar type; both jointly think about this type of experience; in the end, A comes to a deeper understanding of her inner experience through the mediation by B (experiential confirmation). This is the process suggested by Varela and Shear (2002) to overcome some methodological limitations of the first-person form of contemplative practice: "A mediator [Thomas] is eccentric to the lived experience L1 [of Mike] but nevertheless takes a position of one who has been there to some degree, and thus provides hints and further training [understanding]" (Varela & Shear, 2002, p. 8).

Exchange 2

The exchange. In exchange 2, Thomas starts off with an interpretive reflection on a particular first-person contemplative experience:

> What I seem to have observed over the last week, ten days is what we discussed before, that this content, this 'idea wave' pulls me away. This idea wave pulls me away, takes all my energy and then I get all tensed up and excited, and in this excitement I just pay attention to that and not to anything else. Like a sports person gets all focused so much on playing the ball or hitting the puck and being in the game, that you don't really hear the spectators. This is all just a blur and you're so focused.

In response, Mike senses a judgment of the experience by Thomas and challenges this judgment:

But is there anything wrong with this as long as you come back? You ride that idea out and you make the slam dunk, and then you bring yourself out of that state of excitement, and then you realize 'I'm here again and here are my students.'

Thomas accepts this assessment of a negative judgment of his "state of mind when teaching" as understood through his first-person contemplative experience. In his responding, Thomas analyzes the experience in a more complex way than before by linking it to past observations of behavior, which then has him uncover the "deeper" reason for why he (still) believes the experienced "state of mind" is problematic for him for his teaching.

That's a good question, because . . . when we talked last time, I made the point that I find this not ideal, because I feel I'm not attentive enough to the student, and I'm more focused on the issue and the topic and so on and that takes me away from the attentiveness to the student. Well not generally, it might come back, but enough so that I lose some sensitivity and that the danger might lie in that. So the danger that I observed or what seems to be the case is . . . because of what I focus on, but also because if I'm not focused on the student and more on the subject, I seem to, in this excitement, I seem to be more . . . say things, respond in ways that are less, for lack of a better word, less controlled, less thoughtful, less mindful of the student, and they draw out more . . . certain patterns and routines. And it . . . seems to me, there's a pattern from a long time ago going on, when I was teaching high school—it's when I make these certain remarks that I find funny and then I, afterwards, I regret because it wasn't funny for the student. So that's where I see the main challenge. Because . . . I let myself push away. Maybe the challenge is because I have internalized certain patterns of responding . . . that might not be the best, that I find not always the best. That has helped me quite a lot in clarifying that.

What we learned. The learning we see in this exchange is linked to the notion of "being present with others" (e.g., Miller, 2014, pp.

23–26; Senge, Scharmer, Jaworski, & Flowers, 2005). What this specific exchange seems to suggest to us are two things: First, the notion that teaching as a practice is full of long-standing routine behavior and that some of those routines can be in conflict with the teacher being present with her students. Second, the notion that routines that have the potential of undermining the teacher being present with her students do not always have to be problematic if they otherwise benefit students, for instance, their learning of or attitude toward a specific subject matter. This insight provides a good rationale for teaching as contemplative professional practice as conceptualized in Falkenberg (2012).

The structure of the second-person contemplative practice. The structure of the exchange looks to us as follows: A tells of a certain type of a problem identified as part of her first-person contemplative practice; B suggests a judgment and challenges this judgment; through this challenge, A explores further this judgment; in the end A comes to a different understanding of the original problem. The structure of exchange 1 was based on "experiential confirmation." In exchange 2, the interlocutor does not confirm the interpretation of an experience but rather challenges the interpretation of an experience in the approach of a "critical friend," whose wonderings trigger a renewed engagement with a problem.

Exchange 3

The exchange. In exchange 3, Mike initially assesses the level of his noticing of his thoughts and feelings, to which Thomas responds by inviting Mike to think about an explanation:

> *Mike*: I think when it comes to emotions, yes. I've been able to have little snippets of it when it comes to thinking about thinking. But when it comes to the way I'm feeling in the moment or emotions, maybe I had a little snippet of it on the first day. But this was the first time I was able to ride it all the way through. I was able to stay with it for a fair chunk of time.
>
> *Thomas*: Why do you think it was suddenly possible, or maybe it wasn't suddenly, why do you think it was possible?

This prompts Mike to link his experience to a certain aspect of what he taught and is already familiar with, which he suggests allowed him to be able to attend to his inner life at the same time:

> Well, I mean I don't . . . want to overstate it. I don't think I've made a huge amount of progress or anything. . . . I think I have enough experience with the argument [that was brought up in class]. There's been enough time for me to think it over. . . . I think it made it easier for me to step out and be able to practice in that way, I think that was part of it anyway.

In response, Thomas makes a link to a topic we have discussed in preceding exchanges:

> So it sounds to me as if this alludes to what we have discussed over the past couple of conversations, in terms of psychic energy and what's available, because you didn't have to think about a new issue or topic and how you felt about this, the weighing the arguments, etc., because you drew on this and it already existed, and you didn't have to spend as much psychic energy on processing the issue . . . and you had enough available to start noticing.

This linking of Mike's experience he started off reporting on with earlier "theorizing" we have done seems to have led to some insights:

> Mike: Yeah, I think that's it exactly. Yeah, I think that's a good insight. Yeah, I agree.

What we learned. The focus of this exchange is on the challenges we have been experiencing over and over again in our engagement with teaching as contemplative practice, namely, the challenge to attend to our inner life *while* at the same time attending to what needs attention as we directly teach students. Csikszentmihalyi (1988) suggests that we should think of attention as "psychic energy," because "attention is the medium that makes events occur in consciousness" (p. 19). How much we can attend to at any given moment—our psychic energy—is limited. What this specific exchange suggests to us about the notion that we have only limited psychic energy available in a teaching situation to attend to our practice of teaching and to our inner life while teaching is the following: (1) in "mentally complex" situations the psychic energy that is available might not be enough to allow the teacher to also focus on her inner life at that moment (Thomas's reference to past exchanges); (2) in situations that are "mentally less complex," the available psychic energy might be enough to be "normally responsive" as a teacher in the situation while still having enough psychic energy to be attentive to one's inner life; situations for which a teacher has developed certain routines fall into this category (Mike's interpretation of his observation report).

The structure of the second-person contemplative practice. For this exchange the structure looked to us as follows: A tells of a certain type of experience; B interprets the experience with reference to previous discussions; interpreting the situation leads to a deeper understanding of "mindfulness in teaching."

Conclusion: The Role of Second-Person Contemplative Practice for Teaching as Contemplative Professional Practice

We want to conclude with two tasks. We start by elaborating on the way in which we see what we called our second-person contemplative practice is indeed a *contemplative* practice, then we outline in what way our second-person contemplative practice *complements* the framework for teaching as (first-person) contemplative professional practice.

We suggest that our second-person practice (our observations, self-reflections, and engagements with each other) is very similarly *structured* to the first-person contemplative practice we engaged in during our classroom teaching. The latter was characterized by three components: an ethical component ("the ethical imperative of teaching being a moral endeavour for the betterment of all living beings embedded within a holistic view of human living" [Falkenberg, 2012, p. 30]), a noticing component ("using noticing in a disciplined way to change [one's] knowing-to act in the moment in order to change the functioning of [one's] inner life and [one's] professional behaviour" [Falkenberg, 2012, p. 30]), and a mindfulness component (being "in a state of non-judgmental, pre-conceptual conscious awareness of the inner-life experiences in the moment while being engaged in [one's] teaching" [Falkenberg, 2012, p. 31]).

Our second-person practice of engaging with each other and each other's first-person contemplative practice was similarly structured. There is an ethical aspect to our second-person engagement: Our engagement with each other is driven by the ethical imperative of this practice being a moral endeavor for the betterment of each other as teachers and human beings more generally.

There is also a noticing component involved in our second-person practice, as the three vignettes from our exchanges demonstrate. For instance, there is noticing of similarities between each other's first-person experiences (exchange 1), noticing of a judgment of a first-person experience (exchange 2), and noticing of similarities between discussions we had at different times (exchange 3). Similar to the role of noticing in the first-person contemplative practice, it is the noticing that happens in our second-person practice that allows us to envision acting differently in our teaching based on a deeper understanding of our inner life. The noticing in the second-person practice happens in a kind of "common mind space" that we created through our exchange; as in a single person's mind thoughts arise and are replaced by others, so do *expressed* thoughts enter this common mind space and are accompanied, expanded on, or replaced by expressed thoughts by the interlocutors.

Finally, there is also a modified version of a mindfulness component to our second-person practice. We become aware of the components that make up our common mind space that we are jointly creating during our exchanges through our reports of our inner-life experiences and our responses to those reports. Those components of our common mind space are made up of thoughts/ideas that enter the space as thoughts/ideas arising from the report and thoughts/ideas in response to previous thoughts/ideas. Our second-person practice is nonjudgmental and preconceptual in one important sense, namely, in the sense that we do not judge each other's experiences or each other, for instance, in terms of "good" or "bad." Becoming in this sense nonjudgmentally and preconceptually aware of the thoughts/ideas that enter the common mind space is an important component of our second-person practice. However, in our exchanges this awareness does not stay nonjudgmental in the same way suggested in the mindfulness component of teaching as first-person contemplative practice, since our engagement with the thoughts/ideas in the common mind space is partially through judging and conceptualizing those thoughts/ideas (see, for instance, Mike's response in exchange 2). Our second-person practice involves reflection upon what we have become nonjudgmentally and preconceptually aware of, which means judging and conceptualizing these thoughts/ideas and what they might imply for our teaching practice. With this last qualification in mind, we suggest that the second-person practice we have been engaging in is also a contemplative practice in a somewhat similar sense in which our first-person contemplative practice is contemplative.

How does this second-person contemplative practice *complement* the framework for teaching as contemplative professional practice? The purpose of engaging in teaching as contemplative professional practice is to help us align our ethical teacher ideal with our actual teaching practice by using disciplined noticing grounded in being mindful of our inner life while teaching. The framework (Falkenberg, 2012) is mute on ways in which we move from (first-person) inner-life experiences during teaching to a vision of a different practice. The second-person contemplative practice we engaged in and have reported on provides one such way—a way that is quite in line with the contemplative approach to teaching proposed in the framework.

With the three vignettes from our second-person contemplative practice we have illustrated structures of engagement within that practice that have led us to a deeper understanding of the functioning of our inner lives (exchanges 1 and 2) and of the functioning of teaching as a contemplative practice (exchanges 2 and 3). All three started out with some kind of report of inner experiences while teaching. Then each exchange differed in the kind of response provided to the respective report, providing for a different structure: experiential confirmation (exchange 1), being a critical friend and challenging an identified judgment (exchange 2), and linking to an interpretation of the type of inner experience to promote a deeper understanding of mindfulness in teaching (exchange 3). The common mind spaces created within these structures are what provided ways of moving from the inner experiences from teaching as contemplative practice to a greater alignment with one's ethical teacher ideal. The value of creating such common mind spaces is that the understanding they allow to develop and the possibilities flowing from those understandings are not (always) achievable on one's own, as the referenced responses in two of the three vignettes suggest: At the end of exchange 2, Thomas says: "That has helped me quite a lot in clarifying that"; at the end of exchange 3, Mike says: "Yeah, I think that's it exactly. Yeah, I think that's a good insight. Yeah, I agree."

In this chapter, we outlined and illustrated the second-person practice we have been engaging in. We argued that this practice is in a qualified sense a contemplative practice aligned with the framework of teaching as contemplative professional practice that we have been using in our teaching. We also have argued that and discussed how our second-person practice can complement teaching as contemplative professional practice.

References

Csikszentmihalyi, M. (1988). The flow experience and human psychology. In M. Csikszentmihalyi & I. S. Csikszentmihalyi (Eds.), *Optimal experience: Psychological studies of flow in consciousness* (pp. 3–35). Cambridge: Cambridge University Press.

Falkenberg, T. (2012). Teaching as contemplative professional practice. *Philosophical Inquiry in Education* (formerly: *Paideusis*), 20(2), 25–35. Retrieved January 5, 2016 from http://journals.sfu.ca/pie/index.php/pie/index

Gunaratana, B. H. (2002). *Mindfulness in plain English*. Boston: Wisdom.

Gunnlaugson, O. (2009). Establishing second-person forms of contemplative education: An inquiry into four conceptions of intersubjectivity. *Integral Review*, 5(1), 25–50.

Laughran, J. J., Hamilton, M. L., LaBoskey, V. K., & Russell, T. (2004). (Eds.). *International handbook of self-study of teaching and teacher education practices*. Dordrecht: Kluwer Academic.

Mason, J. (2002). *Researching your own practice: The discipline of noticing*. London: Routledge Falmer.

Miller, J. P. (2014). *The contemplative practitioner: Meditation in education and the workplace* (2nd ed.). Toronto: University of Toronto Press.

Senge, P., Scharmer, C. O., Jaworski, J., & Flowers, B. S. (2005). *Presence: An exploration of profound change in people, organizations, and society*. New York: Currency Doubleday.

Trumbull, D. J., & Fluet, K. (2007). Slow research time and fast teaching time: A collaborative self-study of a teacher educator's unexamined assumptions. *Studying Teacher Education: A Journal of Self-Study of Teacher Education Practices*, 3(2), 207–215.

Varela, F. J., & Shear, J. (2002). First-person methodologies: What, why, how? In F. J. Varela & J. Shear (Eds.), *The view from within: First-person approaches to the study of consciousness* (pp. 1–14). Thorverton: Imprint Academic.

Varela, F. J., Thompson, E., & Rosch, E. (2002). *The embodied mind: Cognitive science and human experience*. Cambridge: MIT Press.

6

Awakening to Wholeness

Aikido as an Embodied Praxis of Intersubjectivity

MICHAEL A. GORDON

In April 1993, as a spiritual seeker in my mid-twenties, I joined an Aikido club in the east end of Vancouver, Canada—a decision that would radically reshape the course of my life for years to come. Aikido, known as the "Art of Peace" (*ai* = harmony, *ki* = universe, spirit, love, *do* = path or way), is broadly understood as a defensive art that originated in Japan. It teaches one to *blend with* an attacker's movements and *ki* ("life force" or "energy"). To be precise, the Aikido class I joined belonged to a branch or school of Aikido called Ki Aikido, which emphasizes the dynamics of mind/body unification within oneself, and how the latter impacts and transforms one's daily life.

Having spent a lifetime in Aikido, I have found this Art of Peace to be complex and even paradoxical at its core—one that reflects the double-bind of *intersubjectivity*. This double-bind may be expressed thus: How can dualistic consciousness of subject-object dichotomy apply itself to resolving human conflicts while inherently operating from a position of dualism that creates such conflict in the first place? Put yet another way, if one inhabits a dualistic consciousness, then by the logic of such consciousness, one cannot be intersubjective, and hence, one cannot practice blending or harmonizing with the *ki* of another being. This paradox dissolves when we understand Aikido as a practice of freedom,[1] one that transforms subjectivity from that of the dualistic mind-heart (*kokoro* in Japanese) to that of the nondual *kokoro* through the Art of Aikido. Through such a practice of freedom, we can shift consciousness and thus our habitual actions toward peaceful dialogic interconnectedness, which is true intersubjectivity. This chapter explores in depth this pedagogical transformative process in Aikido, wherein the nature of contemplative intersubjectivity is illuminated. Through a series of vignettes and explication, I will present Aikido as a contemplative way of being and living that *demands* an intersubjective, second-person model of engagement. Thus, this model is based on the view of cosmos as *interdependent relationality*.

The fluid motional engagement in intersubjectivity that Aikido develops is rooted in the kind of localized learning and "tensional and ethical" praxis put forward by Stewart and Zediker (2000). Addressing the broadened use of the term *dialogic* and the risk of the term being weakened by encompassing "all human meaning-making," Stewart and Zediker offer a distinction between the *descriptive* approach to dialogue and "a prescriptive understanding of dialogue as tensional, situationally-accomplished, and inherently ethical" (2000, p. 224). As an aside, their prescriptive model of dialogic practice is based on an Aristotelian distinction between *poesis* and *praxis*. In this sense, Aikido can be seen similarly as a *prescriptive* kind of intersubjectivity—one rooted in what is *situationally* and relationally present.[2] As I will show in the course of this chapter, Aikido shifts the practitioner not only into a mind/body unity of nondual consciousness but also into the realm of full temporal-spatial and global interdependence, whereby one may realize and manifest through the self the nature of the cosmos as interdependent relationality.

Intersubjectivity through Aikido

Aikido is a Japanese defensive art developed by founder Morehei Ueshiba (b. 1883, d. 1969). From its Shinto spiritual underpinnings, Aikido integrates many other martial forms, such as jiujutsu and kenjutsu (sword), comprising a modern form of *budo* or warriorship. However, in its most popularized and widely adapted form, Aikido as we know it represents the culmination of spiritual awakening of the founder through his epiphany about nondual existence, nonresistance, and the realization of inseparability from the cosmos.

The word *aikido* is self-revealing and descriptive. *Ai* can be translated as "harmony" or "to blend"; *ki* represents life force, the Universe itself, or "universal love"; *do* means "way" or "path." Thus, the art represents a *way of harmonizing oneself with all of creation; the cultivation/*

purification of oneself so as to live in nonresistant interdependence with all living beings. Much like *satori* or enlightenment achieved in Zen meditation, where one's "bare attention" leads to the "pure experience" that Nishida describes (Yusa, 1997), Aikido involves a kind of "stripping away" of the preconceptions of self/Other separation, of self-defense, and provides a spiritual approach that suffuses the partner training with an ethos of *mutual liberation*, interdependence, and flowing in intersubjectivity. Beyond any anachronistic setting in *budo* and samurai culture, Aikido is a thoroughly modern art that emerged in its full form after the devastation Japan suffered in World War II. Designated when the founder described it as the "Art of Peace," Aikido itself was born of founder Morihei Ueshiba's spiritual epiphany through not only mind-body unification but also mind-*cosmos* unification: "I *am* the Universe!"[3]

Aikido, while conventionally regarded as an art of tactical self-defense, is a dynamic, relational, and experiential model of contemplative awareness-in-action. It offers practitioners across all walks of life a practical, nuanced, and adaptive approach to cultivating self-actualization in daily life through an embodied practice of nonresistance to conflict, developed reflexively and progressively through emergent and nonreactive human responsiveness. As such, the proposal here is that Aikido represents a second-person model for interrelationality, intersubjectivity, contemplative education, and thus daily life.[4]

As regards second-person of intersubjectivity, which presents an "inter-space" between first-person (the constructed self) or third-person (the constructed other), Yuasa (1987), commenting on Tetsuro, asks: "What does it mean to exist in *betweenness* (*aidagara*)?[5] What Yuasa is addressing here is not merely a phenomenological problem but a *methodological*, even an ethical, one; in an increasingly complex and competitive world, we need relational, collaborative, and dialogic approaches in order to move beyond mindfulness-based practices that risk abetting socially constructed patterns of materialism, exploitation, privilege, or narcissistic self-absorption.[6] Cultivation of "inner" traits of introspection, emotional labeling and self-regulation, and stress reduction—while highly beneficial as interventions against self-harm or one's own outward reactivity—doesn't necessarily engage the *relational* aspect of conflict or imbalances of power that permeate the human world and runs the risk of reinforcing a subjectivist first-person interiority.

What takes contemplative practice from an independent to an *interdependent* worldview is groundedness in intersubjectivity. In Buddhism, for example, meditation is an experiential method of self-inquiry in which one observes the illusory ego-construct of *separateness*, with the ultimate aim of releasing one's self from this illusion. Yet, meditators engaged in introspection of sitting meditation often end up reinforcing the very illusion the meditator is trying to overcome. Aikido is an intersubjective and moving contemplative art, one that implicitly challenges the illusory boundary of the singular self.

Though deeply rooted in metaphysical underpinnings, namely, the animism of Shinto, or *kannagara no michi*, "the continuous way of the gods," Aikido is Morihei Ueshiba's (1883–1969) expression of *budo* principles (historically, samurai warriorship codes). In Ueshiba's words, "True *budo* is the loving protection of all beings with a spirit of reconciliation. Reconciliation means to allow the completion of everyone's mission" (Ueshiba, 1992, p. 179–180). Thus, much like the prescription of mindfulness meditation in Buddhism as a means to embracing principles of interdependence through empathy, Aikido can be seen as the transformation of self, through purification (*misogi*) and training (*shugyo*), from inner aggression (victory over one's "own" aggression") toward an embodied spirit of interdependence and compassion. As such, it holds much in common with enlightened conduct and "right living" through the Eightfold Noble Path laid out in Siddhartha Gautama Buddha's initial teachings. The Eightfold Noble Path is the "fruition" component of the so-called threefold logic of Buddhism (ground, path, fruition) and follows forth from the Buddha's fundamental precepts of the Four Noble Truths. The logic in both of these foundational Buddhist teachings is that: a) suffering is universal and is caused by the clinging to pleasure and aversion to pain (ground); b) that there is a way out, and that way is through the practice of meditation (path); and c) that through "rightful" thought, action, speech, and ethical conduct, one participates in the liberation of all beings from further suffering (path).

How, though, does the preceding constitute a contemplative awareness-in-action related to intersubjectivity? Notwithstanding the deeply rooted spiritual or metaphysical essence of Ueshiba's teachings of the "way" of Aikido, Aikido can be seen as a *transegoic* or transpersonal praxis situated in both the *intra*psychic and *inter*psychic, that is, in the face of real or *perceived* threat when we encounter the Other. In the context of the Buddhist contemplative practice of mindful meditation, this encounter can be fruitfully understood as meta-awareness of one's reactivity, leading to naturally arising wisdom (*prajna*) or "discriminating awareness" and "skilful means" (*upaya*) (Wallace, 2001). In Aikido, with its partner practice of simulated combat encounter, one's self-awareness is actively usurped from resting in a first-person orientation and reaches out toward and engages with another's subjectivity through what can be described as *ki-joining*. (I illustrate this concept of ki-joining in a vignette later in the chapter.)

However, Aikido demonstrates at an experiential level that intersubjectivity still connotes a dualistic view, a *separateness* of being between two subjective cognizers. The resolution of conflict through the joining of *ki* and the harmonization of this dualistic notion is at the heart of Aikido, wherein the subjects-entering-subjectivity are reunited within a continuous ontical and phenomenal field of conscious awareness. It is in this field of consciousness that self/Other and inner/outer dichotomy (and indeed conceptualization of such) is dissolved into liminality and becomes integrated into wholeness. This ontical ground and the "action" of this harmonization in Aikido is *love* (Ueshiba, 1992). I give a phenomenological illustration of the aforementioned principles as follows.

Vignette #1: Harmonizing with the Universe

> "Think here," my practice partner instructs, touching the top of my hand near my thumb; my arm is poised confidently outward as if gesturing a handshake. With steady movement upward from below my wrist, and light backpressure with his other hand atop my elbow crease, my partner unhesitatingly and easily folds my arm and outstretched hand up toward my shoulder.

"Now," he instructs, "extend your mind, out your fingertips." Without effort, as he tests toward my shoulder, my outstretched arm—with light, natural, and relaxed posture—remains unchanged. I have not exerted any greater effort, apart from directing my mind/body to extend out in an unbroken connection to the entire universe.

This exercise, somewhat misleadingly named "unbendable arm," is more aptly a demonstration of the principle of "immovable mind" (*fudoshin*, in Japanese) that results from the joining of self with universal *ki*. Students of Aikido experience, by connecting their mind/body in an unbroken way with the infinitude of universal *ki*, that they are in fact "immovable." As we shall explore later, the systematic pedagogy of Ki Aikido provides multiple ways for students to experientially embody these principles for daily life.

By learning to calm oneself and time a seamless blending of one's movement with an oncoming attacker, the power, intent, and ultimate completion of the aggression are neutralized in a spirit of protection for both *nage* (defender) and *uke* (attacker). This harmonization of opposites is expressed in Aikido terms as *musubi*, *de-ai*, and *ma-ai* (Saotome, 1993). These terms warrant explication and much closer exploration.

Musubi

To paraphrase Aikido master teacher Mitsugi Saotome, *musubi* principle is at the "heart of Aikido." It is translated into English as "unity" or "harmonious interaction" and essentially refers to the attuned communication and *connection* between one and one's partner in and through Aikido training (Saotome, 1989). As Saotome (1989) explains:

> In practice, *musubi* means the ability to blend, both physically and mentally, with the movement and energy of your partner. *Musubi* is the study of good communication. In any interaction between people, communication exists, whether acknowledged or not. It is up to the participants in the interaction to determine whether the communication will be productive or useless, friendly or hostile, true or inaccurate. *Musubi*, as it is refined, can mean the ability to control and alter interaction, changing a hostile approach to a healthy encounter or an attack into a handshake. (p. 9)

Saotome (1989) elaborates that *musubi* is both a principle of learning and teaching, and that the art must be taught with the same principle it espouses. Ultimately, he says, it expresses a spiritual discipline of self-refinement:

> *Musubi* is both a method of learning and the goal of study. *Musubi*, in its ultimate refinement, relates to the achievement of a sense of universal harmony and, in technique, the ability to control encounters for the good. But can such ability be achieved by forcing, coercing, or frightening a person into learning it? No. *Musubi* must be taught and studied according to the principles it exemplifies so that the Aikido student's consciousness may be refined along with his physical movement. *Musubi* must be taught through good interaction and firm but kindly guidance. (p. 9)

In the context of intersubjectivity, *musubi* in Aikido is akin to being highly sensitized to the *ki* of your partner and relates to the Ki Aikido principle of "know your partner's mind" and "respect your partner's *ki*."

De-ai and Ma-ai

In accordance with the principle of *musubi*, which expresses the interconnectedness and, most importantly, the *blending* of one's movement and energy through Aiki, *de-ai* (correct timing) and *ma-ai* (respectful and harmonious distance) are vital components in Aikido training. It is critical to distinguish between *blending* with one's attacker/partner through *aiki* (harmonization with universe, restoring order and *oneness*) and *merging* with the attack. The latter implies a kind of convergence or absorption of the partner's *ki*. To some extent, at least tactically, this is visibly true—one's calmness and nonresistant blending allow the *nage* to neutralize or dissipate the opponent's energy. However, true to its origins in *budo* (particularly *kendo*, or sword training), respectful and proper harmonious distance (*ma-ai*) is integral to ensuring mutual protection. Tactically speaking, *ma-ai* means not allowing the attack to enter and occupy one's spherical center; and *de-ai* refers to the correct timing in order to fulfill *musubi* (blending) and harmonious connection with one's partner. The implications for this training as a metaphor for daily life lived in intersubjectivity are at the heart of Aikido as a "path of love" and are further explicated and emphasized in the pedagogy and praxis of Ki Aikido.

Aikido thus represents a praxis or path moving beyond mere conflict resolution to one of harmony through nondual awareness, and ultimately with what modern Japanese philosopher Nishida Kitaro describes as "pure experience."[7] This kind of prereflective immediacy to experience, within a context of nondual ontology, is pivotal to Ueshiba's vision of Aikido. As such, it offers invaluable insight and methodologies based on interdependence and cooperation that can be adapted to other pedagogical practices toward fostering intersubjective contemplative learning. In the next section, I take a close philosophical look at the experience of intersubjectivity.

Importance of Practice for Experiencing Intersubjectivity

Contemplative Eastern traditions such as Buddhism establish enlightenment, here understood as *bodhicitta*, or "awakened heart," not as a theoretically knowable ultimate Truth, but as an empirically accomplishable goal: one that is cultivated through an experiential path of knowing, doing, and being. A contemplative practice that gains us "oneness of body-mind" (e.g., Aikido, yoga) will invariably lead one to encounter habitual patterns of embodied emotions, thought, and (re)action. Buddhist discourse describes such psychosocial patterns as *conditioning*. It is conditioned psychosocial patterns that are in the way of our being authentically intersubjective. These patterns lock us into the egoic self and prevent us from looking out and opening to the emergent reality of another being or other beings with whom we can practice intersubjectivity. Thus, to practice is to engage with one's *conditioned* nature, to recondition, and thus to re*enact* (Varela, Thompson, & Rosch, 1991), reengage, repotentiate, and reinhabit the lifeworld as a fully present interrelational being.

Aikido, much like mindfulness meditation, is a practice for reconciliation between the dualistic Self (*relative* truth, in "two-truths" theory) and the egoless Self (*absolute* truth)[8] *beyond* dialectical reflection, through *embodied* and *enacted* engagement with the Other in intersubjective connection, that is, in the "betweenness" (*aidagara*) of spatial-*basho*. *Basho* or *topos* (Nishida, in Yusa, 1997) here isn't invoked merely to address the so-called "explanatory gap" between cognitive science and phenomenology. Rather, in the context of Aikido and its cosmological/ontological view of universal existence, *basho* is a lived-world of the energetic field of nonduality. This is central to understanding the core of Aikido's teachings, beyond culturally rooted religiosity or mysticism. What occurs in the intersubjective field in moments of encounter, when Ueshiba suggests that an attack is over before it has begun, is that one who has vanquished aggressiveness and a fighting mind (e.g., separateness of self/Other) within one's self has already defeated the attacker. When a *nage* (the attacked) is able to still himself or herself and *receive* the attack without resistance in a spirit of harmony, there is, in effect, *nothing to attack*—the *uke* (the attacker) is confronted with his own aggressive intent-in-action and shifts from an object-relation with "an enemy" to being *received* and thus protected from himself.

As Yuasa (1987), in his chapter on Japanese philosopher Watsuji Tetsuro, asks: "What does it mean to exist in betweenness (*aidagara*)?" What Yuasa is addressing here is not merely a phenomenological problem, but a methodological one. "If a characteristic of Eastern thought is that a lived experience of cultivation is the methodological route to enlightenment," he posits, ". . . this means that the very character of the dualistic mode in the relationship between the mind and body will gradually change through the process of cultivation" (p. 28). This passage describes the very essence of contemplative practice in Buddhism—to dissolve the illusion of substantive ego-self through the phenomenal meta-awareness of discursive thought and the self-generating narrative of "I" as the flow of mental activity. The following section goes into the actual Aikido training and shows how the experiential, practical path of "harmonization" heals conditioned dualism.

From "Ki-Joining" to Indivisible Wholeness: Aikido Training

The training exercises in Aikido, while ultimately comprising infinitely variable and adaptable techniques for unarmed self-defense,[9] provide a simulation of conflict through which the defender can learn to calmly, lightly, in perfect timing and stable posture, gain control of an attacker. *Ki development* in Aikido training uses mind-body coordination principles and exercises as a way to help students grasp and cultivate the same kind of calm, stable, and determined *states* of readiness, movement, and flow that Ueshiba was able to experience.[10]

Partners team up through physical contact exercises of self-defense not to simply learn body-mechanics to overpower an opponent as seen in Judo, Karate, or similar martial arts, but to develop an acute awareness of the aforementioned energy field (*ki*) within which contact occurs. This practice goes beyond mere proprioception of one's singular subjective movement and agency and requires *inter*subjective awareness and a *meta-perception* of the field itself, indistinct from the *uke* and *nage* within it. In this sense, this "*ki* development" of sensing, joining, and being inseparable from Ki (universe; wholeness) is akin to Bohm's idea of the implicate and explicate order—both are inextricably *enfolded*, or to describe it more accurately, (quantum) *entangled* (Bohm, 1981). Ueshiba defined this dynamic as Love. For our purposes, we can recognize it as moving from *conceptual* intersubjectivity to *engaged* and embodied intersubjectivity.

Now let us talk about the actual *ki* training method. Listed here are the two sets of Ki Development and Ki Aikido principles.

Four Principles of Mind-Body Coordination

1. Think of your one-point.
2. Completely relax.
3. Have a light posture.
4. Extend your mind.

Five Principles of Mind-Body Coordination in Aikido

1. Extend your mind.
2. Know your partner's mind.
3. Respect your partner's *ki*.
4. Put yourself in your partner's place.
5. Perform with confidence.

The first set of principles give students a method for effectively observing the nature of their mind manifested through their body state as regards stability, calmness, and relaxation, while being tested for balance or reaction by their partner. For example, by thinking of one's virtual center at their abdomen, the "one-point," the mind and the body align in a natural way to become "immovable" (*fudoshin*), which results from *ki*-joining and harmonization. Similarly, with these principles in place as embodied awareness and state-based calmness and relaxed movement, practitioners can engage in Aikido exercises in motion—attack and defense—with the relational aspects of Other (e.g., "respect your partner's *ki*") as a means of blending or harmonizing their movement with the attack. In doing so, *aikidoka* (participants of Aikido) are thus engaged in shared meta-awareness of dynamics that transcend dualism, experiencing firsthand that a lived experience of inseparability from the *ki* field brings to fruition a felt-sense of the "oneness of body-mind," as referred to in Zen training. This "oneness" experience is most starkly demonstrated in *shugyo*.

Shugyo is the enhancement of a student's increased capacity for presence, to be witnessed as *tada ima*, "only now . . . there is only this moment" (Saotome, 1993, p. 162) or *ichi go ichi e*, "one life, one meeting" (p. 173). Thus, *budo* training is not so much about preparation for the destruction of war, but the preservation of life, and the fearlessness of one's indomitable spirit in engaging the liminality of life and death in any encounter. In the martial context of such a liminal and martial encounter, it is the calmness and concentration, and the harmony of one's *ki* (*aiki*), the absence of any "spiritual separation" that leaves one vulnerable to injury, that ultimately secures protection of life. This liminality can be seen in the expression *sei shi ichi ryo*: "life and death are one" (p. 165). Saotome (1993) writes:

> Standing on the edge of life and death, you cannot make a lie. Standing on the edge of life and death, your physical and your spiritual vibration can only speak the truth, and your deepest self will appear. A master understands this and he awaits an imbalance, an opening in the other's defense. He surrounds the emptiness, the negative space in which to catch the enemy's spirit and vibration, with his presence. (p. 169)

In essence, then, Aikido is a spiritual path or *do*, through *shugyo* (cultivation), of cultivating mind-body coordination that results in calmness, readiness, relaxation, presence. One cultivates for an embodied and *felt* sense of calmness and so on through partner training for the continuously lived experience of liminality that dissolves the duality of life-death and self-Other in daily life. Training with a partner thus becomes a canvas of relational dynamics on which a spiritual exercise in moving from singular subjectivity to relational intersubjectivity, in which physical confrontation constitutes one's own encounter with ego. The cultivation of nonresistance, of joining in and blending with the other, takes place at such a point of contact.

Vignette #2: Mirrorboxing: From Self-Projection to Reflection and Synchrony

I shall now slip into another first-person narrative to describe a teaching experience in the Aikido *dojo* (training hall, in Japanese) that leads to a deeper understanding of intersubjectivity.

> The *ikkyo undo* (first principle exercise) instructs students to "raise hands to eye level": from the *hanmi* stance (basic Aikido posture: one foot forward and turned out slightly, the rear foot at almost a right angle to the front) the student bends the knee to allow a forward movement from the body/hips, leading to a swinging up of the hands, with her fingertips directed toward an imaginary partner's eyes. Imagine bringing your hands and arms up as if to make applause at eye level.
>
> In a very direct application of this exercise (which one does repetitively on one's own, such that it becomes natural and effortless), the synchronized raising of the hands/arms,

anchored with the mid-point in the abdomen or "one-point" (Jap.: *hara*) allows the *nage* to make contact with an attacker's strike to the top of the head (*shomenuchi*)—done with a weapon or edge-of-hand. The contact with the strike blends with it in an upward motion, redirecting the attacker's hand or weapon strike in a matched "cut" back toward them in a circular movement, forcing the attacker to turn away and protect her balance. In this way, the strike is redirected such that the attacker's cut turns on *herself*. Ultimately, this is done with the least physical movement necessary: the raising of hands with a "directing" of *ki* blends and "extends" the same kind of sword-like feeling to the attacker, diverting or interrupting the attack, which in effect "moves" the attacker's mind subconsciously, forcing the attacker to miss the target, or at least to create an opening (*suki*), a weakness, in the attacker's *ki*.

In studying this exercise recently with my students, I emphasize how one's calmness as the defender (*nage*) allows one to be "one step ahead" of the attacker and thus move in perfect unison with the opponent's raised arm attack. To demonstrate this principle, I stand in front of the large windows in the *dojo*, which now looking out to darkness offers a reflective black surface for my body in motion.

I speak of the principle of "knowing your partner's mind," while taking the Aikido posture to draw/receive the *shomen* strike (making my body oblique to the attack, not square-on). Since the "attacker" in the reflection is *me*, I highlight how it is impossible to escape an awareness of my own intention to attack. First detected is the impulse to attack; what follows is the slightest impulse to move my body in succession. As if to respond to my reflection's attack, I raise my hands in *ikkyo undo*, obviously in perfect coherence with my "shadow" partner.

This, I explain, is perfect *aiki*. My internal awareness makes it impossible for me to *fool myself* through my own reflection. Thus, being in stillness, open, ready, and attuned with the Other, I am able to instantaneously perceive the attacker's mind (or the energy-intention-thought to attack) and thus effortlessly, and without hesitation, move in perfect matched synchrony to diffuse the attack without a clash.

In addition, the attacker's intention and aggression has already put her out of her own synchrony. This reveals two critical points. One, the attacker is already out of sync with her self (here I use the analogy of a four-color printing process in a newspaper, where the color register is off and the printed version shows off-register color shifts in the reproduced photograph). This disharmony shows, as O Sensei taught, how one "has already been defeated." Second, to follow the latter, that his asynchronous mind/body betrays his attack, thus allowing me to move imperceptibly in perfect timing with him. This is in fact precisely what occurred when Ueshiba was able to preemptively evade his sword challenger's strikes in the aforementioned encounter, leading to his epiphany from which Aikido was born.

The preceding vignette reflects the multilayered aspects of inter-subjectivity, also understood as *dependent co-arising* in Buddhist discourse, encountered via our phenomenal perception. Coming back to our main concern in this chapter, Aikido can be seen as contemplative practice *in action*; it is inherently relational, thus second-person oriented. At the same time, one cultivates a state of nonreactive responsiveness and readiness that produces, as the saying goes: "minimal effort for maximum efficiency." Much like in meditation where practice highlights and then diminishes one's habitual mental discursiveness, partner practice makes one first aware of, then adaptive to, one's own reactivity when faced with the "challenge" of a partner entering one's space. Within the value framework of conflict resolution, harmony of dissonance, and the unification of the "human family" as envisioned by the founder, Aikido echoes the pragmatism of Buddhist contemplative practice: in order to fulfill the practical and soteriological goals of resolving conflict arising from dualistic separateness, one must first examine and overcome one's own egoic defensiveness and aggression. In this sense, Aikido goes beyond the first-person mind-body unification of contemplative practice to directly relational self-Other unification. The primary focus of the art is to make one aware of one's own dualistic nature and how we are out of accord with one another due to our *inner* separateness and discord, which is mirrored in our reactive aggression to the Other.

Wallace (2001) brings in a similar relational view concerning the conceptualization of the self going beyond first-person:

> . . . the self is brought into existence by the power of conceptual imputation. . . . Buddhism maintains that conceptual frameworks are not private. They are public and consensual. So the ways in which I perceive and conceive of myself and others are inextricably related to the community of language-users and thinkers with whom I share a common conceptual framework. (p. 2)

Wallace describes seeing how others see us as a kind of *reiterated empathy* "in which one views one's own psychophysical processes from a "second-person" perspective (p. 5), and that this is as "real" as our "first-person" perspective—neither exists independently of one another. Wallace further points out that in Buddhist methodology, the realization that interior and exterior existence are inherently unreal, therefore that no distinction exists, is achieved through *dzogchen*[11] practice.

I offer another vignette that illustrates Aikido's potential for pedagogical leadership as follows.

Vignette #3: Aikido as Embodied, Nonresistant Leadership

From the "mirrorboxing" example, we move to a partner-to-partner exercise. Facing each other in *seiza* (kneeling position, ankles under), one partner extends his arms to be held. The *uke* holds the sides of the *nage*'s wrists (like the *nage*, who is holding wide handlebars, the *uke* is, in turn, holding the *nage*'s wrists). With a spirit of honesty, the *nage* cannot make any conscious effort without encountering resistance, especially as the *uke* is exhibiting stable mind/body coordination.

Rather, with the *uke* "following" lightly—that is prepared for any movement so as to follow through their control/attack/test—the *nage* must in fact "follow" her tester's *ki*, joining with the forward movement of the *uke*'s grip/intention. And like the mirrorboxing analogy, the *nage* moves in a synchronous and unbroken fluidity that will end up with the *uke* in an unstable position, thus having to "escape" (*ukemi*) in self-protection. Simply put, the *nage* lowers her elbow in a relaxed manner, swooping in with her wrist (and her partner's), such that the partner, still holding, is "lifted" up (mind and body) in a continuous, destabilizing motion. This is called "leading" or "moving" your partner's mind.[12]

If we return to our primary concern here, how might Aikido model a praxis of relationality in such a contemplative way? How might this translate as *warriorship* for educators? Etymologically, the word *educate* has its roots in the Latin *educere*, "to lead out." This has radical implications if taken to heart in pedagogy, suggesting its core mission or purpose is to lead *by example*, and to inspire. From the vantage point of working toward interpenetration via contemplative practice, to be "educated," then, means to be led to self-awareness, to an awakened state. Within the values of contemplative traditions such as Aikido and Buddhism, to be awakened is to be aligned with self-evident truth, to overcome the fear of being awake, and thus the fear of looking within.

Aikido cannot be reduced to merely tactical training, nor should its potential contribution to pedagogy be reduced to matters of tactic. Rather, Aikido offers pedagogy the concept of *warriorship* as a process of learning to become intersubjective and co-developmental through relational encounter.

Closing: Transformative Pedagogy as Human Interdependence

While Western and Eastern philosophy share similar aims in terms of knowing, doing, and being, a preoccupation with an objectivist approach to epistemology and ontology continues to dominate Western philosophical discourse. This is largely the result of the problematic theoretical circularity encountered in the subject/object split, despite voluminous advances in phenomenology by the likes of Levinas, Buber, Merleau-Ponty, and others. However, in Eastern approaches, pragmatic and achievable traits and tasks are facilitated through cultivation of the self for "body-mind oneness" (Easai, in Yuasa, 1987). In the principles and training of Ki Aikido and Shambhala Buddhism, as examined here, one can see a soteriological ethos for enlightenment through "peaceful warriorship."

In relation to pedagogy, the discussion serves to humanize educators in their roles not only as pedagogues but also as human beings tasked with the "tensional, ethical" praxis of dialogue (Stewart & Zediker, 2000). Leadership exemplifies praxis by privileging the relational over the individual, humanness over objectivity and productivity. If indeed, as O'Byrne (2005) says, the function of pedagogy is to "teach revolution," then, as Freire (2000) says:

> A revolutionary leadership must accordingly practice co-intentional education. Teachers and students (leadership and people), co-intent on reality, are both Subjects, not only in the task of unveiling that reality, and thereby coming to know it critically, but in the task of re-creating that knowledge. As they attain this knowledge of reality through common reflection and action, they discover themselves as its permanent re-creators. (p. 69)

While Aikido is not presented here as an idealized or singular path to praxis, it does point the way to knowing-being through intersubjectivity as *do* or "way," through nonviolent presencing and interconnectedness. Aikido thus represents a praxis or path moving beyond mere conflict resolution to harmony through nondual awareness, intersubjectivity, and ultimately with nondual "pure being."

Notes

1. See Fornet-Betancourt, Becker, Gomez-Müller, and Gauthier (1987). "Practices of freedom" is in reference to Foucault's thoughts on the correlation between freedom and ethics, as expressed in late life interviews, as regards his theory on "care of the self" and how it impacts ethical relations with action toward others.

2. I have written about this elsewhere, as regards Aikido as praxis, and the implications for pedagogical application regarding intersubjectivity. See Gordon (2016).

3. This, following a challenge Ueshiba accepted, unarmed, from a naval officer student who attacked him with a wooden sword. Ueshiba's famous epithet arose from his ability to effortlessly evade his attacker while simultaneously protecting him, the challenger, from harm—arising from an embodied nonduality with the flow of nature, the Universe, both conceptually and physically.

4. As Gunnlaugson (2009) defines it: "second-person approaches to contemplative education involve exploring contemplative experience from an intersubjective position that is represented spatially as between us, in contrast to inside us (subjective position) or outside us (objective position)" (p. 2).

5. Yasua guides us here that the Japanese term *between* (*aida*) connotes a physical sense of space, "between a thing and a thing," such that our

"betweenness" implies our existence in a definite, spatial *basho* (place, *topos*, field). "Naturally," he says, "this *basho* is not a position in a neutralized, physical space that obliterates any human significance; rather, it is the life-*basho* in which we find the interconnected meanings of the life-world" (Yuasa, 1987, p. 38).

6. See this site: http://www.salon.com/2015/09/27/corporate_mindfulness_is_bullsht_zen_or_no_zen_youre_working_harder_and_being_paid_less/and http://www.buddhistpeacefellowship.org/white-privilege-the-mindfulness-movement/?blm_aid=6718486.

7. Feenberg (1999) comments: "Nishida shared this concept of pure experience with D. T. Suzuki, who popularized the identification of enlightened consciousness with a kind of immediacy prior to all reflection. Suzuki's influence, in turn, is explicitly present in Nishida's later theory of Japanese culture where he writes that 'No-mind (*mushin*) can be considered the axis of the Oriental spirit (Suzuki Daisetz)'" (Nishida in Feenberg, 1999, p. 29).

8. Kapstein (1997). This is a reference to the Buddhist theories of "emptiness" and "two-truths" (*śūnyatā*) explicated by highly influential Indian philosopher Nāgārjuna (ca. 150–250 AD) of the "middle way" (*madhyamaka*) tradition. These two paradigms can be expressed (cognitively and ontologically) as a dialectical tension between what "is" (absolute truth) and what "appears to be" (phenomenal, or "relative truth"), leaving us with a "both/and" paradox in his teaching of Emptiness (that the relative and absolute truth are interdependent).

9. Aikido movements revolve around two general principles: in *tenkan*, one enters into the center of an attack (in the attacker's "place," accelerating the centrifugal or centripetal force; in *irimi*, the *nage* or defender enters into the attack, redirecting *uke*'s force to cause *uke* to turn. In either general countermovement from the *nage*, the *uke* is—by the nature of his continued attack—forced to make *ukemi*: escape. In essence, this ultimately forces the *uke* to question his aggression. In its most advanced form, suggested Ueshiba, the attack is over before it begins. Thus exists the axiom about Aikido that it is "winning without fighting."

10. Koichi Tohei (b. 1920; d. 2011) was an early student of the founder, eventually becoming chief instructor and the first awarded the highest rank of 10th Dan. Tohei keenly observed that while many students were emulating the founders' movements, they were incapable of throwing and controlling their *ukes* with the same effortlessness. Ueshiba, it seems, was unable to transmit in a cohesive, accessible way, the deeply embodied esoteric spiritual principles— coupled with years of rigorous and highly integrated martial training—through a singular pedagogy. After the war, Tohei studied the principles of mind-body coordination of yoga-influenced teacher Tempu Nakamura. He was soon to discern from Tempu's approach that what Aikido students were unable to replicate from Ueshiba's movements (and what Ueshiba was unable—or unwilling—to explicate) was the founder's powerful *feeling*: his *Ki*. In other words, what made Ueshiba the embodiment of his own art was his exquisitely tuned flow-state of mind-body unification, his capacity to move freely and in totally harmonized

timing with an attack—in essence, to defeat the attack before it arose. After the founder's death in 1969, Tohei (1980) began to adapt Ki Development into Aikido training, using mind-body coordination principles and exercises.

11. From Tibetan Buddhism, also translated as "Great Perfection," *dzogchen* aims to attain and cultivate a natural primordial condition, considered a liberatory achievement in the Nyingma tradition.

12. Spiritually speaking, this aspect of self-awareness, linked to the Buddhist concept of *karma*, is absolutely central to Aikido. There is not ample space here to explore this inter-spiritual pedagogical aspect of Aikido, where the *nage* is—without being destructive, but rather nonresistant and protective—leading the *uke* to face his or her own choice to attack. This is effectively a kind of *karmic* encounter. In a spirit of loving protection, the aikidoist seeks to dissolve the seed of aggression in the attacker's mind or conditioned nature. This is the highest spiritual aim of Aikido, which led Ueshiba to deem it a "path of love."

References

Becker, H., Fornet-Betancourt, R., Gomez-Müller, A., & Gauthier, J. (1987). The ethic of care for the self as a practice of freedom: An interview with Michel Foucault on January 20, 1984. *Philosophy & Social Criticism*, 12(2–3), 112–131.

Bohm, D. (1981). *Wholeness and the implicate order*. London: Routledge & Kegan Paul.

Feenberg, A. (1999). Experience and culture: Nishida's path "to the things themselves." *Philosophy East and West*, 49 (1), 28–44.

Freire, P. (2000). *Pedagogy of the oppressed* (30th anniversary ed.). New York: Continuum.

Gordon, M. A. (2016, March). Towards pedagogical warriorship: Aikido as contemplative education through relational praxis and the primacy of other. Paper presented at the 60th annual conference of the Comparative International Education Society, in Vancouver, Canada

Gunnlaugson, O. (2009, December 14). Exploring presencing as a contemplative framework for inquiry in higher education classrooms. Unpublished doctoral dissertation. University of British Columbia, Vancouver.

Hahn, T. N. (1998). *Interbeing: Fourteen guidelines for engaged Buddhism* (3rd ed.) (F. Eppsteiner, Ed.). Berkeley: Parallax Press.

Kapstein, M. (1997). Buddhist perspectives on ontological truth. In E. Deutsch & R. Bontekoe (Eds.), *A companion to world philosophies*. (pp. 420–433). Oxford: Blackwell.

O'Byrne, A. (2005). Pedagogy without a project: Arendt and Derrida on teaching, responsibility and revolution. *Studies in Philosophy and Education*, 24(5), 389–409.

Saotome, M. (1989). *The principles of Aikido*. Boston: Shambhala.
Saotome, M. (1993). *Aikido and the harmony of nature*. Boston: Shambhala.
Stewart, J., & Zediker, K. (2000). Dialogue as tensional, ethical practice. *Southern Journal of Communication, 65*(2–3), 224–242.
Tohei, K. (1980). *Ki in daily life*. Tokyo: Ki No Kenkyukai.
Ueshiba, K. (1985). *Aikido*. Tokyo: Hozansha.
Ueshiba, M. (1992). *The art of peace* (J. Stevens, Trans., Ed.). Boston: Shambhala.
Varela, F. J., Thompson, E., & Rosch, E. (1991). *The embodied mind: Cognitive science and human experience*. Cambridge: MIT Press.
Wallace, B. A. (2001). Intersubjectivity in Indo-Tibetan Buddhism. *Journal of Consciousness Studies, 8*(5–7), 209–230.
Yusa, M. (1997). Contemporary Buddhist philosophy. In E. Deutsch, & R. Bontekoe (Eds.), *A companion to world philosophies* (pp. 564–572). Oxford: Blackwell.
Yuasa, Y. (1987). *The body toward an eastern mind-body theory* (T. P. Kasulis & S. Nagatomo, Trans.; T. P. Kasulis, Ed.). Albany: State University of New York Press.

7

Self, Other, and the System

IAN MACNAUGHTON

Introducing My Pedagogical Work in Its Context

The focus of this chapter is the intersubjective domain of learning. In proposing to explore this topic, I must first mention that new paradigms have evolved to enhance learning effectiveness. There has been a noticeable transition from a linear, top-down approach (teacher to student) to include a bottom up and lateral, holistic, collective experience. Discussion replaces lecture, visceral experiences with an emphasis on the intuitive and on the felt sense are supported alongside the cognitive aspects of learning, and movement is integrated in class experientially. Therefore, the intersubjective relational field between teacher and the student involves a dynamic interplay.

Ninety percent of my students are licensed therapists with 20 to 30 years in clinical practice. Students offer unique and different points of view. Part of my process is to incorporate my own and the students' similarities and differences, and bring them to life in an explicit, constructive way to enhance learning through mindfulness, somatic practices, and the theories of Systems-Centered Training® (SCT) (Agazarian, 2012). My students come to learn more about how to integrate mindfulness practices—the integration of the body-mind—into more effective ways to alleviate human suffering. In that process many become interested in learning about my ability to sense within my own body to know whether or not the "other" has experienced a resonant system with me. They attend my classes to explore the experience of learning this skill, and to develop their own capacity of coming into resonance with self and other. They practice first by experiencing it with me (interpersonal neurobiology, IPNB), and then with others, and then with the class itself, the collective.

I teach resonance in the class field so that the group itself learns how to develop a feeling, sensing, thinking collective that creatively processes what each voice offers to construct a new whole. My focus is on the interrelationships between the self and individual students and then between the self and the collective experience such that students feel seen in their entirety. In educational settings, I model and teach students how to allow learning to be a cocreative emergent process (dynamic versus linear) (Agazarian, 2012; Fosha, 2002, 2003, 2005; Schore, 2001; Tronick, 2003; Tronick & Beeghly, 2011). In that way, we connect with what the self brings to the group, and we see how the group's wisdom becomes re-expressed as a new shared wisdom that emerges from the group experience via dialogue, presence (somatic and energetic sensing), modeling, and direct instruction. We may end up in a very different place from where we, including myself, all started. Combining physically interactive approaches such as movement and role play with a cognitive interplay of language patterns (SAVI: Systems of Analyzing Verbal Interactions®) and Focusing (Gendlin, 1969, 1981, 1996) allows students to shift perspectives within the context of the interpersonal field and somatic attunement and resonance.

Indeed, the lack of resonance is sometimes "sensed" below the "water line" of consciousness. With improved sensate capacity and awareness, discord in the resonance can be sensed and addressed with curiosity and in relationship. Without the awareness within the person that something is misaligned in themselves, the teacher, other classmates, or in the group itself, there is no opportunity to dialogue and learn individually and together.

Intersubjectivity in Educational Settings

I teach students (or whomever I am engaged with, in relationship with, or work with) how to know themselves more deeply, fully, and richly. At the same time, they learn how to engage more constructively with others' developing selves, and they learn group interaction skills. That is, by looking at a "between-us" perspective for learning versus a subjective or objective consciousness (the life task of moving from internal perception and data to the relationship field), we take the time to experience contemplative human consciousness.

As I will show, intersubjectivity in individuals is not only about the art of personal reflection; nor is it solely about practicing how to listen to one's personal way of being in life and work. It also involves knowing how to be with presence and resonance in order to attune to the somatic experience (with "somatic" defined as the body experienced from within) with a group, with a larger sense of human-to-human interpersonal intersubjectivity, and with the even larger expanse of our interbeingness (Bai, Scott, & Donald, 2009; Gunnlaugson, 2009). My work speaks to "being with" oneself and to having done the "work" to become sufficiently self-regulated in order to sense both oneself and the other(s), and to develop the ability to know more accurately what experience is ours and what is another's. I will discuss being able to "be" with others in different roles—interpersonally and as a teacher—in such a way that mutual connection and harmony (that is, "safety" in the psychobiological system) can enhance the students' and the group's emergent mutual discovery and learning. This speaks to system dynamics: the reality that we are immersed in a nonlinear dynamical universe and that we ourselves—our brains and our whole personal system—are operating in the same way. Our task with respect to intersubjectivity is to discover a flexible stability within the factual uncertainty of life itself. In this capacity, I am proposing that the interpersonal relativity field can positively or negatively influence learning for both teachers and students. Current brain science supports my thesis that the connection between intersubjectivity and contemplative practice is key to facilitating learning.

In the next section I will begin by summarizing a few findings in current brain science that support my thesis about the connection between intersubjectivity and contemplative practice, and then I will discuss how this connection is key to facilitating learning.

What Brain Science Tells about Learning

Research into neuroscience (brain imagining), psychology, and education offers a clearer understanding of how the human brain actually "learns." Joseph LeDoux (1996), who first traced the emotion of fear throughout the brain, offered the proposition that emotions engage many parts of the neocortex. Our emotions and cognitions are inseparable processes from our nervous system; brainstem and limbic areas of the brain serve as the source of our emotional life and stimulate our motivational drives

(Panksepp, 2010). Educators will benefit from understanding how these systems function. For example, knowing that the amygdala (which is located deep in the brain's medial temporal lobe and forms part of the limbic system) scans for signals of safety or threat, and is poised to cue sympathetic activation (fight or flight) if necessary while simultaneously signaling the neocortex to contemplate the current situation and assess a true threat, allows educators the means to physiologically structure classroom environments, interactional processes, and so forth. I am assuming here awareness that while there is a vertical dimension to the brain's organization (and our experience), there is also left and right hemisphere differentiation to consider and include in learning enhancement (the right brain being more linear and the right brain being more holistic). In addition, there is the discovery of mirror neurons that fire off when there are changes in each person that emulate or indicate safety, as a counterpoint to the alarm of the amygdala.

Thus, a fundamental precept in contemplative education must be awareness or the intention of developing present-centered awareness, that is, to be able to notice what is actually going on in both the cognitive and somatic reactions within the body itself by the person who is residing in this body. This speaks to the ability to track—discriminate various energies, sensations, feeling tones, emotions, and cognitions—in a spectrum of awareness that fills out the sense of self and enhances the ability to engage with others in a learning context. In the next section, I speak more about tracking and other pedagogical abilities.

Essential Pedagogical Abilities

Effective teaching and learning experiences—in fact, all close interpersonal relationships—involve tracking, alignment, and resonance as a means to attunement and utilizing affective resources. For example, feeling that our emotions are understood by another supports self-regulation and a sense of safety, which helps to settle the nervous system and affords a greater possibility of learning.

Tracking

When I say I track a student's signals, I am in actuality focused in the present, watching state and trait changes moment-to-moment with an open and curious mind. I listen to the words as well as the intonations, watch how gestures enhance or belie what is said. At the same time, I am sensing what my visceral experience is and how it is engaging me or removing me from connection to myself and the student: for example, being lost in thinking, being bored, overstimulated, or experiencing discomfort. Tracking allows me to align my current state with the student's.

Affect Attunement

One person having the capacity to attune sufficiently with another person to be able to approximately match their internal state, energy, sensation, their feelings (open, closed, tight loose, etc.), with the state of the other person at a feeling level, is what I reference here as affect attunement.

Alignment

Alignment is one component of affect attunement. It occurs when "the state of one individual is altered to approximate that of the other member of the dyad" (Siegel, 2012, p. 280). Alignment is both unidirectional and bidirectional, with one matching the other or both working to tune into one another and making necessary state shifts. "Feeling felt" supports the attunement experience with the overall effect described as "resonance."

Resonance

Resonance evolves beyond alignment of states to include how the interpersonal interactions affect the individuals involved. Our mirror neuron system allows us to feel another person's experience in ourselves, as if it is happening to ourselves. Our brain fires in response to what we see and sense in the other person (Gantt & Agazarian, 2006, p. 78).

Intersubjective Relational Field

Thus, the intersubjective relational field involves many pieces that the teacher must know and subtly integrate within his self or her self and within the methodology. This sets the stage for how the teacher comes to the classroom embodying the intersubjective contemplative approach to instruction. These components must be in place to support students as I challenge them to participate in the process, as well as they support the expansion necessary for the self to become part of a learning dyad and then part of the collective experience. This speaks to the concept of self-regulation. If there is not sufficient clarity of the context and roles and goals for learning, learning is diminished. With reduced capacity to utilize relationships to enhance learning, the safety, confidence, and curiosity to learn are greatly reduced.

Self-Regulation

Self-regulation requires another person. In other words, we need to be in relationship with others to learn how to self-regulate. Steven Porges's (2001, 2007), Allan Schore's (2001), and Edward Tronick's (2003) research all support the supposition that we cannot truly self-regulate ourselves in the best sense of the word without "another." According to De Jaegher, Di Paolo, and Gallagher (2010), social interactions are accurately viewed as a "co-regulated coupling" that results in an "autonomous self-sustaining organization" (p. 442). To self-regulate with another, however, a sense of safety must exist. How does a sense of safety come about in terms of our nervous system?

Neuroception

We are geared to automatically and intrinsically notice "safety," a sense wired in neurobiologically since the caveman. Porges (2001) proposed a "social engagement system," which is part of our global social nervous system. Within this system, Porges proposed a mechanism that he called "neuroception" that functions to trigger or inhibit defensive strategies outside of our conscious awareness. This ongoing monitoring process assesses safety or threat and determines whether it is safe for spontaneous social engagement or if the sympathetic nervous system needs to prepare for a flight, fight, or freeze response. Detecting safe and/or trustworthy features from the face (features and gestures), voice (tonality), and movement (gestures) then activates a neural circuit projecting from the temporal cortex to the central nucleus of the amygdala that inhibits defensive limbic functions. This circuit signals a "brake" to inhibit the limbic defense systems responsible for organizing and regulating our fight, flight, and freeze behaviors; it also enables the pathways in the brain that regulate social engagement behaviors.

When our nervous system determines that the external environment is safe, we have more resources to draw from—we are more creative and more likely to interact at an intimate level. The absence of danger, however, does not support a sense of safety. Receiving cues from other people triggers our sense of safety. This calming state starts with our ears—tonality overrides the content of a conversation. When we hear words that have melodic intonations, the muscles in our ears relax. From here, the muscles in our eyes and our face release tension. Our breath deepens. Our heartbeat slows. Our sympathetic nervous system can down regulate, and we are able to socially interact. Porges estimates that 80 to 85% of efferent nerves move from the body upward and only 15 to 20% downward. These percentages indicate what we should pay attention to in our lives—developing the capacity to feel comfortable in our bodies and, when something is awry and we're sensing danger, developing the ability to track what is going on and forming alignments with others around safety. Restoring resonance is imperative for safety.

When social engagement breaks down, learning breaks down. As an educator, I must address how students move beyond their own implicit needs for safety, belonging, and expression to learn what they bring to a group and how they bring it to a group such that they are part of the emergent work of the collective. My role involves the creation of a "safe enough" forum/context that facilitates interpersonal safety, thus allowing learning to take place. Donald W. Winnicott (1953) presented a parallel concept in his discussion of the "good enough" mother; he noted that her key role is to adapt to the baby, thus giving the infant both a sense of control and connection (to the mother). Just as mothers allow infants to transition at their own rate to a more autonomous position, with micro interactions between them central to the development of their internal world, teachers support students in a similar way.

It is my responsibility, as a teacher, to reflect back to the person, the dyad, and the group, information I notice coming into the discussion and to reframe differences as an opportunity to learn. My job is to be congruently able to connect with students around what they are trying to bring into the group. I hold a container for the group and resultant functional subgroups to reframe the differences as a contribution that is yet to be fully understood. We move from individual learner to functional subgroup learner to a group-as-a-whole-learner. What I really do is give the empowerment for the learning to the group; the group is learning to become a functional, self-regulating learning community.

Learning Communities: A Dynamic Process

Initially, students under my direction explore the actual goal of the group beyond the explicit goal that has been presented (usually by the teacher, not the students). Additionally, we touch on the implicit goal that may well be to "avoid" vulnerability, which is always the first phase of group development. This occurs within a context, and each person has a role: that of student, teacher, learner, and so on, and the "work" then is for each person to learn how to bring in their own authority toward actualizing their role within the goal of the context (Agazarian, 1997, 2001, 2012).

It is part of my role to deliver a structure for the learning field. I provide not only the context but also the skills and the process for mutual outcomes. I incorporate focusing skills and role-playing to create an embodied connection with the content, as well as movement, noting that "learning only occurs primarily through movement" (Sheets-Johnstone, 2011). The process involves subgroups that support each other in their differences, while within the "group," members practice staying in "enough" eye contact to be able to "join" in what is similar enough without taking things "personally" (Agazarian, 2001, 2012). All this speaks to having developed a personal presence that is secure within the students and in the interpersonal field, allowing everyone to express themselves in ways that are appropriate for learning. This starts with members being with themselves and developing an embodied presence.

I offer some concrete tools to support the work of creating learning community as follows.

Tools for Creating a Learning Community

To create a learning community that also develops the learner and the field of relationship in community, I incorporate an array of approaches based on numerous schools of thought, including but not limited to the following: Gestalt therapy, Accelerated Experiential Dynamic Psychotherapy (AEDP) (Fosha, 2002, 2003, 2005), attachment theory (Bowlby, 1988; Bretherton, 1992), Systems-Centered Group Psychotherapy (SCT) (Agazarian, 1997, 2001, 2012; Agazarian & Byram, 2009; Agazarian & Gantt, 2005; Simon & Agazarian, 1967, 2000; O'Neill et al., 2013), family systems theory (Bowen, 1966), Focusing (Gendlin, 1969, 1981, 1996), Bodynamic Analysis (Payne, 2006), and Reichian Vegetotherapy. I also interweave mindfulness and other contemplative practices (Buddhist, Qigong-Taoist) with energetic practices, shamanic work, developmental resourcing through psychomotor patterns, psychodrama, behavioral language systems, Somatic Experiencing® (SE), and Eye Movement Desensitization and Reprocessing (EMDR) (Shapiro, 1989). I detail two particular systems approaches that I find effective and widely useful as follows.

1) THE SYSTEM FOR ANALYZING VERBAL INTERACTION (SAVI)

Communication becomes key, and the System for Analyzing Verbal Interactions (SAVI) offers one pathway to effective interactions. SAVI categorizes the way we talk—it distinguishes the differences between opinions and questions, and between sarcasm and facts or feeling statements. Through using SAVI, we explore the verbal behavior in play and the tonality used to deliver the content. SAVI evolved as a research tool in the 1960s to track a group's potential to process information and solve problems. Yvonne Agazarian (1997, 2001) noticed that specific language patterns impeded the flow of helpful information. For example, when someone says, "Well that may be true but . . . ," the positive agreement gets lost in the quickness of trying to bring in additional information and it doesn't feel like it builds on the conversation (Simon & Agazarian, 2000, 1967).

The goal of the SAVI model is to assist in analyzing whether the apparent goals and the implicit goals of the communication task at hand are being met. Specifically, it helps ascertain whether the language and totality are moving "toward" or moving "away from" the goal, or alternatively, if the conversation is rather neutral and nothing is getting "done," that is, learned toward agreement. I help students separate the two things out, which means we have to calm down (any sympathetic activation) to be able to notice in our body where can we find the curiosity rather than feeling that the other person just disagreed with us. This process provides a way to think about and to describe communication that enables understanding; it provides an explanation for what is happening in the discussion or interaction, and it predicts what is likely to come next and what you have to do to try to change the events. From this foundation, students can learn what to ask or how to say things differently to gain the results they want.

2) SAFETY THROUGH RESONANCE WITH SIMILARITIES: SYSTEMS-CENTERED TRAINING (SCT)

The field of interpersonal dynamics works effectively as long as we are talking about things that we find similar enough. But when there is any degree of significant difference, or perception of difference, people often react by either dropping inside themselves in withdrawal or by expressing more assertion/aggression in their opinions and demeanor. As the differences get bigger, it becomes not just a breakdown in communication but also a situation where people start to become anxious and tend to create a story about themselves or the other person (typically a negative narrative). And if the anxiety and the resultant negative story dominate the person's perspective, then any learning between them disappears. People move away from connection and intersubjectivity, and do not try to move toward how to learn together as curious learning partners.

Systems-Centered Training (SCT) was founded on the premise that systems survive, develop, and transform by discriminating and integrating differences within themselves, others, and groups as a whole. It is a useful model in helping groups move from individual concerns to embracing how to become a learning community. I address teaching and learning approaches (as well as therapeutic interventions) within the member system to affect both the inner person and the whole person: group dynamics influence individual dynamics.

Phases of Working Groups and Their Process

It is important to keep in mind that all groups go through certain phases in their learning and their capacity to be in the intersubjective field, both with each other in the group as well as with a teacher/instructor. These phases have been fairly well documented. It is also important to consider that in the beginning all groups start off with a certain degree of discomfort and anxiety about both the group and their place in it. Understanding this anxiety can reduce the teacher's expectation of how quickly the group can learn together. Enough safety has to be created around the students' self-awareness in tracking, in their capacity for alignment, and in personal and interpersonal resonance for that to occur. Supporting joining through similarities, building on similarities, and allowing subgroups to discuss differences can support safety in the group and move toward cohesiveness.

If the group is safe enough and they have reduced at least some of that first phase of anxiety or dampened it down, social engagement is more present. They are going to feel that it is much easier to initially bring in their questions and statements, and then distinguish between questions that are disguised as statements or statements that are disguised as questions.

When students see themselves as a group member, they can access more curiosity to explore and learn. They can cross their boundary into the member system and thus relate to external context as well as personal. In the learning context, transitory subsystems develop within the member system as students come together around similarities and separate when differences are determined. Subgroups, then, can be both a driving motivational force and a restraining force.

Subgroups

I introduce subgroups as a technique to deepen academic content and learning through discussion. Through this process I can engage students at an emotional level and enhance their cognitive learning, engage them in meta-cognitive processes, and help them develop listening skills. The goals are to allow students to learn something new by listening deeply to their classmates, to explore the different thoughts and feelings around an issue or content, to deepen their understanding, and to generate creative thinking and problem-solving strategies.

We inherently seek others who are similar enough to us. With this sense of connection, the hardwiring in our brain does not activate the sympathetic system or the amygdala. When we can discover greater capacities to connect with others while still maintaining our own individual selves, we move to more resonance in our own systems. From this place of resonance, we can then introduce things that are similar enough and add to what is being discussed, and still manage to maintain connection; that is, attuning enough to another person while introducing something that is not too different. Within this process, we make sure to maintain enough similarity to enhance learning.

Students learn how to think about what they bring to the group, what they agree with and differ with. The process offers a way to support new information that builds on what has already been said. Within any group you always have more than one opinion. My role is to assist people to subgroup around ideas, concepts, feelings that are similar to them, so no one is working alone, so they know that they are not the only one in the group. Concurrently I support the other people, who present a difference, so they have the opportunity to speak.

For example, if someone says something divergent, or too different, I intervene, usually by slowing the dialogue down. I want to honor and respect what individual students offer and support what has been said. The idea is to bring the difference into conscious awareness, to have the person restate his or her opinion (feeling, information) and then ask, "Anybody else?" This SCT phrase stimulates the core construction of subgroups with the emphasis on what are called functional subgroups where people recognize differences and integrate them (an effective conflict resolution methodology), versus stereo subgroups where people gather due to similarities and reject or scapegoat those with differences. As the teacher, I make sure both groups get the opportunity to discuss both similarities and differences.

A Demonstration: The Process in Action

It is not unusual for a student to become activated—emotionally distressed—from one of the personal and interpersonal learning exercises we used in an interaction field. With conscious awareness, I attune to the student's emotional state by both listening and clarifying so that the student believes I understand his distress. The attunement requires both the student and me to be mindful and present. We often make an agreement about how to use the current situation as an in-class, live example of what to do to alleviate distress and reframe it into increased personal resources for learning. As we work together, the student also instructs me in terms of what is needed moment-to-moment to allow him to move to more resources and to facilitate an enhanced ability to stay in the present time. The experience can diverge into a subgroup experiential exercise or into dyads to discuss what students learned, before a whole class discussion including responses, questions, and outcomes. This typically leads students to feel less anxious, more curious, and to become passionately engaged with the process of learning; it helps them understand how being mindful and present with centered awareness connects them to their somatic resources of centering and grounds their learning in experience.

Centering

Our bodies—our biofeedback systems—juggle between centeredness on self and connection to the other. If we feel tension, it will shift us into ourselves, and a little bit away from the other. To the degree that we feel tension or the sort of rush of anxiety and the sensation of that energy, we move away from social engagement and away from others because our system is saying danger. Something is wrong.

The ability to be aware of when one is more centered is important in the intersubjective field of learning because people can have strong opinions or they can feel resigned. Both situations have parallels in the connective tissue and the muscular system. People can't sense their connective tissue as easily as they can their muscles, so working with the muscles and areas of tension or lack thereof is useful. If they can't find the impulse and/or the words to express themselves, it is helpful to contract the muscles or notice if they are resigned or weak, indicating that there isn't a core impulse guiding their way. It isn't supported by the muscles.

Centering exercises always begin with an embodied awareness. Students are first directed to notice their weight on the chair, then their back supported by the chair, their feet on the ground. Then to notice their breathing, to be more present. From that, depending on the group and where we are, several exercises may be used (from Bodynamics, ROST).

USING OUR MUSCLES TO CENTER: AN EXAMPLE EXERCISE

To begin this exercise, I have students notice whether they feel present and centered, or not. Have them put a little weight on their feet and notice if it feels as if they are being athletic and trying too much. Are they actually trying hard or are they just a little floaty, as if they are not feeling enough of the inside of the bottom of their feet and their shoe? Have them notice if they can sense the sensation at the bottom of their feet.

I usually work with a group of 15 to 30 students, and occasionally there will be someone who actually feels worse after this exercise. To alleviate this situation, have them stretch those muscles out. Have everyone stretch out their feet instead of putting pressure on them. I gesture with my hands, put my foot up and point out what the leg would be doing, and have them replicate my actions with both feet and notice if anything shifts. Ninety-nine percent of the time, people will say, "I feel a lot better."

I also ask if anyone in the room noticed anything on the inside of their legs or pelvic floor. Somebody will usually say, "Yes it went right up, I felt my pelvic floor," or "Yes, there was something in my abdomen." This is the ideal, and if they practice this exercise over time, they will find that it will become easier. However, instead of bringing themselves back to being centered, they will start noticing when they start to lose it, which is the other side. Then they are truly centered. But, like the rest of us, it wanes depending on how we feel and what is going on in our lives.

Centering and Intersubjectivity in Contemplative Education—A Portrayal

I now offer a narrative account of how I conduct my pedagogic work in the classroom.

Say, for example, that "Jane" expressed difficulty with the centering exercise. I would ask whether other people agreed with Jane and what she said or some part of it. If everybody is quiet, I'll say, "I know there must be some people here who agree. Would you raise your hand? You won't have to say anything, you just need to raise your hand." Three or four will raise their hand. I'll say, "Jane would you look at those people. What is it like to look at those people knowing that some of these people agree with you at least in part? What happens for you in your body when that happens?" Typically, the person will say, "Well, I don't know what it is, but I just felt . . ."

And then our process begins. I attune, reflect, listen for language patterns, model, and interact. Once we feel complete, I turn to the group and introduce the theory behind the experiential exercise. I explain that when we bring things up, we cross the threshold from ourselves to making a group contribution. Sometimes, after someone speaks, there is no recognizable response from the group, and a sense of feeling alone occurs. When we feel alone, we go inside. In an instance like this, I ask other people to join with this student, to reflect on something in what the student said that they agreed with. I emphasize that the student went from taking the risk to cross the boundary of just their individual self to take up active membership in the group by attempting to contribute something and the group was silent. I nudge it a bit. I try to support group members to join in a way that feels comfortable for them and then I ask the student to recognize it. With recognition she will feel more connected to those people. I explain that there were most likely a couple of more people in the group who just didn't raise their hands for a number of reasons, which is fine and normal. In doing so, they actually feel more connected in the group and more available for learning because they are not as preoccupied with whether anybody else understands what they are saying.

Then I return to the student. "Did what I say make sense. Did I say too much?" She might say, "Yes," or "I didn't understand this part," or "No, it was okay." If I sense that it still might not be okay, I might say, "Well, the reason I'm asking is because I have this feeling in myself that maybe I got a little vague, so I just wanted to check whether there was something in the way I explained it that just was too much information?"

Initially, I suspect she may have needed to process internally because it was too much new information beyond what she could integrate, so perhaps we now are back in connection. My job is to really notice if there is a breakdown in the interpersonal field and check it out. Sometimes I will make statements such as, "So I'm feeling that . . ." or, "It could be . . ." or, "Is it me or is it you or is it both of us?" And the student might reply, "Well, I think it is a bit of both of us." And then I say, "I wonder what I missed. I'm just going to stay with that for a minute."

Now I am modeling how to have a conversation about differences that doesn't put the other person in an anxious place because I am taking responsibility for my own felt/intuitive somatic sense.

There is a model that differentiates between being centered and grounded. And there are various parts of the body that are specific to each sense. When teaching I don't want to make it too complicated so I use the words interchangeably. However, there are times when a student will say, "Well, you said centered, but I felt more grounded." With that statement, somebody has now introduced a difference. I know they are, of course, bringing all their history and what they know and the words that I'm using. Another learning experience has presented itself for potential discussion.

Boundaries

Another important process that I work with is sensing boundaries. Boundary sensing between self and other enables us to feel contained, centered, and grounded, thereby promoting emotional safety. Our first concrete boundary between self and other is the skin.

If I am in a diffused energy state, a disassociated state, there are going to be parts of my body where I don't notice the skin. We have to create awareness so it is felt as something that is really tangible. You can feel your skin by lightly tapping; bring some actual sensation in those areas. If students are in a chair, they can push the inside of the chair's legs with the outside of their heels. This movement starts to bring in the outside of the legs—the quadriceps are all about boundaries. If you hold the outside of your legs and have the legs exert a counterforce toward the centerline of your body, not athletically and not too little, you can sort of kick in the tensor fascia on the lateral side of your thighs. That is an area that tends to act as a container and it is like containing the self, a felt sense of containment for the self. If you have an actual felt sense of containment that is centered and grounded, you can contain a steadier flow energy in your body because it is not leaking out as water in a cup with holes in the side or bottom of it; instead, the water stays in the container.

We all need our own sense of containment. If we don't have that, we are not in ourselves. If we are not in ourselves, we are either going to be rigid or not have a way to connect in the group, or in the learning situation. Students may be too "over-boundaried" or "over-coupled," if you will, in Peter Levine's terms (1997). Also, if their boundaries are diffused, you are going to have people who too easily merge with other people's experiences and become followers. They are not coming from a place that is centered. They are diffused or overconnected with other people as a means of stabilizing themselves. In SCT we say, "You have fallen into a pair bond." Energetically you are overconnected to the extent that your safety depends on the other person staying within a certain range that you can follow. If this other person introduces too much difference, all of a sudden you don't have any place that you are resting in yourself. You go into reactivity or disassociation or something like that. The danger in that is if the other person changes too quickly or goes away, you are left because you don't have your own center, your own grounding or sense of who you are in containment.

One easy boundary exercise I use with students is to take my hands and put them together, palm to palm. First, I push too much, athletically like I am exercising. Then I place them together in a sort of floaty way, your hands are not close enough. You are diffused. You are spaced out. Then I have them find a place between the extremes, where they are not really pressing very hard, but it brings in something from the muscles on the side of their trunk. There is just a slight resistance. I get people to just do that a little bit and they often remark that something happened, that they feel a little better. From here I can help them track that to be more refined. I remind them that if they want to do this when they don't feel too contained, even in a group, all they have to do is put their hands down on their lap and do the movement. Nobody will notice.

You can actually get more containment, which will help you get more centered and help you get more grounded. Some people will do this and say, "Oh I don't like it." Once again, more energy is being put in some resigned muscles. So, I say to them, "Okay, let's do the opposite. Instead of pushing together your hands, pull them apart. Pull too much, then too little, and find the place in the middle." Using these simple movements, we are triggering our safety mechanism. That is a key point. We are trying to help the person feel safe in themselves by reducing anxiety.

Summary and Final Thoughts

How we communicate—between the individual student and me, and how the students communicate with each other—allows us to build coherence in the group so that people feel comfortable to address their learning concerns. The main thing is whether the group is moving toward agreement or away from it, depending on the language and tonality. I weave together attention to language with SCT to create an integrated system. I pay attention to the tonality of language in individuals and use it as a marker as to how the group is doing in terms of the follow: Are they feeling comfortable, taking in learning, not being anxious, or are they in a flight or fight phase? Is the communication working? Is the information transformative or is it too ambiguous? Is there noise in the system or is the signal getting though?

In this SCT model, then, with awareness of language and tonality (SAVI), my role is to help the students who initially found something to agree to discuss that. The discussion begins with one student offering a thought or feeling related to some issue. Classmates then reflect on the response to see if they have a similar thought or feeling.

When a group of people start to become a learning community that feels safe, they have a model or a way to start introducing their differences when they come up. The differences will be heard by me, and others in the group will agree with them. If too much is introduced at once, it shuts down the social engagement except within their own group. People start to get worried about saying anything because now there is a conflict.

From a foundation of self-centeredness and present awareness, each member of the group can now expand from an inner perspective to an intersubjective experience. The "I" becomes more of a focal "we" experience as the group begins to associate and interact, first as part of a dyad with the teacher and then as part of the collective. This leads to the third phase noted as actions that arise "out of," or an emergent quality from the relationship with the teacher, the student, and the collective: the "emergent" qualities that are "discovered" from the process.

In system science if you perturbate, that is, flex, a steady-state system into a living system sufficiently, for example, the learning context between the teacher and the students as well as the students and each other, the system loses some degree of its self-organization and there is an emergent quality that is discovered. If you don't introduce enough novelty, nothing changes too much, and chaos ensues. Somewhere in "just enough," transformation and evolution occur. However, it is impossible to delineate what that emergent quality will be with any true predictability as it is a function of the dynamics of the interaction of the system. Afterward, the organizing principles of the emergence can be understood through the meaning created and a new "map" of realty occurs; then we are in a new stable platform discovered through the autopoietic "self-organizing" process of life itself.

The process of understanding the context in which all learning takes place then is not in isolation; it involves others. As we see in emergent brain science, we travel a path with others, and that is wired neurologically and biologically. The formation of resonance within ourselves, and our centered, grounded presence with appropriate boundaries, are essentially created in both a cognitive and in a Mind-Body Integrated process—what we may call a somatic reality. The theories and evidence-based practice of Bodynamic Analysis, Mindfulness, SCT, and SAVI can enhance the sense of safety and reinforce the learning situation.

An intersubjective contemplative pedagogue utilizes a Mind-Body perspective and practice, increasing the probability that learning will be enhanced though creating safety and yielding self-regulation. A more self-regulated individual can connect with themselves and others, optimizing their effectiveness in different learning contexts.

References

Agazarian, Y. M. (1997). *Systems-centered therapy for groups*. New York: Guilford.
Agazarian, Y. M. (2001). *A systems-centered approach to inpatient group psychotherapy*. Philadelphia: Jessica Kingsley.
Agazarian, Y. M. (2012). Systems-centered group psychotherapy: Putting theory into practice. *International Journal of Group Psychotherapy*, 6(2), 171–195. doi:10.1521/ijgp.2012.62.2.171

Agazarian Y. M., & Byram, C. (2009). First build the system: The systems-centered approach to combined psychotherapy. *Group* 33(2), 129–148.

Agazarian, Y. M., & Gantt, S. P. (2005). The systems perspective. In S. Wheelan (Ed.), *Handbook of group research and practice*. Thousand Oaks: Sage.

Bai, H., Scott, C., & Donald, B. (2009). Contemplative pedagogy and revitalization of teacher education. *Alberta Journal of Educational Research*, 55(3), 319–334.

Bowen, M. (1966). The use of family theory in clinical practice. *Comprehensive Psychiatry* 7(5), 345–374. doi:10.106/S0010-440X(66)80065-2

Bowlby, J. (1988). *A secure base: Parent-child attachment and healthy human development*. New York: Basic Books.

Bretherton, I. (1992). The origins of attachment theory: John Bowlby and Mary Ainsworth. *Developmental Psychology*, 22, 759–775.

De Jaegher, H., Di Paolo, E., & Gallagher, S. (2010). Can social interaction constitute social interaction? *Trends in Cognitive Sciences*, 14(10) 441–447. doi:10.1016/j.tics.2010.06.009

Fosha, D. (2002). The activation of affective change processes in AEDP. In J. J. Magnavita (Ed.), *Comprehensive handbook of psychotherapy, vol. 1: Psychodynamic and object relationship in psychotherapies* (pp. 309–344). New York: John Wiley & Sons.

Fosha, D. (2003). Dyadic regulation and experiential work with emotion and relatedness in trauma and disorganized attachment. In M. F. Solomon & D. J. Siegel (Eds), *Healing trauma: Attachment, trauma, the brain, and the mind* (pp. 221–281). New York: W. W. Norton & Company.

Fosha, D. (2005). Emotion, true self, true other, core state: Toward a clinical theory of affective change process. *Psychoanalytic Review*, 94(4), 513–552.

Fosha, D., & Yeung, D. (2006). AEDP exemplifies the seamless integration of emotional transformation and dyadic relatedness at work. In G. Stricker & J. Gold (Eds.), *A Casebook of integrative psychotherapy* (pp. 165–184). Washington, DC: APA Press.

Gantt, S. P., & Agazarian, Y. M. (2006). *SCT in clinical practice*. (EDS). Livermore: WingSpan Press.

Gendlin, E. T. (1969). Focusing. *Psychotherapy: Theory, research & practice*, 6(1), 4–15. doi:10.1037/h0088716

Gendlin, E. T. (1981). *Focusing* (2nd ed.). New York: Bantam.

Gendlin, E. T. (1996). *Focusing oriented psychotherapy*. London: Guilford Press.

Gunnlaugson, O. (2009). Establishing second-person forms of contemplative education. *Integral Review*, 5(1), 25–50.

LeDoux, J. E. (1996). *The emotional brain*. New York: Simon and Schuster.

Levine, P. (1997). *Waking the tiger: Healing trauma*. Berkeley: North Atlantic Books.

Northoff, G., & Panksepp, J. (2008). The trans-species concept of self and the subcortical-cortical midline system. *Trends in Cognitive Science*, 12(7), 259–264.

O'Neill, et al. (2013). Are systems-centered teams more collaborative, productive, and creative. *Journal of Team Performance Management, 19*(3/4), 201–221.

Panksepp, J. (2010). Affective neuroscience of the emotional BrainMind: Evolutionary perspectives and implications for understanding depression. *Dialogues of Clinical Neuroscience, 12*(4), 533–545.

Payne, H. (2006). Tracking the web of interconnectivity. *Body, Movement and Dance in Psychotherapy: An International Journal for Theory, Research, and Practice, 1*(1). doi:10.1080/17432970500468117

Porges, S. W. (2001). The polyvagal theory: Phylogenetic substrates of a social nervous system. *International Journal of Psychophysiology, 42,* 123–146.

Porges, S. W. (2007). The polyvagal perspective. *Biological Psychology, 72*(2), 116–143.

Schore, A. (2001). Effects of a secure attachment relationship on right brain development, affect regulation and infant mental health. *Infant Mental Health Journal, 22,* 7–66. Retrieved February 14, 2016, from http://www.trauma-pages.com/a/schore-2001a.php

Shapiro, F. (1989). Efficacy of the eye movement desensitization procedure in the treatment of traumatic memories. *Journal of Traumatic Stress, 2,* 199–223. doi: 10.1002/jts.2490020207

Sheets-Johnstone, M. (2011). *The primacy of movement.* Amsterdam, Netherlands: John Benjamins.

Siegel, D. J. (2012). *The developing mind: How relationships and the brain interact to shape who we are.* New York: Guilford Press.

Simon, A., & Agazarian, Y. (1967). *SAVI: Sequential analysis of verbal interactions.* Philadelphia: Research for Better Schools.

Simon, A., & Agazarian, Y. (2000). SAVI: The system for analyzing verbal interaction. In A. Beck & L. Lewis (Eds.), *The process of group therapy: Systems for analyzing change* (pp. 357–380). Washington, DC: American Psychological Association.

Tronick, E. (2003). "Of course all relationships are unique": How co-creative processes generate unique mother-infant and patient-therapist relationships and change other relationships. *Psychoanalytic Inquiry, 23,* 473–491.

Tronick, E., & Beeghly, M. (2011). Infants' meaning-making and the development of mental health problems. *The American Psychologist, 66*(2), 107–119. doi:10.1037/a0021631

Winnicott, D. W. (1953). Transitional objects and transitional phenomena: A study of the first not-me possession. *International Journal of Psychoanalysis, 34*(2), 89–97.

8

Walking Steps

Contemplative Wanderings with Humanbecoming

DEBORAH SALLY THOUN, ANNE BRUCE,
AND COBY TSCHANZ

Walking Step

Close your eyes
Let earth's energy wash over you
Empty the self to fill the spirit.
Warmth. Birdsong.
Things of meaning lost in the minutiae.
Close your eyes. Walking step.
Rhythm. Flow.
Guide towards meaning, in pursuit of
Nothingness
I feel my breath. In, out.
I feel my being. Grow, grow.
I am, I am not.
There is nothing without something.
And every something avoids the nothing.
Quiet now. Close your eyes.
Walking step.

—Ashley Chee, from "Integrating Learning and Life"

Contemplative approaches to teaching and learning call us into spaces where we can listen and notice. As this opening poem reflects, when students wander into spaces where they learn to simply be, they cultivate intersubjective awareness, presence, and bearing witness to human being that are central to nursing practice. In this chapter, we attend to our growing recognition that "creativity-rich and contemplative development" are "essential facets of the more complete education called for in our time" (Sarath, 2015, p. 314) and in our profession of nursing.

We begin with a snapshot of how we came to honor and incorporate this view within our teaching of nursing practice. An overview of select literature related to contemplative pedagogy and intersubjectivity as well as changes to our pedagogical approach in light of this recognition follow. Next, we provide an example of a nursing inquiry course and the synergistic resonances we found among and between contemplative pedagogical approaches, course content, and the deeply connected philosophical ground of each. Finally, personal reflections and student accounts are presented.

Honoring and Incorporating Contemplative Pedagogy and Practice

For the last two years we have openly drawn on contemplative pedagogy to guide the development of a "nursing inquiry" course in an academic nursing program. This signaled a change from a participatory, constructivist pedagogy situated within diverse nursing theoretical knowledge to guide professional practice, to one of personal awareness, insight, creativity, discernment, and a single nursing theory. This reorientation was motivated by many experiences, not least of which was frequent feedback from students who did not recognize the relevance of using nursing theoretical knowledge for clinical practice and so-called real-life experience.

We made an explicit choice to apply contemplative pedagogy to advance our values of whole-person education and our hope that inclusion of contemplative practice would help students recognize and challenge dominant discourses of productivity, utility, and immediacy found in health care and academic settings. Within nursing education, attention on and value for empirical knowledge, fact and reason, circulates with ease. Educators and students often hear the imperative to provide information, answers, and explanations (as responsible preparation for licensing exams) rather than to explore human experience, pose questions, and contemplate values that are at the "core of what it means to be a truly educated individual" (Sarath, 2015, p. 311). Our decision to incorporate contemplative pedagogy into our classrooms was fourfold. We wanted: (1) to foreground student well-being and creativity, (2) to introduce experiences of abiding with the ambiguity of human being, (3) to question taken-for-granted understandings of dualistic ontology with empiricist epistemology, and (4) to refine our personal visions of nursing education.

How Are Contemplative Pedagogy and Contemplative Practices Understood?

Contemplative pedagogy is a (re)emerging field of interest across disciplines in higher education. It is a philosophy of education that promotes contemplative practices in teaching, learning, and research (O'Donnell, 2015). Contemplative pedagogy aspires "to cultivate student attention and emotional balance, compassion, empathic connection, and altruistic behaviour" and develop "pedagogical approaches that support student creativity, insight and learning course content" (Zajonc, 2013, p. 83). In a brief history of contemplative pedagogy, Morgan (2015) traces the presence of contemplation in education and concludes that it is essential for understanding both who we are and how we learn. Similarly, Hart (2004) defines contemplation as a way of knowing through silence, looking inward and witnessing the contents of one's consciousness. And, Harris (2014) describes contemplation more broadly as "investigating the nature of consciousness directly through sustained introspection" (p. 209).

While contemplative practices are more easily introduced into North American classrooms than previously, such practices are nuanced in their associations with religious instruction or training within wisdom traditions. Burack (2014) tackles the question of whether integrating contemplative approaches in secular educational institutions infringes upon the value of separating church and state. He reassures and reasons that when educators are clear and transparent about pedagogical goals (e.g., offering diverse experiential learning opportunities) and take steps to maintain the safety of learners (e.g., offer voluntary engagement with alternative activities and instructions to stop as needed), then educators can effectively maintain classrooms free of perceived coercion, indoctrination, or conversion. However, Burack and others (Barbezat & Bush, 2014) caution that as with any new body of knowledge, teachers must be sensitive, self-aware, and teach within their scope.

Reflective practices have been developed across cultures and over time to concentrate and deepen conscious awareness of our personal life experiences. Many meditative and reflective practices have been adapted into educational settings under the umbrella of contemplative practices. Posted on the website for the Center for Contemplative Mind in Society (CCMS) is a "Tree of Contemplative Practices" (Dueer & Bergam) outlining current practices used in academic contexts. These activities are considered contemplative if they remind learners to slow down, focus, and feel more connected to self, work, and the environment. Contemplative practices described by CCMS include a range of activities such as reflective writing, breath meditation, and improvisation.

Although contemplative pedagogy has been explored in many disciplines (Barbezat & Bush, 2014; Todd & Ergas, 2015), it has only recently been visible in nursing. We found a small but growing body of scholarship on this topic in nursing, wherein most research is in the area of mindfulness meditation as a therapeutic intervention or stress management for students (Beddoe & Murphy, 2004; Goff, 2011; Shirey, 2007; Young, Bruce, Turner, VanderWal, & Linden, 2001). However, opportunities to develop contemplative ways of knowing and being hold promise within nursing education, beyond those of therapeutic intention.

In particular, central to nursing practice is the importance of being with patients and families that draws on and honors an ever-expanding awareness of diverse human experience and interactions. The ability to live with awareness and "be with" people in ways that are unobtrusive—not focused on managing or changing situations and people—is vital to providing patient and family-focused care. When doing so, nurses transition into experiential spaces of intersubjectivity, which we find difficult to articulate and teach. Although such spaces are core to nursing, our earlier attempts using participatory, constructivist pedagogy and ways of knowing met with only limited success.

How Is the Concept (or Experience) of Intersubjectivity Understood?

Intersubjectivity is used in diverse ways across disciplines and affords an ontological notion that literally means "between subjects." Teunissen (2014) draws on the work of sociologists Zlatev et al. in defining intersubjectivity as: "Our ability to sense what other people intend, think, feel and to imagine what effects our actions (might) have on them . . . and that this ability lies at the core of the shared reality we create through our interactions" (p. 349). Within nursing, Pierson (1999) nuances this understanding through her examination of relationship as an intersubjective process integral to nursing care.

Pierson (1999) introduces intersubjectivity as an important contrast to traditional Cartesian and human sciences approaches to nurse-person relationships. Drawing on Heshusius and others, Pierson conceptualizes intersubjectivity in light of dialogic connection that generates a third space, "a co-unity or a 'selfother'" (p. 300). She explains how intersubjectivity between nurse and patient arises through an interdependent process of relationship:

> The individual cannot independently perceive the self (Holquist, 1990; Macy, 1991; Witherell, 1991). The self must be perceived by another. Consequently, there is a necessary interdependence that exists between individuals. This notion merits some attention in terms of the profound and intimate relationships . . . within the domains of professional nursing practice. It is a paradox that the connection between individuals begins with distance. There must be a space, a place in-between individuals, so that they may come together (Witherell 1991). Closing the intellectual and emotional distance between individuals and creating a co-unity or a "selfother" (Heshusius, 1994, p. 17) moves past the notion of allowing the self to be present with the other. (Pierson, 1999, p. 300)

Pierson cautions that a new unity where identities blur can also be interpreted as intrusive. She goes on to say that intersubjectivity in the context of nursing care must remain attached to a sense of otherness while at the same time cocreating "a place in-between individuals so that they may come together" (Pierson, 1999, p. 300). The emergence of contemplative pedagogy however, provides language and experiential activities that go beyond Pierson's caution and enables us to explore the tension between notions of unity and otherness. Perhaps more importantly, contemplative practices offer an alignment with ways of being articulated in some nursing theories—in particular, humanbecoming theory (Parse, 1981, 1998, 2014) that is discussed later in the chapter.

Course Example and Pedagogical Changes

In this section we introduce a case example of integrating contemplative pedagogy into a required third-year course in a Bachelor of Science in Nursing program. While the course content has been taught many times before, integrating a contemplative approach has had remarkably positive effects for students and faculty alike. The course, entitled Nursing Inquiry, is one of six courses addressing professional practice and examines knowledge development in and for the nursing profession. Most often, course goals have been met by introducing a wide range of nursing theories, including their scope, philosophical bases or assumptions, major tenets, concepts, related practice methodologies, and research approaches. Coverage of course material has tended to include conventional dialectic approaches, small- and large-group discussion forums, and student presentations.

Our changes to the design and delivery of the course, Nursing Inquiry, began by moving away from studying numerous nursing theories to adopting an in-depth exploration of one nursing theory. This shift toward depth over breadth was predicated on our wish to mitigate the superficiality of exploring diverse theoretical perspectives in one course. Our intent was not to narrow students' understanding of nursing perspectives but to slow down and thoroughly investigate one theory through sustained and focused exploration where meaningful theory-practice linkages could be made to nursing practice.

Pedagogical Changes

Four key curricular changes were implemented and are identified here with detailed descriptions. First, we introduced and defined our approach to contemplative pedagogy in the course syllabus, ensuring that our rationale and relevance were explicit. Second, we created an "Awareness Notes" reflective assignment that was not graded but linked to class preparations and discussions. Third, we experientially engaged pedagogical practices with an assignment structured to support in-depth exploration. And fourth, lest we be charged with indoctrination (Burack, 2014), we asked students in a final assignment to develop insight into, knowledge of, and meaning related to a rival theory that was informed by their deep learning throughout the course.

Introducing the Pedagogical Approach

To support transparency, we defined contemplative pedagogy in the course syllabus as a type of teaching-learning that "cultivates inquiry about what is deeply meaningful, develops discernment, gives rise to an ethical frame, enables students to hold different views simultaneously, and focuses on student well-being" (Thoun & Tschanz, 2015). Explicit connections were made for students to understand how this approach aligns with the overall principles of the School of Nursing where the teacher-student process is at the center of learning.

Awareness Notes

We created an "Awareness Notes" project to support students in cultivating concentration, attention, and deepening conscious awareness. Students were asked to keep a notebook in which they recorded observations, ponderings, and reflections on their well-being, their experiences with the contemplative practices, and any thoughts associated with the course and beyond. This could include drawings, pictures, photos, quotes from things they read or overheard, songs, poems, reflections on their assumptions, crafted questions to share in class, or almost anything.

While the awareness notebook was private (and not submitted), we also expected students to compose responses to the course readings each week. This requirement assisted students to prepare for class and was periodically submitted to the professor. Students were encouraged to notice, observe, and be aware of their experience during their readings. They were encouraged to pose questions such as: What do I notice (perhaps boredom, distraction, confusion, excitement, or particular emotions)? Do these experiences seem related to the content of the reading or context (physical setting, time of day, other experiences preceding reading, etc.)? Instructions foregrounded how reflections should highlight meaningful observations, insights, challenges, as well as be guided by a sense of inquiry, attention, and compassion. Notebook entries were made by students and professors on an ongoing basis, as desired. Opportunities to do so were also provided during class time. We emphasized how the quality and comprehensiveness of one's notebook would contribute to the quality and comprehensiveness of assignments.

Contemplative Practices

> When I closed my eyes, the sky was stormy outside the window.
> Sometime later, I opened my eyes to blue sky. Rain had passed without my hearing and drops of water shone everywhere with sun.
> One drop eased free of its yellowing leaf, loosing its sparkle.
> Was that drop forsaking the light? I thought: No, no. It was simply living the slow and insistent rhythm of Fall.
>
> —Coby Tschanz, "Awareness Note"

Each class began with a 5–10-minute contemplative practice led by either the professor or a student volunteer. If students did not wish to participate, they were invited to remain in silence. If they were unable to arrive to class on time, they remained outside until the practice was concluded and the door was opened.

In addition, starting in week five of the 13-week course, students chose a contemplative practice to engage 10 minutes (minimum) daily for the following month. This provided students greater depth with a practice that was introduced during class or any practice they found meaningful. Reflections on their chosen practice, along with challenges or outcomes of their daily practice, were recorded in their awareness notebooks. Choosing three words to describe experience was one way of approaching such a description.

Examples of contemplative practices that students practiced included: guided meditation, meditation on an object, contemplation of a painting, walking meditation, mindful eating, knitting, yoga, body scans, silence, contemplative reading or writing, and focused breathing.

Aligning Content and Process

The humanbecoming (HB) school of thought posited by Rosemarie Parse (1981, 1998, 2014) was chosen as the theory of focus for the course. It seemed an appropriate choice because it offers a critical examination of scientific materialism and a contrasting view of more familiar materialist views to which nursing students had been exposed in previous courses. In addition, we believed that ideas germane to contemplative pedagogy and those of humanbecoming theory are similarly conceptualized, marking the potential for an extraordinary experience of coherence (interweaving) for students and teachers alike. The following draws attention to some of the parallels we are seeing and sheds light on resonances between humanbecoming metaphysics, theoretical concepts, and contemplative pedagogy.

Interweaving, Resonating, and Parallel Discussions

A shining light in this course has been my contemplative practice. Cody (1994) speaks about the challenge of knowledge arising outside of nursing being called nursing knowledge. However, Rogers (1970) suggests that if we are transparent about our influences, we can see how our engagement with other disciplines informs and enriches nursing science. Poetic inquiry is one way that I examine my influences and chart how I integrate and synthesize new ideas. It is a useful tool for me and one that brings me great joy. As someone with an arts background, it is very important for me to find ways to bring creative practice into the new-to-me world of nursing. The gift of time to spend on a creative process this term enriched not only my understanding of nursing inquiry but cued me to the ways in which I was making assumptions, constructing concepts, reacting to challenges, and making meaning. It removed the proposed separation between science and art, opening up a boundless world of becoming. (Wignall, 2015—third year nursing student)

A discussion of parallels between the metaphysics of Parse's humanbecoming and those of contemplative pedagogy helps to illustrate the implications (importance) of such resonance for our teaching-learning experience and nursing education overall. For example, numerous authors conceptualize mindfulness as "a way of being" (Grossman & Van Dam, 2011, p. 234) that calls for an "open-hearted, moment-to-moment, non-judgmental awareness" (Hyland, 2015, p. 178) and a focused attention on moment-by-moment experiences (Kabat-Zinn, 1990). Similarly, Parse (2014) posits nursing practice as a way of being marked by reverence and awe, where personal hopes and fears are respected without judgment.

One student pondered such practice through the use of awareness notes:

> Through true presence, nurses can care beyond the biomedical task-focused approach, and provide holistic care that enables

understanding of patients (Parse, 2010). With true presence, a nurse silently bears witness to patients' experiences, and enables or opens space for meaning to emerge (Parse, 2010). In contemplative practice, this concept became a theme that gave me the insight to see that I have often felt too stressed about school to be truly present with the people I value most. Lack of presence, in my experience, causes people to grow apart, the exact opposite of what we as nurses strive for. (Munro, 2015—third year nursing student)

This student expresses an expanded view that differentiates nursing practice from interventionist, predetermined, and measurable actions (reductionist instrumentalism) where professionals are considered experts in another's health. Rather, the student is able to see how both practices (humanbecoming and contemplative approaches) are embedded in specific ethics fostering a way of being that is cultivated rather than marked for improvement. We began to see further resonances between the purpose and practice of contemplative approaches and key concepts of humanbecoming theory. We have selected three postulates of the theory—illimitability, freedom, and paradox—for illustration.

Illimitability

According to Parse (2014), illimitability is "the indivisible unbounded knowing extended to infinity, the all-at-once remembering and prospecting with the moment" (p. 26). Unbounded knowing begets a creative or innovative departure from normative interpretations and limits, conventional values that are often placed on one's own thoughts and understandings.

Through contemplative practices, students learn to stop, and stop to learn (Brady, 2007), beginning with openhearted and nonjudgmental listening to their own thoughts and ideas. Through slowing down and paying attention, students become aware of their habitual patterns, how they come to know, and the choices they face from moment-to-moment. Barbezat and Bush (2014) argue that contemplative practices develop intelligence(s) through stabilizing awareness, concentration, synthetic thinking (awareness of multiple possibilities), and pattern recognition. Through recognizing patterns, students learn to choose alternatives to habitual responses or to rest nonjudgmentally, observing, and simply paying attention to whatever is arising in the situation (Hyland, 2009), "the all-at-once remembering and prospecting with the moment" (Parse, 2014, p. 26).

As they integrate contemplative practices, students find themselves at the center of their learning. Barbezat and Bush (2014) allege that this experience transforms teaching and learning "into something personally meaningful yet connected to the world" (p. 6). As students recognize personal patterns, habits, and reactions, they strengthen reflective and prereflective awareness of moment-to-moment situations as well as their attitudes.

As one student shared:

> I remember having a discussion in class concerning documentation using the humanbecoming theory. We talked about compliance/non compliance and I remember a time when I wrote that my patient was non compliant because she refused to take her medications. I felt an overwhelming amount of disappointment in myself for writing something dehumanizing. However, I was grateful for the opportunity to realize why labeling takes dignity away from the patient. (Warren, 2015—third year nursing student)

Freedom

Freedom is another concept central to the theory with resonances in contemplative practice and pedagogy. In humanbecoming, "situated freedom" is a core concept drawing on scholars of existential phenomenology. From this standpoint, freedom is understood as inherent in being human; we have freedom, whether knowingly or not, "in choosing situations as well as attitudes about situations" (Parse, 2014, p. 15). While choices may be unquestioned, culturally engrained, or situationally prescribed, Parse (2014) draws on Sartre in asserting that humans always choose, even if that choice is to not choose. Such freedoms are also embedded in paradox—"there is freedom only in a situation, and there is a situation only through freedom" (Sartre qtd. in Parse, 2014, p. 33).

The importance of understanding freedom in this way calls nurses to trust each patient and the choices they are making, to follow a patient's lead in understanding the meaning that situations hold for him or her. We see resonances of situated freedom within contemplative practices and pedagogy. For example, O'Reilley (1998) writes of teaching as contemplative practice and highlights the importance of attending, what she calls radical presence and its expression through deep listening. O'Reilley laments that deep listening and attending to another is a capacity humans require, asserting, "People are dying in spirit for lack of it" (p. 19).

Similarly, one student shared:

> Parse's theory of humanbecoming . . . emphasized the notion that patients are their own experts on their own health and that nurses assist patients in making healthcare decisions rather than making decisions for them. I think as nurses we get caught up in the medical model, in thinking we know what is best for our patients, when in reality, the patients are the ones who know best. (Warren, 2015—third year nursing student)

Paradox

Parse (2014) identifies paradox as central to the theoretical principles and concepts of humanbecoming and explicates human experience as paradoxical in this way:

> the inherent living experience of hope is only known in light of no-hope, and the experience of joy in light of sorrow, birthing in light of dying, being in light of non-being, courage in light of cowardice, and others. Paradox is the living moments surfacing with insightfulness that can only unfold with the contradictory. (p. 32)

As such, paradox offers a primary understanding of human being and "an inherent aspect of everyday life" (Mitchell, 1993, p. 47), living and dying all-at-once (Hutchings, 2002). Paradox is also threaded through discussions of contemplative pedagogy.

Coburn (2011), Palmer (1980), and others (e.g., Brown, 2011, 2014; Zajonc, 2013) suggest the tensions of contradiction, ambiguity, and paradox are more easily endured and, even necessary within education. Zajonc writes of a practice of sustaining contradiction, claiming that "it is often better to maintain and even intensify the experience of how two opposites can be true at the same time" (p. 86). Similarly, within humanbecoming, paradox is not something to be deliberately diminished or enhanced. For example, Parse conceptualizes the all-at-onceness of hope–no hope, rather than a spectrum or continuum of hopelessness to hope. Rather than favor a state or condition of hope, nurses guided by humanbecoming might bear witness to expressions of hope–no hope without needing to encourage patients to revise their hopes or diminish expressions of hopelessness. In line with contemplative practice, the process of being, without need to fix or change, is supportive of paradox.

One student expressed her understanding in this way:

> The HB explanation of humans relating in rhythmical patterns gave me insight into my own nursing experience with a patient who had admitted himself voluntarily to the mental health unit. This patient had enabled himself to heal, while limiting himself to the restrictions of the hospital at the same time. His choice, grounded in his unique values and beliefs, resulted in a rhythmical pattern of enabling-limiting that sowed the seeds of his life path. (Munro, 2015—third year nursing student)

Student Ponderings

Reflected by excerpts from their awareness notes, students ponder experiences with contemplative practice and understanding of humanbecoming theory.

One student expressed learning in this way:

> In my first awareness exercise I was asked the question, "What would you most like to take way from this course?" I believe I wrote something like, "an even greater awareness of myself so that I can teach and be an example to others in my nursing profession and in life." I believe this goal was achieved, because what I learned most about myself is that just because something is hard, and difficult to understand, it shouldn't make me resist it. Instead of telling myself that Parse's theory was too hard, too confusing, and too wacky for me to understand, I worked hard, and now I feel more accomplished, more scholarly, and proud that I was able to

achieve the level of understanding that I did in Parse's theory. This course taught me to honour people's experiences and to search the meaning behind the things I don't understand. With new awareness about myself and others, I can go into [my practice experience] with more confidence than before, because now I have knowledge that is unique to nursing and I am looking forward to how my relationships with patients will change. (Williams, 2015—third year nursing student)

Students developed deepened understandings, investigating their own lives through the theory and learning process. Their reflections articulated and explored assumptions about human being. They pondered topics that were difficult, at times affirming or shifting their personal values and beliefs.
One student wrote:

The awareness notes regarding these practices, although sometimes difficult to write, led to a creativity, which I did not know I possessed. I filled my notebook with drawings, pictures, quotes, and this led to deeper conscious awareness of my ideals. I wish I could have had the courage to share some of these insights in class but find I am much too shy. (Brown, 2015—third year nursing student)

Another student shared:

I was disconnected from my spiritual self for a long time. This class rekindled my connection with my spiritual side through the contemplative exercises and personal reflections in the awareness notes. Therefore, my expectations for the course were far exceeded. I expected to learn about nursing theories and theorists and how they could be applied and integrated into my nursing knowledge. I certainly did not expect my entire philosophy on how I view nursing to be challenged, as well as my existential beliefs to be revitalized. (Wrona, 2015—third year nursing student)

The beliefs and values of humanbecoming were meaningful to individual students as the experiential context of contemplative practices shed light on the abstractions of the theory in new and different ways. For example, one student described her experience in this way:

The integration of contemplative practice in my life and into the art of humanbecoming has determined aspects of my lived experiences in a new light. My priorities have changed, and what I now value is not necessarily what I did value. There is a new awareness of my inner self when I am able to awaken my sleeping mind, my ideas and beliefs about humanity change. My sleeping mind—which is the subtle state of thinking, a higher form that allows thought to flow—can recognize aspects of my life that I value most, thoughts that I never knew I had or valued so much. (Ulaszonek, 2014—third year nursing student)

Students engaged in searching questions that bridged their personal and professional selves. Their willingness to broach topics of their mortality, religious beliefs, addiction, abortion, grief, and death invoked compassion and insights for professional practice. One student's poetic expression of working with a patient reflects this:

Woman Lost

Her mind was a haze, memories lost deep in the maze,
Of an illness from which she'd never be free
Frustration touched her gaze, and she sank back in malaise,
Because the lock on her mind had no key
As the mind begins to fray, we have only fear to convey,
Complete powerlessness no matter our plea
For the body betrays, when we reach life's final phase,
A fate from which we struggle but cannot flee

(Chee, 2015—third year nursing student)

Faculty Ponderings

We were very fortunate to be able to create space in our busy lives to come together to share our own ponderings and explore the richness of experience that took place for each of us in using contemplative pedagogy in a nursing course. These opportunities surfaced a number of our own insights (aha moments) and deep learning as teacher-learners. We were surprised and encouraged by the depth of experience many students shared. We questioned if this was reflective of our new approach to teaching-learning or perhaps something more. What seems unclear in contemplative literature is whether disparate metaphysics among pedagogical approach and course content are desirable or even possible to work/teach within. In other words, does a metaphysic that is inconsistent with the subject matter being taught impede the educational process? Based on our reflections in this chapter, we believe that resonances within ontology, theory, and pedagogical approach reinforce teaching-learning and offer a transformational power for student and teacher alike.

In a similar vein, rather than considering intersubjectivity as a relational process that is bound to discursive, dialogical, and social formations, we found the combination of humanbecoming theory and contemplative practices reinforced our view of intersubjectivity as happening in the oneness of all that goes beyond discursive and constructionist positions. Using the skillful means of contemplative practices, we shifted a focus onto being (as is) rather than fixing, altering, or changing—an honoring of what is without judgment rather than an urge for comparison, mastery, or critique.

Finally, we pondered the living quality of the classroom and the possibility it held for offering respite in the context of teaching-learning. We noticed a respite—from busyness, from pressures to perform and produce, from surveillance—that we as well as students experienced. We noted that personal worries and feelings of being pressured would sometimes ease upon entering the classroom, greeting students, and beginning with a practice that focused our attention. This is not to suggest that things were utopian but rather to highlight the contributions that contemplative pedagogy offers in opportunities for feeling at peace and experiencing solace, momentarily free . . . within our intense academic and professional lives.

References

Barbezat, D., & Bush, M. (2014). *Contemplative practices in higher education: Powerful methods to transform teaching and learning.* San Francisco: Jossey-Bass.

Beddoe, A. E., & Murphy, S. (2004). Does mindfulness decrease stress and foster empathy among nursing students? *Journal of Nursing Education, 43*(7), 305–312. Retrieved from http://www.healio.com/nursing/journals/jne

Brady, R. (2007). Learning to stop, stopping to learn: Discovering the contemplative dimension in education. *Journal of Transformative Education, 5*(4), 372–394. doi:10.1177/1541344607313250

Brown, M. (2015). Integrating learning and life. (Unpublished paper, Professional Practice IV: Nursing Inquiry) University of Victoria, British Columbia, Canada.

Brown, R. (2011). The mindful teacher as the foundation of contemplative pedagogy. In J. Simmer-Brown & F. Grace (Eds.), *Meditation and the classroom: Contemplative pedagogy for religious studies* (pp. 75–83). Albany: State University of New York Press.

Brown, R. C. (2014). Transitions: Teaching from the spaces between. In O. Gunnlaugson, E. W. Sarath, C. Scott, & H. Bai, *Contemplative learning and inquiry across disciplines* (pp. 271–285). Albany: State University of New York Press.

Burack, C. (2014). Responding to the challenges of a contemplative curriculum. *Journal of Contemplative Inquiry*, 1, 35–53.

Chee, A. (2015). Integrating learning and life. (Unpublished paper, Professional Practice IV: Nursing Inquiry) University of Victoria, British Columbia, Canada.

Coburn, T. B. (2011). The convergence of liberal education and contemplative education—Inevitable? In J. Simmer-Brown & F. Grace (Eds.), *Meditation and the classroom: Contemplative pedagogy for religious studies* (pp. 3–12). Albany: State University of New York Press.

Dueer, M., & Bergam, C. The tree of contemplative practices. Retrieved from http://www.contemplativemind.org/practices/tree

Goff, A. (2011). Stressors, academic performance, and learned resourcefulness in baccalaureate nursing students. *International Journal of Nursing Education Scholarship*, 8(1), 1–20. doi: 10.2202/1548-923X.2114

Grossman, P., & Van Dam, N. T. (2011). Mindfulness by any other name . . . : Trials and tribulations of sati in Western psychology and science. *Contemporary Buddhism: An Interdisciplinary Journal*, 12(1), 219–239. doi:10.1 080/14639947.2011.564841

Harris, S. (2014). *Waking up: A guide to spirituality without religion*. New York: Simon and Schuster.

Hart, T. (2004). Opening the contemplative mind in the classroom. *Journal of Transformative Education*, 2(1), 28–46.

Hutchings, D. (2002). Parallels in practice: Parallel nursing practice and Parse's theory of human becoming. *American Journal of Hospice & Palliative Care*, 19(6), 408–414. Retrieved March 12, 2017 from http://journals.sagepub.com/doi/pdf/10.1177/104990910201900612

Hyland, T. (2009). Mindfulness and the therapeutic function of education. *Journal of Philosophy of Education*, 1(43), 119–131. doi: 10.1111/j.1467-9752.2008.00668.x

Hyland, T. (2015). On the contemporary applications of mindfulness: Some implications for education. *Journal of Philosophy of Education*, 2(49), 170–186. doi: 10.1111/1467-9752.12135

Kabat-Zinn, J. (1990). *Full catastrophe living: Using the wisdom of your body and mind to face stress, pain and illness*. New York: Delacorte.

Mitchell, G. (1993). Living paradox in Parse's theory. *Nursing Science Quarterly*, 6(1), 44–51. Retrieved from http://nsq.sagepub.com/

Morgan, P. F. (2015). A brief history of the current reemergence of contemplative education. *Journal of Transformative Education*, 13(3), 197–218. doi:10.1177/1541344614564875

Munro, R. (2015). Integrating learning and life. (Unpublished paper, Professional Practice IV: Nursing Inquiry) University of Victoria, British Columbia, Canada.

O'Donnell, A. (2015). Contemplative pedagogy and mindfulness: Developing creative attention in an age of distraction. *Journal of Philosophy of Education*, 49(2), 187–202. doi: 10.1111/1467-9752.12136

O'Reilley, M. R. (1998). *Radical presence: Teaching as contemplative practice*. Portsmouth, NH: Boynton/Cook.

Palmer, P. J. (1980). *The promise of paradox: A celebration of contradictions in the Christian life*. Notre Dame: Ave Maria Press.

Parse, R. R. (1981). *Man-living-health: A theory of nursing*. New York: John Wiley & Sons.

Parse, R. R. (1998). *The human becoming school of thought: A perspective for nurses and other health professionals*. Thousand Oaks: Sage.

Parse, R. R. (2014). *The humanbecoming paradigm: A transformational worldview*. Pittsburgh: Discovery International.

Pierson, W. (1999). Considering the nature of intersubjectivity within professional nursing. *Journal of Advanced Nursing*, 30(2), 294–302. doi: 10.1046/j.1365-2648.1999.01081.x

Sarath, E. (2015). Improvisation and meditation in the academy: Parallel ordeals, insights, and openings. *Journal of Philosophy of Education*, 49(2), 311–327. doi: 10.1111/1467-9752.12143

Shirey, M. (2007). Educational innovations: An evidence-based solution for minimizing stress and anger in nursing students. *Journal of Nursing Education*, 46(12), 568–571.

Teunissen, P. W. (2014). When I say . . . intersubjectivity. *Medical Education*, 48(4), 349–350. doi:10.1111/medu.12299

Todd, S., & Ergas, O. (2015). Introduction to special issue. *Journal of Philosophy of Education*, 49(2), 163–169. doi: 10.1111/1467-9752.12143

Thoun, D. T., & Tschanz, C. (2015). Nursing 341 professional practice IV: Nursing inquiry [Course syllabus]. University of Victoria, British Columbia, Canada.

Tschanz, C. (2014). Awareness notes. (Unpublished paper, Professional Practice IV: Nursing Inquiry) University of Victoria, British Columbia, Canada.

Ulaszonek, S. (2014). My learning. (Unpublished paper, Professional Practice IV: Nursing Inquiry). University of Victoria, British Columbia, Canada.

Warren, N. (2015). Integrating learning and life. (Unpublished paper, Professional Practice IV: Nursing Inquiry). University of Victoria, British Columbia, Canada.

Wignall, A. (2015). Integrating learning and life. (Unpublished paper, Professional Practice IV: Nursing Inquiry). University of Victoria, British Columbia, Canada.

Williams, D. (2015). Integrating learning and life. (Unpublished paper, Professional Practice IV: Nursing Inquiry) University of Victoria, British Columbia, Canada.

Wrona, J. (2015). Integrating learning and life. (Unpublished paper, Professional Practice IV: Nursing Inquiry). University of Victoria, British Columbia, Canada.

Young, L. E., Bruce. A., Turner, L., VanderWal, R., & Linden, W. (2001). Student nurse health promotion: Evaluation of a mindfulness-based stress reduction (MBSR) intervention. *Canadian Nurse, 7*(6), 23–26. PMID: 11868216

Zajonc, A. (2013). Contemplative pedagogy: A quiet revolution in higher education. *New Directions for Teaching and Learning, 134,* 83–94. doi:10.1102/tl.20057

9

Contemplative Learning

A Second-Person Approach to Physical Fitness

SALLY K. SEVERINO AND M. ANDREW GARRISON

Integration of contemplative techniques into teaching, especially second-person approaches, may be met with confusion and even resistance. Advances in neuroscience that arise from the more traditional approach to education offer support for these efforts. By providing "legitimacy" from mainstream academia, scientific research can encourage efforts to bring contemplative practices into learning settings. Increasingly, classrooms where teachers and students engage in fully participatory exchanges are being praised for the flourishing of ideas and insights that cocreative processes engender. Collaborative sharing among students is valued for its ability to enable students to develop new identities (Gergen 2009).

In this chapter, we focus specifically on second-person intersubjective learning. We begin by reviewing the scientific literature that provides the groundwork for understanding a second-person approach to contemplative learning. We then present a case study that shows the second-person approach applied to becoming physically fit. We conclude with a summary and a description of settings where a second-person approach may not be successful.

Neuroscientific Groundwork

Intersubjectivity, defined in the 1970s as interpersonal communion, is a "sharing of experiential content (e.g., feelings, perceptions, thoughts, and linguistic meanings) among a plurality of subjects" (Zlatev, Racine,

Sinha, & Itkonen, 2008, 1). Educational psychologist Ann Cale Kruger (2011) writes,

> Sharing psychological states with others is more than, but may include, empathy (a matching of moods), perspective-taking (a shared reference), embodied synchrony (a mirroring of behaviors), theory of mind (an imputation of mental states), or common ground (shared background knowledge). It is having joint thoughts and feelings with another person about some aspect of reality when each is aware of the other's role in the commonality. (p. 113)

Intersubjectivity can be differentiated from imitation by comparing human children with apes. Apes and children differ in social cognition in at least three ways. First, apes can understand motivations, perceptions, intentions, goals, and knowledge of others, but they cannot understand that others have mental representations of the world. Human children instinctively develop the ability to understand that others have mental representations as exemplified in understanding others' false beliefs about the world. Second, apes copy another's use of a novel tool by reproducing the same end, but they do not copy the means to the end. Children reproduce every detail of the other's means to the end. Third, apes do not enter into joint attention with others. Children present objects to another for the sole purpose of enjoying the experience together.

As Ann Cale Kruger (2011) points out,

> This seemingly modest difference between great-ape and human social cognition makes human culture possible. . . . The human power to create and transmit culture is the result of the synergy of our common primate cognitive capacities and our uniquely human desire to enter into communion with others. By entering into shared [psychobiological] states, we are able to learn and transmit the cultural practices and products that are distinctive of the species. (pp. 117–118)

For readers who seek a more detailed description of cultural learning, which distinguishes between imitative learning that arises from intersubjectivity and other simpler cases of imitation, for example, mimicking and emulation, a publication entitled "Cultural Learning" (Tomasello, Kruger, & Ratner, 1993) is a good source.

Intersubjectivity can also be differentiated from imitation by the differences in what we do. When we imitate, we copy another person's behavior or the function of another's behavior. We adopt another's perspective. When we engage in intersubjectivity, we cocreate a shared experience. We learn *through* another. Intersubjectivity is the psychobiological act whereby two people share psychobiological states—attention, emotion, and/or thought (Kruger 2013; Tomasello, Kruger, & Ratner, 1993).

Intersubjectivity is made possible by our mirroring bodies. Mirror neurons—first reported in the mid-1990s—are nerve cells that reside in specific anatomical areas of our brain. They fire when people *watch* mouth, hand, and foot movements and when they *perform* those actions (di Pellegrino et al., 1992; Gallese, Fadiga, Fogassi, & Rizzolatti, 1996; Gallese, Fadiga, Fogassi, & Rizzolatti, 2002; Mukamel et al., 2010; Rizzolatti, Fadiga, Gallese, & Fogassi, 1996). Thus, mirror neurons are thought to be bodily mediators of the coding for actions performed by the self and by another person (Gallese 2001; Rizzolatti & Craighero 2004).

What is going on is more than the preparation for and production of actions. Direct bodily understanding also includes recognizing, anticipating, predicting, and interpreting the actions of others. It is the way human beings directly understand another's intentions without reflecting on them (Blakemore & Decety, 2001). Human infants learn through direct resonance soon after birth (Bråten & Trevarthen, 2007). When this direct resonance with another's expression of actions and emotions is a reciprocal subject-to-subject sharing of psychobiological states rather than merely copying the other, the process has been named *primary intersubjectivity*.

Primary Intersubjectivity

Primary intersubjectivity is a dance-like proto-conversation that is observed as an infant's facial imitation of another's smile or tongue protrusion. An infant 42 minutes old can express this innate tendency of all human beings to connect with another in dyadic engagement—in interactive action synchrony and affective attuning (Meltzoff, 2011). "The 'function' of imitation might be its effect on the other and the interpersonal dialogue it promotes" (Reddy 2008, p. 65). These mutual gaze communions are a central component in the formation of attachment bonds. Our mirror neuron-mediated resonance allows infants to access their caregivers. This access is what attachment theorists view as essential for making contact and thriving. This motor and emotional attuning to others gives birth to our earliest sense of self—our bodily self (Gallese & Sinigaglia, 2010). This body-to-body attuning shapes the self-experience of infant and other; it is a reciprocal interactive process.

Understood in this way, our earliest self is "an experienced self, understood only in-relation-to-the-other" (Reddy, 2008, 143). Our self begins with our early emotional and physical experiences in engagement with another. As professor of developmental and cultural psychology Vasudevi Reddy puts it, the "other's attention is first *felt* by the infant ... as a *response* to receiving it from others in engagement" (Reddy, 2008, 90). Then, as we grow, our self becomes able to experience later forms of self-conscious emotions and bodily expressions such as shame and pride, which in turn, lead to an expanded sense of self and self-awareness. Here, let us underscore again a uniqueness of human beings. The magnitude of our self-consciousness—originating in neonatal experiences—is a profound aspect of human beings that distinguishes us from other creatures. Human beings can participate in the minds of each other.

Primary intersubjectivity operates at a prereflective (before thinking) motor and emotional intentionality. Not only can infants imitate immediately an act that they have seen, but when they are not allowed to respond immediately, they can also delay their imitation until later. Nine-month-old, six-month-old, and even six-week-old infants can delay imitation for 24 hours. Twelve-month-old infants can delay imitation for over a month (Nadel & Butterworth, 2010). The motive for imitation seems to be, first, communication (beginning at birth), and, second, learning (beginning around the fifth month of life). As infants grow and develop, their capacity for intersubjectivity becomes increasingly complex.

Secondary Intersubjectivity

Secondary intersubjectivity is where an object is the focus of joint attention and emotional referencing within a trusting relationship. It appears from about nine months of age. It is a triadic (infant, caregiver, and object) engagement of "cooperative awareness" (Trevarthen, 2005, p. 70) of the world we share. Expert on infant and child development Andrew Meltzoff and his colleagues have studied gaze following in children (Meltzoff, 2011, pp. 61–63). They ask adults to turn to a target with eyes open for one group and with eyes closed for another group. Infants follow the adult significantly more often when the adult's eyes are open than when the adult's eyes are closed. It is as if the eyes of the adult transform the object into one that the infants desire.

Tertiary Intersubjectivity

Tertiary intersubjectivity expresses collaborative engagement. It is attained in the second year of life when infants can engage in symbolic conversation, can share goals with others, and can share unspoken intentions. Sharing unspoken intentionality has been demonstrated in 18-month-old infants (Meltzoff, 2011, pp. 64–66). Infants are shown adults successfully and unsuccessfully pulling an object apart. When the adult fails, the infants understand the adult's intention and complete the act of pulling the object apart. Infants are also shown an inanimate device successfully and unsuccessfully pulling an object apart. In the unsuccessful event, infants do not attribute intentions to the movements of the inanimate device and do not pull the object apart. With the attainment of tertiary intersubjectivity, thus, we can *share* the minds of others.

Fourth Level of Intersubjectivity

A fourth level of intersubjectivity—*understanding* minds—is achieved in year four (Allman, Watson, Tetreault, & Hakeem, 2005). "This implicit and pre-theoretical, but at the same time contentful state enables us to directly understand what the other person is doing, why he or she is doing it, and how he or she feels about a specific situation" (Gallese 2011, p. 100). Once we can *understand* the minds of others, we have acquired a theory of mind (ToM). Having acquired a ToM, children can predict another's behavior based on intuiting attributes of the other's mental state.

To clarify what ToM is, let us digress and look at the Smarties test that is used scientifically to determine if children have acquired a ToM. In this test,

> Child A is shown a box of Smarties candy. A researcher asks the child what he or she thinks is in the box. The child naturally replies "candy." The researcher then shows the child that in fact there are pencils in the box. After putting the pencils back in the box, the researcher then asks the child, "Your friend, Child B, is about to come into the room. What will Child B think is in the box?" If the child responds "pencils," she indicates a lack of understanding of the thinking, or mental state, of Child B. But if Child A can infer the mental state of Child B, the correct answer should be "candy." (Keenan, Gallup, & Falk, 2003, p. 94)

Some posit that the acquisition of ToM relates to the acquisition of a special kind of mirror neuron called von Economo neurons (VENs). VENs emerge after birth and reach their peak number at age four when the fourth level of intersubjectivity is achieved. VENs are "a recently evolved cell type which may be involved in the fast intuitive assessment of complex situations" (Allman, Watson, Tetreault, & Hakeem, 2005, p. 367).

Thus, neuroscientific and developmental psychology studies are showing that human beings enter life prepared to connect intersubjectively, that is, with a potential to learn *through* others (Severino, 2013; Morrison & Severino, 2009). Indeed, our bodies are neuroanatomically designed to connect openly with others. Human beings understand the *actions* of others by embodied simulation—the direct mapping of the visual representation of the observed action into a motor representation in our brains of the same action (Gallese, 2001; Gallese, 2003; Gallese, Eagle, & Migone, 2007; Rizzolatti & Craighero, 2004). Human beings also understand the *emotions* of others intersubjectively, possibly mediated by mirror neurons. These scientific findings lend credence to the innateness of human intersubjectivity and provide the "how" for second-person contemplative learning.

Moreover, these scientific findings point to an important observation: Intersubjectivity is the starting point for human development. "We are multiple from the start" (Haidt, 2012, p. 109).[1] Humans begin life as, what Martin Buber (1937) named, an I-Thou. "Every instantiation of mirroring or interpersonal resonance—that is, embodied simulation—is always a process in which the behavior of others is metabolized by, and filtered through, the observer's idiosyncratic past experiences, capacities, and mental attitudes" (Gallese, 2011, p. 101).

Case Study

To shift from neuroscientific groundwork to case study, we need to shift from third-person to first-person language because this case study comes from the life of one of the authors. Here is his story.

My name is M. Andrew Garrison. I am a recently retired wellness professional who enjoyed a 27-year career in Bernalillo County government in Albuquerque, New Mexico. In 2006, one of my duties was to validate and implement physical readiness standards for corrections officers at the

Metropolitan Detention Center (MDC for short). The validation began with a survey of 100 veteran officers to rank the frequent (standing, walking, sitting, lifting, etc.) and critical (restraining inmates, running to an assistance call, etc.) tasks of their job.

From the various fitness components, we developed a series of physical fitness tests: 1.5-mile run, 300-meter run, vertical jump, push-ups, sit-ups, Illinois Agility Test, and one-repetition maximum bench press. After putting a stratified random sample of 150 sworn personnel through each of the events, statistical analyses of their results determined the cut-off scores. This resulted in a fitness battery, a one-job/one-standard for cadets and veterans. All aspiring cadets were required to pass the full physical fitness test battery in their training academy in order to become sworn officers.

Professor of psychology Louis Cozolino has noted that teachers can positively influence the well-being of their students by establishing optimistic expectations of them (Cozolino, 2013, p. 149). I attempted to do so by role modeling my personal belief, as a lifelong athlete, that one should be prepared to do one's best and to improve one's self continually. I committed to competing with the cadets in the complete physical fitness test battery and scored in the top 10 percent on all events. As I had hoped, my role modeling set expectations for achievement, which positively influenced the learning and health of the cadets, many of whom were 20 years younger than me. At the same time, some of the veteran officers, who had not experienced the team-building of the validation testing, misperceived the physical readiness standards as looming punishment intended to push them out the door to retirement.

To change their misperceptions, we adopted Verbal Defense and Influence methodologies to increase officer safety by voluntary compliance from inmates. Because persuasive de-escalation techniques require calm minds and mouths, professional officers quickly learned that they needed to be in a homeostatic physical state in order to maintain control of the aggressive emotions traditionally provoked by inmates. Demonstrating how this homeostasis worked with inmates had the effect of stimulating all facets of the officers' minds, brains, and bodies, convincing them that physical fitness was not just a standard, but it was also an integral part of their ability to perform, to keep everyone safe and secure, and to defend against their own stress, exhaustion, and burnout.

All our hard work, however, almost ended at 9:35 p.m. on September 25, 2008. I suffered a motorcycle accident on my Buell XB12R and awoke, with an uncertain future, in the Intensive Care Unit at the

University of New Mexico Hospital. My head was lacerated front to back. My right shoulder was torn out; my left rotator cuff was damaged. I had six broken ribs and bruised lungs. My left foot hung tenuously. Six days later I left the hospital an amputee.

Early in 2009, I was scheduled to meet with Byron Gardner who would assess my residual left limb for healing and weight-bearing capability and cast a new foot for me. Byron's office was located far in the back of Carrie Tingley Hospital, which is primarily a children's hospital. This required making my way down winding hallways to get to him. Filling those hallways, I saw quadriplegic children in motorized wheelchairs. Some were grossly disfigured, having lunch fed to them through a tube. My heart churned.

Hung in frames all along the walls were haunting narratives telling the stories of these children. I had originally assumed that they suffered from congenital conditions, but I soon learned differently when I read the horror of one healthy five-year-old girl who was rendered forever dependent by a trampoline accident. My empathy with her experience thrust me into a respect for intersubjectivity—a respect for learning *through* others. In experiencing her fragility and pain through her story, I came to see myself in a new way.

While she was surviving through resilience, I was imperfectly well. Compared to what happened to her, I felt that absolutely nothing had happened to me. Even without a prosthetic, I was already limping around on my residual limb. No longer able to compete with top athletes, I embraced simply competing with myself. In hindsight, my old mantra of "be prepared to do your best and improve yourself continually" still applied. But now it meant more than pushing employees to pass fitness standards. It became part of my *being image*, a person who engages employees in healthy-weight and stress-reduction strategies that could improve the quality of their lives at work and at home. As I internalized my new image of myself, my *being image* became that of a cocreative agent with people who choose to enhance their *being image* through a sense of purpose.

Being Image

A *being image* is an internalization of relationally embodied talents and passions for the core purpose of connecting with and serving the community. It is a proactive process of expanding knowledge through service within second-person intersubjectivity. It is purposeful, and its purpose is service. In short, *being image* is what we experience as our body and self in interaction with others. This is distinguished from *body image*, which is what we individually see as our physical self in comparison to others, and from *self-image*, which is what we individually think about our abilities and appearance in comparison to others.

When I returned to MDC with a new foot, I committed to passing the full physical fitness test battery myself. This was a commitment to change my *body image* from "the one-footed fitness guy" to a *being image* of "the physically fit MDC team guy." In other words, I changed my *body image*—my bodily internalization of "the one-footed fitness guy"—to a *being image*—a purposeful interrelational internalization of "the physically fit MDC team guy."

I couldn't do it alone. It would ultimately be a process of second-person intersubjective cocreation, although my training in preparation for passing the fitness standards required first-person efforts to control pain.

First-Person Efforts

Of the six tests required of all corrections officers, the 1.5-mile run promised to be the most difficult for me. The validated cut-off time for the run was 19 minutes and 53 seconds. I had been in a wheelchair for the bulk of four months. I couldn't even walk without pain in my residual limb, much less jog for a mile and a half on a marked course made up of pavement and hard gravel. While I did not know where my effort would end, I knew what my first step must be. I just had to begin.

Since I couldn't run yet, I walked. Since I couldn't walk for a full mile and a half, I walked half of that (.75 miles). After a couple of months, I employed light interval training alternating between walking fast and jogging. All of these adjustments allowed me to continue training at a level of pain that I could endure.

Three months later I timed the .75 mile at 10 minutes. Assuming I could maintain the same pace in a second half, it would take me 20 minutes to complete the 1.5-mile course. I then made a deal with myself. I would segue into the full course if I could complete the .75 mile in nine minutes flat. Since my residual limb still could not support a consistent jog, I continued to train with my interpretation of what is called Fartlek Training, alternating walking fast with slow jogging.[2] This allowed the pain of jogging to subside during walking. These first-person efforts, established upon my *being image* of a cocreative agent, readied me for cocreative participatory learning.

Second-Person Collaborative Participation

The moment had finally arrived. Almost a year from the time I became an amputee, I joined a group of 20 cadets to run the 1.5-mile test. I was about to establish a staunch belief in my body as an essential way to create synergy through others. To do this, I needed another person with whom I could cocreate collective success. I engaged one female cadet who was jogging well under the validated cut-off time. I would jog past her, and then walk. When she cruised by me, I would again jog and pass her. In the end, I completed the 1.5-mile test in 17 minutes and 45 seconds. The female cadet passed the finish line about 30 seconds ahead of me.

We were engaged in what psychologist Kenneth J. Gergen (2009) calls "synchrony in action." Our synchronic coordination of jogging was the essence of our understanding that we were helping each other pass the test. We transcended our individual selves by running for both of us and for all the cadets that day. It didn't matter what we looked like, what our body fat percentage was, or how tan our legs were. It only mattered that we collectively met the standard of the organization. We functioned cooperatively rather than as individuals. As a result, we cocreated our *being images* as persons with the physical capacity required of law enforcement officers in a detention center.

Passing the fitness test was not only to prove something to myself. The exertion also demonstrated the power of intersubjective learning. First, the cadet and I cocreated new *being images* of wellness by "opening ourselves to becoming something other" (Bauman, 2014, p. 150). Second, our enhanced *being images* connected us more intimately with the entire security workforce. In my instance, the security workforce appreciated my success in demanding of myself what I demanded of them, and I appreciated their success in meeting the physical fitness standards for correction officers. Together our energies fueled each other. We all cocreated new *being images* of successful, physically and purposefully fit people.

In my larger role at Bernalillo County and now as a wellness consultant, I focus on reframing perceived intimidations employees may carry about wellness education. The message is clear that the short-term objective of wellness education is to cocreate behavior change that is good for you, good for me, and good for our community. The long-term objective is collective becoming, continually cocreating new beings. In this process, we openly discuss wellness dreams and then assess the challenges to that vision of wellness within the socio-ecological model.[3]

In classroom teaching, whether in the field of public safety or in wellness seminars for county employees, I use case studies to show how second-person intersubjectivity works, emphasizing the power of brain-to-brain transmission of resonant relationships (Bovatzis, 2012). I supplement this with techniques that are successful with students who are new to collaborative learning, such as the "Think-Pair-Share" activity. This activity described by Barbara J. Millis, director of the Teaching and Learning Center at the University of Texas in San Antonio, and Phillip G. Cottell Jr., associate professor of accountancy at Miami University, Ohio (1998), begins with the instructor posing a question. After a minute for formulating an answer, students pair with a neighbor to discuss their ideas. After several minutes, the instructor invites group sharing of answers to the question that the pairs have cocreated. The benefits of this activity are manifold. The active pairing interaction exposes students to alternative ways of approaching what they do and do not know. The sharing activity enhances students' oral communication skills as they interact with one another. And the discussion experience threatens students less because if the answer is wrong, embarrassment is shared.

Challenges

The unique culture of MDC and the organizational rollout of physical fitness training created officer mistrust of management; officers misperceived "ominous training" as a reflection of their work as inadequate. Early classroom efforts, therefore, focused on endorsing positive views of officers' abilities to perform in homeostatic physical states that established safety for themselves and for inmates. It is becoming increasingly appreciated that teacher expectation is an active agent in student achievement (Cozolino 2013, p. 152).

Similar to MDC, other organizational environments may present challenges for second-person intersubjective learning. Difficulties may arise, for example, with groups experiencing internal conflict or in settings where employees have perceived inconsistencies with the oversight of organizational regulations. These antagonistic settings are not conducive to sharing or cocreating.

Finally, second-person intersubjectivity may be too demanding of employees with high stress levels or burnout who cannot access their higher learning centers for problem solving. This is because, "People process, store and retrieve information and then respond to the world in a manner that depends upon their current physiological state" (Perry & Szalavitz, 2006, p. 249). Even with the same IQs, calmer people can access their neocortex for problem solving whereas people who are alarmed react reflexively and use their lower brain centers for problem solving.

Summary

We are convinced that advances in neuroscience offer support for efforts to integrate contemplative techniques into teaching and training curricula. We present the neuroscientific groundwork on intersubjectivity that underpins second-person learning followed by a case study that demonstrates how second-person contemplative learning facilitates the cocreating of a new *being image* in the realm of physical fitness. We close by delineating those settings where this approach may be challenged and/or may not be successful.

Notes

1. This idea of being "multiple from the start" was originally stated by cultural anthropologist Richard Shweder (1991, p. 5).

2. *Fartlek* means "speed play" in Swedish. It is a method that blends continuous training with interval training. The intensity and/or speed of the training vary according to the athlete's needs. Most Fartlek sessions last a minimum of 45 minutes. They can include both aerobic walking and also anaerobic sprinting.

3. The socio-ecological model recognizes the interwoven relationship between each person and his or her environment. The most effective approach leading to healthy behaviors combines efforts at all levels—individual, interpersonal, organizational, community, and public policy.

References

Allman, J. M., Watson, K. K., Tetreault, N. A., & Hakeem, A. Y. (2005). Intuition and autism: A possible role for von Economo neurons. *TRENDS in Cognitive Sciences*, 9(8), 367–373.

Bauman, W. A. (2014). *Religion and ecology: Developing a planetary ethic*. New York: Columbia University Press.

Bovatzis, R. (2012). Neuroscience and the link between inspirational leadership and resonant relationships. *Ivey Business Journal*, 76(1), 26. Retrieved February 3, 2016, from http://www.iveybusinessjournal.com/topics/leadership/neuroscience-and-the-link-between-inspirational-leadership-and-resonant-relationships-2#.U4OcfaXvb1r

Bråten, S., & Trevarthen, C. (2007). Prologue: From infant intersubjectivity and participant movements to simulation and conversation in cultural common sense." In S. Bråten (Ed.), *On being moved: From mirror neurons to empathy* (pp. 21–34). Philadelphia: John Benjamins.

Blakemore, S.-J., & Decety, J. (2001). From the perception of action to the understanding of intention. *Nature Reviews Neuroscience*, 2, 561–567.

Buber, M. (1937). *I and Thou*. New York: Free Press.

Cozolino, L. (2013). *The social neuroscience of education: Optimizing attachment & learning in the classroom*. New York: W. W. Norton & Company.

di Pellegrino, G., Fadiga, L., Fogassi, L., Gallese, V., & Rizzolatti, G. (1992). Understanding motor events: A neurophysiological study. *Experimental Brain Research*, 91(1), 176–180.

Gallese, V. (2001). The 'shared manifold' hypothesis: From mirror neurons to empathy. *Journal of Consciousness Studies*, 8(5–7), 33–50.

Gallese, V. (2003). The roots of empathy: The shared manifold hypothesis and the neural basis of intersubjectivity. *Psychopathology*, 36(4), 171–180.

Gallese, V. (2011). The two sides of mimesis: Mimetic theory, embodied simulation, and social identification. In S. R. Garrels (Ed.), *Mimesis and science: Empirical research on imitation and the mimetic theory of culture and religion* (pp. 87–108). East Lansing: Michigan State University Press.

Gallese, V., Eagle, M. E., & Migone, P. (2007). Intentional attunement: Mirror neurons and the neural underpinnings of interpersonal relations. *Journal of the American Psychoanalytic Association*, 55(1), 131–176.

Gallese, V., Fadiga, L., Fogassi, L., & Rizzolatti, G. (1996). Action recognition in the premotor cortex. *Brain*, 119, 593–609.

Gallese, V., Fadiga, L., Fogassi, L. & Rizzolatti, G. (2002). Action representation and the inferior parietal lobule. In W. Prinz and B. Hommel (Eds.), *Common mechanisms in perception and action: Attention and performance XIX* (pp. 334–355). New York: Oxford University Press.

Gallese, V., & Sinigaglia, C. (2010). The bodily self as power for action. *Neuropsychologia*, 48, 746–755.

Gergen, K. J. (2009). *Relational being: Beyond self and community*. New York: Oxford University Press.

Haidt, J. (2012). *The righteous mind: Why good people are divided by politics and religion*. New York: Pantheon Books.

Keenan, J. P., Gallup, G. G., Jr., & Falk, D. (2003). *The face in the mirror: The search for the origins of consciousness*. New York: HarperCollins.

Kruger, A. C. (2011). Imitation, communion, and culture. In S. R. Garrels (Ed.), *Mimesis and science: Empirical research on imitation and the mimetic theory of culture and religion* (pp. 111–127). East Lansing: Michigan State University Press.

Kruger, A. C. (2013). Personal email, June 25.

Meltzoff, A. N. (2011). Out of the mouths of babes: Imitation, gaze, and intentions in infant research—the 'like me' framework. In S. R. Garrels (Ed.), *Mimesis and science: Empirical research on imitation and the mimetic theory of culture and religion* (pp. 55–74). East Lansing: Michigan State University Press.

Millis, B. J., & Cottell, P.G., Jr. (1998). *Cooperative learning for higher education faculty*. Phoenix: American Council on Education and The Oryx Press.

Morrison, N. K., & Severino, S. K. (2009). *Sacred desire: Growing in compassionate living*. West Conshohocken: Templeton Foundation Press.

Mukamel, R., Ekstrom, A. D., Kaplan, J., Iacoboni, M., & Fried, I. (2010). Single-neuron responses in humans during execution and observation of actions. *Current Biology, 20,* 750–756.

Nadel, J., & Butterworth, G. (Eds.) (2010). *Imitation in infancy*. New York: Cambridge University Press.

Perry, B. D., & Szalavitz, M. (2006). *The boy who was raised as a dog: And other stories from a child psychiatrist's notebook*. New York: Basic Books.

Reddy, V. (2008). *How infants know minds*. Cambridge: Harvard University Press.

Rizzolatti, G., & Craighero, L. (2004). The mirror-neuron system. *Annual Review Neuroscience, 27,* 169–192.

Rizzolatti, G., Fadiga, L., Gallese, V., & Fogassi, L. (1996). Premotor cortex and the recognition of motor actions. *Cognitive Brain Research, 3,* 131–141.

Severino, S. K. (2013). *Behold our moral body: Psychiatry, Duns Scotus, and neuroscience*. London: Versita.

Shweder, R. A. (1991). *Thinking through cultures: Expeditions in cultural psychology*. Cambridge: Harvard University Press.

Tomasello, M., Kruger, A. C., & Ratner, H. H. (1993). Cultural learning. *Behavioral and Brain Sciences, 16,* 495–552.

Trevarthen, C. (2005). Stepping away from the mirror: Pride and shame in adventures of companionship—Reflections on the nature and emotional needs of infant intersubjectivity. In C. S. Carter, L. Ahnert, K. E. Grossman, S. B. Hrdy, M. E. Lamb, S. W. Porges, & N. Sachser (Eds.), *Attachment and bonding: A new synthesis* (pp. 55–84). Cambridge: MIT Press.

Zlatev, J., Racine, T. P., Sinha, C., & Itkonen, E. (2008). Intersubjectivity: What makes us human? In J. Zlatev, T. P. Racine, C. Sinha, and E. Itkonen (Eds.), *The shared mind: Perspectives in intersubjectivity* (pp. 1–14). Philadelphia: John Benjamins.

10

Teaching Creativity and Building Community in the Undergraduate Classroom

Self-Awareness, Empathy, and Character through Relational and Contemplative Practice

SEAN PARK

Interdisciplinary Expressive Arts

I had the opportunity in 2013 to teach a few undergraduate courses in the Interdisciplinary Expressive Arts (IDEA) program at Kwantlen Polytechnic University in Surrey, British Columbia. Founded and developed by Dr. Ross Laird—a creative writing instructor with a background in counseling psychology, Eastern contemplative practices, addictions, technology, and mythology—IDEA courses offer undergraduate students unique and transformative learning experiences.

One of the courses I taught as a sessional was IDEA 1100—Interdisciplinary Foundations. The course, capped at 35 and open to all undergraduate students, asks: What's the point of university? Why are we here? What should we do? These questions are explored through the lens of interdisciplinary inquiry and creativity. Led by the initiatives and interests of students, the course included a diverse number of current interdisciplinary approaches to help students ask—and answer, in their own ways—questions about purpose, meaning, and direction. Dr. Laird encouraged me to design and offer these courses in my own way within a framework of student-designed projects, individualized curriculum, purposeful play, and other innovative approaches that would make possible the creation of collaborative learning environments in which students discovered their own paths and purposes.

At the time, I was a doctoral student at Simon Fraser University, studying contemplative education with my supervisor Dr. Heesoon Bai. As part of my study and research with Dr. Bai and others (Bai, Park, & Cohen, 2016; Bai et al., 2014; Park & Cohen, 2010), contemplative practice and intersubjectivity in education was a prominent area of focus. It became clear in our work together that the community dimension of the classroom was of great significance in fostering learning environments animated by respect, compassion, connection, presence, and creativity. It is in the relationships educators and learners cultivate, more so than the teachers themselves, that the deepest teaching happens. By engaging in contemplative practices in ways that explicitly focus on the interpersonal dimensions of teaching and learning, it becomes possible to attend to our *shared* human multidimensionality, which includes the full spectrum of fears, desires, dreams, suffering, and joy we all bring to the classroom. To cocreate such an environment is to build community in the classroom, and it is the community dimension that offers teachers and students innumerable opportunities for growth.

I wanted to learn more about the potential and relevance for relational contemplative practice and community development in the classes I was teaching. The Interdisciplinary Foundations course would be my first opportunity to do so in a practical way. My aim in this chapter is to illustrate how I attempted this in terms of course design, facilitation, and what some of the reflections were on the experience, both from the students and myself. I offer a brief overview of interdisciplinary expressive arts education, and the course design, assignments, and assessments of one iteration of the course to show the context of building the classroom as a contemplative, creative community. These elements help frame how themes of belonging and acceptance were addressed as part of building self-awareness, character, and empathy in the classroom. Descriptions of how mindfulness meditation, interpersonal mindfulness practice, group dialogue, and Japanese *ensō* painting were offered to students serve to illustrate how these themes were held and explored within the broader framework of the course.

Self-Awareness, Empathy, and Character

I situate my approach to joining contemplative practice and community development in the broader context of a vision for interdisciplinary expressive arts education that I have been exploring with Dr. Laird. Interdisciplinary expressive arts education focuses on the integration of personal and professional development using creative methods, experiential learning, outdoor trips, self-awareness practices, cultural immersion, student-built content, and many other approaches. The expressive arts—which include poetry, movement, music, film, drawing, theater, among others—are seen as critical to learning and interdisciplinary inquiry because they connect us to different ways of knowing and enable all of our different faculties to participate. In addition to rational thought, movement, emotion, intuition, touch, sight, sound, and rhythmic awareness are part of how we humans orient and make sense of the world. Creative writing, movement, storytelling, meditation, and many other practices support the ability to think and act in multidimensional ways.

In the process of exploring various ways of inquiring and approaching problems, learners not only broaden and deepen their knowledge and skills, but they also learn to see who they are as individuals and where they stand in the world. Personal purpose and meaning in what we do with our lives becomes part of our search for truth and identity, and what it means for these things to be provisional and fluid.

Interdisciplinary expressive arts education focuses on integrating three core values—self-awareness, empathy, and character—that can cut across domains and disciplines. Self-awareness is what we know—about ourselves, our interests, our capacities and where we feel stretched beyond our comfort zones. Empathy is what we feel—toward others, the state of the world, toward nature. Character is what we do with our self-awareness and our empathy—how we act, express, and lead. Awareness, emotion, behavior. Or, to put it another way: being, feeling, doing. As a set of skills, these three areas break down into the following set, although many other lists could be created:

Self-awareness

- Developing experiential awareness of one's own mind, body, and emotions and a path for working with and transforming them as a whole.

- Following the search for knowledge and meaningful answers.

- Developing creativity through play and imagination.

- Thinking clearly and critically.

- Situating one's self with respect to history and social location.

Empathy

- Opening oneself to empathy and compassion.
- Communicating effectively in speaking, listening, writing, and performing.
- Building trust, emotional safety, and a culture of collaboration.
- Being open to giving and receiving feedback and accepting others.
- Embracing and resolving conflicts.

Character

- Engaging in the reciprocal process of mentorship.
- Creating useful solutions to complex problems or reframing problems in new ways.
- Joining and contributing to communities.
- Modeling and teaching ethical practices.
- Opening to, and learning from, other cultures.
- Being a lifelong learner.

These are more holistic, integrative, and focused on the general goals of personal and community development than university programs tend to be. The skills do not align themselves with any particular academic domain or content area, although many contribute to them. Their development does not require lectures or exams and the interdisciplinary expressive arts instructor is a facilitator rather than a content expert. Communities of learners who use creativity, play, and personal development are created to build the skills of self-awareness. Empathy is deepened through community engagement, and character is built through the challenges of experiential learning, collaboration, and mentorship.

IDEA 1100—Interdisciplinary Foundations

In my iteration of Interdisciplinary Expressive Arts (IDEA) 1100—Interdisciplinary Foundations, students were asked: What's the point of university? Why are we here? What should we do? This course explored these questions through the lens of interdisciplinary inquiry and creativity. Led by the initiatives and interests of learners, the course included a diverse number of current interdisciplinary approaches to help students ask—and answer, in their own ways—questions about purpose, meaning, and direction. The course included a variety of learning experiences contingent upon regular attendance and dedicated participation. Because authentic interdisciplinary inquiry is an interactive process, much of the class time was devoted to group experiential exercises, individual reflective tasks, collaborative endeavors, and practical assignments. Some of these activities, including mindfulness meditation and contemplative painting, are described later in this chapter.

The course was structured around the following constructs and tasks:

Learning Contract

Students identified skills from each value domain (self-awareness, character, empathy) that they wished to work on over the term. They were asked to identify why they wanted to work on these areas and the kinds of opportunities and resources they think would help them. Students were asked to write a two-page learning contract during the first two weeks of class that I helped them refine. It was considered a work-in-progress and was revisited at the end of the course during a final exit interview and evaluation.

Classroom experiences, experiences outside the classroom, and the individual and group project (described later) were opportunities for students to work and develop in the areas they wished to grow. Invariably, students could start to see that the skills required for self-awareness, character, and empathy applied to many areas outside the boundaries of the course, and they were encouraged to consider their learning contract in other contexts. The learning contract helped students to see, create, and engage in any opportunity to develop the skills. Students that needed more focus could complete a scoped individual project comprised of any type of expression (writing, music, imagery, dance, movement, photography, etc.) that explored the values of self-awareness, character, and/or empathy and developed the skills they identified.

Students demonstrated their growth by collecting "evidence" that showed how they had been working on their skill area and what the outcomes were. Evidence could take many different forms and would not usually be of the formal, scholarly kind. For example, an email exchange between students might illustrate where they are practicing new approaches to communication and conflict resolution.

Weekly Reflections

Once a week, the evening before class, students submitted an online reflection using a range of creative modes, including poetry, drawing, song, and so on, that concerned the skill set, what they were struggling with, where they saw growth, and what questions were arising for them.

Group Project

Each student was a member of a group of about six; each group would present in the second half of the course (roughly 30 minutes) on a topic of choice. Significant class time (one out of three hours) was given for working in groups, although groups were required to find time outside of class to work with each other. The central idea of the group project and presentation was to give students opportunities to practice interdisciplinary thinking and expression. As such, the presentations needed to use multiple presentation strategies and modalities, including (but not limited to) storytelling, poetry, music, dance and movement, film, photography, web content, craft and art work, reflection, meditation and health practices, creative processes of any kind, cultural practices, and nature experiences. Students self-assessed and assessed other group members halfway through the course and again at the end using a rubric to rate participation and contributions to the group.

Peer Tutors

Four upper-year students that had taken the foundations course and had a deep commitment to self-awareness, character, and empathy (based upon the recommendation of other instructors) were recruited to be peer mentors. The peer mentors served many roles in the course. They spoke to students about their experiences with interdisciplinary expressive arts education, how they were making sense of university a few years in, and their process of thinking about their next steps after completing their degree. They also served as facilitators in each of the small groups that met during and outside of class time. Their role was to be a facilitator and resource to the groups as they worked to figure out their purpose and direction. The peer tutors received credit for their role by enrolling in the IDEA 3300: Creativity and Leadership in Groups course. We met multiple times throughout the term to discuss their own growth as facilitators and how to effectively facilitate group development.

Text

The required text for the course was *The Element* by Sir Ken Robinson, and it needed to be read in the first three weeks of the course. The book offers an array of stories of how people came to find their unique passions, the challenges they faced, and how others supported them. It served as a starting point for asking questions about the purpose of education and developing individual and group projects that explored questions about enacting meaningful education.

Assessment and Final Skills Interview

Assessment took several forms; I assessed individual and group projects, students assessed themselves, and they assessed each other in their small group and class presentations. The values of self-awareness, character, and empathy and their skill sets were the focus of assessment. Students needed to demonstrate to themselves and to me, objectively, that they had changed (better skills) from the start of the course to the end of the course. It was really that simple, in principle. I had several discussions with students individually, in small groups, and as a class about this. The skills and a student's level of improvement were translated into a letter grade (the evaluation) using a simple rubric demarcating poor (C, C–, C+), good (B, B–, B+), and excellent (A, A–, A+) with descriptions of skill demonstration for each level. The grade was negotiated with each student during a 30-minute exit skills interview and focused on the original learning contract, self and peer assessments, a final reflection, and the student's presentation of the evidence of growth.

The Personal and Relational Context of Creating Together

The course approached the teaching and learning of creativity as a way of being, feeling, and doing. It included our movements, feelings, imagination, hunches, and our capacity for reasoning and planning. As a whole-person endeavor focused on transformation, creativity was nurtured through iterative, pragmatic action and learning through experience, feedback, and reflection. We read an essay on creativity and the soul by Isabella Colalillo Kates (2005), who shared:

> To create is to transform; but the basic issue is what is being transformed. It may be raw materials (clay, wood, words, pigments or the patterns of social behaviour) to which a more integrative and meaning-realising form is given; but it also could be the consciousness of human beings and their capacity to respond effectively to the challenge of a greater life. (Rhudyhar, 1977 qtd. in Kates, 2005, p. 194)

When we engage in inquiry and creation, we bring all of our perceptions, expectations, and habits with us and there always exists the possibility that we will be changed by what is created. If we have a glimpse of the frames we impose upon the world, we can be either more deliberate or more open to how we proceed. To open this conversation, I asked students the following four questions as part of creating their learning contract:

1. What do you want to feel, be, or experience in life?
2. What do you not want to feel, be, or experience in life?
3. What are your expectations of this course?
4. Are you open to the outcomes of this course being different from what you expected?

The responses were quite rich, and the following list is a composite of the diversity of reflections. In the interest of space and the focus on intersubjectivity, I focus on responses to the first two questions:

> I want to continue to feel loved and blessed with the people in my life.
>
> I want to get more comfortable not only with myself but also around other people.
>
> I want to be genuinely good to other people.
>
> I don't want to feel taken for granted or lonely
>
> I want to be a successful individual who works in a career I am passionate about.

- I want to be a happy, stress-free individual as much as possible, which I feel will be accomplished once school is complete.
- I don't want to be continuously stressed like I usually am, and I don't want to be someone stuck in a job I hate.
- I don't want to live in a routine, but rather live each day to the fullest and enjoy the unexpected.
- I don't want to feel or experience a sense of disappointment in myself.
- I want to connect with people emotionally, intimately, and in other ways.
- I want to experience a feeling of connection with God.
- I don't want to be a disappointment to myself, but mostly to my mother. She sacrificed a lot to bring me to this country.
- I want to feel secure with myself.
- I want to feel that I am complete and that I am not just good enough, but better than good.
- I want to be able to inspire others.
- I want to be a role model, and I want my younger sister to be able to look up to me.
- I want to be able to live my life the way I want to live it, without always having to worry about what others will think.
- I don't want to let the fear of how others may perceive me keep preventing me from living.
- I seek to feel belonging, confidence, acceptance, love, and support.
- I seek to experience good friendships, a healthy relationship, and a family of my own in the upcoming future, as well as the experience of finding myself rising above challenges and being able to see myself grow as a person.
- I don't want to feel like a failure.
- I am seeking to be independent, genuine, honest, and kind-hearted.

> I am not seeking to be someone who relies on others for happiness, or someone who is associated with conflict or tension.
>
> I do not want to feel unwanted, to feel lost, abandoned, or incompetent.
>
> I am seeking to not experience unhealthy relationships, and to not experience myself trying hard to achieve my goals, just to witness failure.
>
> I would hate to go through life feeling like I am nothing, and that I don't matter.

These responses are brief, candid, and human responses. They are common responses that I see in almost every undergraduate class where I have asked these questions. The questions and the responses were not directly addressed in the classroom, however a class-wide conversation about the questions provided an opportunity to talk about a dominant theme that impacts the development of creativity, namely, relationships and the desires and fears of being seen or not being seen. These desires and fears shape a great deal of how we engage in expressive work and play, both alone and in groups. We read again from Kates (2005), who points out how the Inner Critic can shut us off from connecting to our creativity and the aesthetic:

> The Inner Critic, the composite voice of the many external critics that try to govern our life, wants us to obey its overbearing commanding voice. The more we do so, the more victimized and uncreative we feel. Our resident Critic uses our creative energy to machinate against the will of the Inner Creator. . . . Its main role is to protect us from taking risks, from overreaching our dreams. In its attempts to spare us from failure, usually through shame and fear, the Critic cuts us off from the creative energy of the Creator. (Kates, 2005, p. 202)

During the second week of class, I asked students to come up with a classroom contract of commitments—what we will do and *not* do—to create a learning environment that helps us deal with the Inner Critic and tap into the energy of the Inner Creator. To do so, we used an activity or *liberating structure* called 1-2-4-All. Liberating Structures are a set of interventions designed to involve all participants in maximal and efficient ways (Lipmanowicz & McCandless, 2013). In this application of 1-2-4-All, students were given a minute on their own to come up with what is important to a learning environment that helps work with the Critic and then to elaborate with a partner for two minutes. Groups of four then met for two or three minutes to elaborate further. Finally, we debriefed with all the groups to fill out the contract and sign it.

The contract varies from course to course, but it invariably includes items such as letting others speak without being interrupted, treating others as they would like to be treated, speaking with each other and me as concerns arise, turning off cell phones, coming to class on time, and creating a fun, welcoming, and supportive environment. I ask them if we can refer back to the contract, elaborate on it, and change it as we need to. My intention in helping them create the contract is that it keeps them invested in honoring, developing, and taking responsibility for it.

Interpersonal Suffering and Relational Mindfulness

Building off the theme of being seen and accepted, I offered a short talk about the work of Theravadin Buddhist teacher Gregory Kramer, who writes and teaches on the relational and interpersonal aspects of Buddhist teachings and points out that a great portion of our feelings and emotions arise in relationship to others (Kramer, 2007). Whereas distress at feeling physical pain can be experienced as personal suffering, our fears about what others will think of us (or not think of us) are interpersonal suffering. We experience both immense joy and suffering in relationships because we are relational and social beings. Human brains and cultures evolved in groups that survived as a result of being able to stay connected with each other. Our sense of self is formed in the relational context of other human beings, learning at an early age what is me and what is not-me. We learn with whom we feel safe and attached and with whom we need to hide parts of ourselves to be accepted.

In the interpersonal domain, Kramer writes that the Buddha's teachings point to the existence and causes of human suffering as originating from the hungers for this sense of self to be preserved; the hunger to be and the fear of nonbeing. The hunger to be is essentially the basic drive to live, to exist. Relationally, this hunger is the desire to be seen and accepted by others. The hunger to be is also strengthened by the fear of not being seen, of being unworthy of love and unacceptable.

The flipside of the hunger to be is the hunger to avoid being and the fear of being seen. This hunger is the drive to escape situations and circumstances that threaten our safety, enjoyment, or basic sense of self. Fear of intimacy or public performance can bring about a great deal of discomfort because of not wanting to be fully revealed where the possibility exists that we will be rejected and seen as unworthy.

I shared with students that in my own life, I recall a strong desire in my earliest years of school and into graduate school to be seen as a smart, articulate, and visionary person. I wanted people to respect me, and I strove to accomplish many things to secure this respect. But underneath this was often a sense of lack, an Inner Critic that could not be satisfied by trying to create this image of myself in other people.

One way of working with the Critic, the hungers, and their attendant fears as they arise in our relationship with others is to examine and become aware, firsthand, of our inner experience of being in relationship with others. Grounding my instructions in the Theravadin practice of Insight meditation (*vipassana*), I introduce mindfulness as a practice of pausing, noticing, and resting with moment-to-moment experience in everyday actions (Kramer, 2007). Developing awareness of one's own bodily sensations, emotions, and thoughts is practiced primarily by stilling the body in an upright and relaxed posture in classroom chairs and repeatedly bringing a compassionate and open stance to phenomena that arises and dissipates in the present. Inspired by the work of Gregory Kramer on the relational hungers to be seen and not seen, I invite students to relax their bodies and dispassionately disengage from internal chit-chat as they notice themselves feeling distressed about their relationships with others.

The lesson that Kramer offers is that mindfulness practiced in this way helps us become less impulsive in our attempts to escape the hungers and make space for acting more compassionately toward ourselves and others. Mindfulness also allows us to be present with others, appreciate their perspectives, work with our uncomfortable and judgmental reactions toward them, and skillfully handle conflicts.

The Practice: Mindful Speaking/Listening and Class Check-In

The class met once a week for three hours. Each session began with a five-minute mindfulness practice, such as observing the breath, listening to sounds, or a walking meditation focused on paying attention to the felt sense of the body in motion. The practices were framed as self-regulating activities for increasing concentration, reducing stress, and entering into a state of embodied curiosity. Before engaging in some version of a classroom "check-in" in which students could speak about their present-moment experience, I gave instructions in mindful listening and speaking based on guidelines developed by Gregory Kramer in his text *Insight Dialogue*. For example, I would speak something like the following to students as part of the meditation.

> Rest
> To rest is to pause and relax and by inviting ease and comfort to the body. Shoulders are relaxed, we soften the musculature in our face, chest, and torso. We feel the weight of our body resting upon the ground and notice the natural flow of the breath. Resting slows our intentions and movements so that we can get a handle on what we're experiencing inside and what we perceive around us.
>
> We temporarily suspend any agenda to accomplish something so that a wider space of awareness and possibilities can open up. The rest is the necessary gap to consider what might be a priority in the moment, to make space for another perspective, to notice your own.
>
> By inviting the mind and body to rest, we are no longer expending energy trying to accomplish something. We catch our breath amid our usual hustle and bustle of activity.
>
> As you rest here, take a few moments to notice if there is a word that somehow fits with how you're doing in the moment. Take some time to notice inside if the word resonates for you, if it feels true. Notice if there are any other words that come to you that feel more accurate.
>
> In a few moments I will ring the bell and you will have an opportunity to share your word with the class. As you speak, I invite you to rest before you say your word, as you speak, and after you speak. Take your time. Feel your body resting. Notice your breath. And as you listen to others sharing their word, experiment with resting as well. Notice what it is like to relax your body and breath as you wait for your turn. Notice the sensations and thoughts that arise inside to what others are saying. See if you can rest with these sensations and thoughts.

On some weeks, we would practice the mindfulness meditations and do the check-in in a large group circle. On other weeks, I used the

Liberating Structure 1-2-4-All to run the check-in. In this 1-2-4-All, each student had a minute or two to reflect on how they were doing in the moment, where they were feeling stuck in their individual or group project, and where they were progressing. Students then formed dyads to share and elaborate on their reflections for two minutes and then moved into groups of four to share and elaborate for a few minutes. Then, as the whole class, we quickly had each group of four debrief with the rest of the class for five minutes on anything that was noteworthy. These small groups gave students a safer container for sharing, especially for those who have difficulty speaking up in a larger group. This intervention also prevented dominant voices from taking over the space.

No interpretations or explanations were offered and problem-solving cross-talk by other students was discouraged. Occasionally, I would comment on certain themes, questions, and issues that were arising—usually to do with the stress of being in university—and we had a brief dialogue on how our work together in the course could be of support to students in working with some of the challenges they were facing. As often as I could, I referred to the skill set and posed questions about how these skills could be helpful. This conversation lasted between 10 and 15 minutes. A few students remarked in their final reflections on the value of spending this time together each week:

> It felt as if the controls were handed to the class.

> To me it is a space that never lets you be comfortable but just enough so that you want to stay in the moment.

> It's a space where screwing up is alright because life isn't perfect, why should you be?

> It's a class that not only gives you permission to laugh at yourself but encourages it.

> It's a space where you can share your story without any strings attached, you share it because you want to.

Teaching Creativity through Group Contemplative Arts Practice

This introduction serves as a way of helping orient students to being in a creative space and ready to engage in reflective, creatively interactive, and interdisciplinary activities that are often a sharp contrast from the heavily disciplinary, cognitive, and individually focused assignments in other classes. More importantly, the mindful speaking and listening practice and check-in served to both normalize the diverse range of experiences students were having and to build a classroom community where students feel capable to bring more of themselves into the classroom, feel welcomed by others, and take risks.

The short assignment, classroom contract, a weekly mindfulness practice, and check-in help establish vast creative ground. They are ways of preparing, orienteering, and softening us all up to go even further into transformative space. The classroom space becomes primed and charged to then start cooking up the raw materials, both experiential and material. From here, we engage in expressive arts practices that are instructor-led for a period of time before groups begin to direct classroom activities. There is no set outline for what we might explore. In the past, we have read some sections from composer John Cage's (1961) *Silence* and watched his famous performance of *4:22*. Following this, we go on a nature soundscape walk inspired by composer and music educator R. Murray Schafer and then move into collective wonderments that use journaling, a classroom mural painted in silence, or short improvised performances to pull out the perspectives, questions, reflections, and experiences that arose in the process. On other weeks, we have explored some partner movement exercises from Augusto Boal's (1992) Theatre of the Oppressed work and a reading on empathy, attachment, and attunement to set up interdisciplinary conversations on embodiment, theater, performance, and research into helping relationships.

What I will describe, in some greater detail, is how the vast creative ground is created using the contemplative arts practice of *ensō* painting. I describe the relational focus of what might otherwise be viewed as a purely subjective, individual practice and share a summary of reflections for the ensuing class conversation. Of note in these reflections is how the intersubjective space holds a range of voiced responses and reactions about acceptance, being seen, and creating inclusive community—themes that emerged in the first reflective assignment.

Ensō Painting

Before we would engage in the painting practice, I offered students a brief introduction to Japanese contemplative arts. In Zen Buddhism, the *ensō* (円相, circle) is a hand-painted or hand-drawn circle that expresses a moment in which mind and body are united and unfettered in movement. The circle may be drawn with one or two strokes and is usually done with a paintbrush using black ink on white paper. Typically, the circle is drawn in one fluid stroke and it may be left open or completely closed.[1] The *ensō* is not altered once it is drawn and stands as a momentary expression of the creator and the context of creation. The art of drawing *ensō* as a spiritual practice is called *hitsuzendō* (筆禅道, way of the brush) and cultivates natural, graceful, simple, and tranquil thought and action in the practitioner (Yoshiko, 2007).

Dō is the Japanese equivalent of Dao in Chinese and refers to the path or way of life. When associated with a particular practice such as tea ceremony (*chadō*) or calligraphy (*shodō*), an art understood as a *dō*, or Way, tells us that this activity has "surpassed its utilitarian purpose and been raised to the level of art" (Davey, 2007, p. 8). Here, an art as a Way is practiced not to achieve a practical end, but "to understand the ultimate nature of the whole of life by examining ourselves through a singular activity of life: to arrive at the universal through studying the particular" (p. 8). The universal concerns the dynamics of birth, death, growth, evolution, emergence, decay, and change, and the arts have the potential to teach us how to live, move, and dance with these dynamics. Davey (2007) writes that understanding the Way through one art gives one insight into the "principles, aesthetics, and mental states common to all the Ways" (p. 31). The key to any *dō* is that we are actually engaged in some kind of physical action with mindful awareness of what we are do-ing!

Now for the practice. I have students prepare themselves before painting. First, we loosen our wrists, shake our hands, and extend our fingers out fully. We then practice good brush posture. Approaching the paper from above, I have students hold the brush vertically. Wrist, elbow, and shoulders are relaxed. Breathing is slow, calm, even, and smooth. The body can be felt resting on the ground through the feet. I ask the students to close their eyes and first imagine everyone else in the room drawing an exquisite, spontaneous, and natural circle on their page. I also ask them to consider that their presence in the room supports and encourages all others to paint in such a beautiful way. I then ask the students to imagine that everyone else's presence in the room is supporting them in an exquisite, spontaneous, and natural circle.

Before students are to paint their circle, I emphasize to them that it is a single act that happens all at once. Mind and body move as one and there is no attachment or idea of a particular outcome. Whatever is drawn is neither good nor bad, only an expression of the moment. Painting in this way is an ongoing practice. Part two is called "just paint" and lasts less than a minute. The students complete their painting by using a Chinese *chop* (stamp) to make a red *inkan* (seal) on their painting or making their own mark.

In the activity debriefing, one student said she didn't feel alone in the act and it was if they were all painting as one. Another echoed her comments and felt that he was helping others by focusing intently on his piece. A woman was very disappointed with her circle saying that it turned out crooked and wondered if it meant she was crooked too! Others in the class laughed in a lighthearted way at the suggestion and, in response, a student said he liked the circle because it was extremely unique. The appreciation seemed well received for someone who was struggling to express herself confidently.

The warm atmosphere allowed others to express their feelings. "It's just a circle, who cares?" was followed by laughter and a short conversation about how such a simple thing could bring up so many feelings and reflections. So too came the comparisons as students shared their perceptions at how much better they thought other drawings were. Most students shared that they were either very relaxed or very anxious during the practice, and virtually every student wanted to keep practicing their circles. We practiced one more drawing together, and as a closing one student suggested to wild cheering that everyone put their circles together as part of a larger circle and take a photo of evidence of their learning together. This debriefing exemplifies, I believe, the expression of community development in the classroom. Student willingness to express vulnerability, care for each other, appreciation of others, humor, confidence in directing the flow of activity, enthusiasm for practice, and whole-class collaboration are evident.

End of Course Student Reflections

The painting exercise was only one part of whole host of activities over the course of 12 weeks. There were many different ways of measuring the impact of the course on students. The individual and group projects all provided strong evidence about how the container, community, and activities in the course supported their growth. What was perhaps most striking were the reflections that students offered to me in writing before they came in for their final interview. The following reflections—which are composites of multiple students—illustrated the ways in which students felt about the class, their relationships with other people, and the skills associated with self-awareness, character, and empathy. In the interest of space, I only share a few of these reflections:

> It's about the overall experience of forging real connections and friendships as the class progresses. As opposed to other classes where you might go through an entire semester sitting beside the same person the entire time and not even talk to them.
>
> I'm proud that every week, I came more and more out of my shell. I communicated more and more, in person and online, with my classmates. I always actively participated during discussions and came up with really neat collaborations during group meetings, and I took risks even when I was nervous or felt severely self-conscious for some of the group activities we did.
>
> I took a deeper look at what it means exactly to be an assertive and forward-type personality. I have always had this fearful perception that self-assurance means that you're somewhat of a "bitch" and a cold-hearted mean person to others. In fact, it's not. Through some careful contemplation, I realized that assertiveness means that you know what you want by just being honest with yourself first.
>
> I guess I have always been extremely mindful of other's feelings. I automatically took the same steps in regard to their experiences but not my own. I realize this just now at the end of the semester. I understand that now. It is matter of practicing this new skill at this time.
>
> The most difficult task by far was becoming a better communicator in class. I am dreadfully shy and this was extremely challenging. One of the first things I did to make friends in the class was I sent an email to everyone in my small group. In this email I shared that I was trying to overcome my anxiety and make new friends. I asked if anyone would like to have coffee or hangout—I had three responses that felt good. Our small group began meeting every week before class to work on our group project, and it was in this time that I grew to be quite close with everyone. I began enjoying class more now that I had a couple people who helped me

feel more comfortable. As a result of having this comfort, I was able to look forward to coming to class and truly began enjoying being a student. I always left my cell phone in my backpack when I was in class to allow myself the opportunity to be fully engaged.

Constructive Alignment

These comments reflected my own intention to have a high degree of alignment between the curriculum—explicitly articulated in terms of self-awareness, empathy, character, creativity, community development, and so forth—and real practices experiences that explicitly develop these areas across the curriculum (assessments, in-class activities, assignments). I believe that bringing contemplative practices into the undergraduate classroom that emphasize intersubjectivity, relationship, and community must be aligned with the intended outcomes of the course, the assessment and evaluation, and the assignments and activities that students will engage in. Such an approach, called "constructive alignment" appreciates that effective teaching aligns the teaching method and course assessment with course objectives (Biggs, 1996, p. 353). With a detailed description of learning outcomes (i.e., the skill set) written to specify the desired actions by students, the instructor then chooses teaching and learning activities that are likely to lead to students engaging in those performances. Focus on student actions are key as "what the student does is actually more important in determining what is learned than what the teacher does" (Shuell, 1986, qtd. in Biggs, 1996, p. 349).

Constructive alignment requires assessments to reinforce the course objectives by providing opportunities to engage in actions that correspond to the learning outcomes. Assessment and evaluation have a dominant influence on outcomes, and irrespective of instructions or opportunities to aim higher, tests or assignments that privilege memorization or other low-level cognitive activities will shift the behavior of most students toward performing at "lower cognitive levels" despite opportunities to (or instructions to) practice "higher level" learning activities (Frederiksen & Collins, 1989, qtd. in Biggs 1996, p. 350). The key, then, is to work with students to create an environment that values and nurtures connection, self-awareness, empathy, and compassion as the highest aims and to offer practices, assessments, and assignments that align to these aims.

Such alignment is not an easy task, evidenced by the frequency with which undergraduate students tell me how much they hate hate working in groups and will go to great lengths to avoid working in them. The classroom can be a hostile environment for students, and opening to vulnerability, fears, and desires is often not safe (Bai, 2001). The view I take is that building a classroom community capable of attending to the human dimension of relationship can be explicitly developed through grounded and repeated practice done with mature guidance and clear intention about the ultimate educational aims of such practices. Most students have never received such training nor have most educators been equipped to facilitate such an environment.

Contemplative and relational practices like the ones described in this chapter offer ways of inquiring into, resting with, speaking about, and artfully navigating the shifting and frequently uncomfortable domain of interpersonal existence. The intersubjective turn takes time and repeated practice—it is nurtured through repeated acts, not rushed through as one part of the curriculum to cover before moving on.

As Depraz, Varela, and Vermersch (2003) point out:

> We need training because we are not experts regarding the objects which make up our experience and toward which we can turn ourselves . . . any more than we are botanists because we can turn our attention to the plants in our gardens! The content of subjective experience is not any more directly given to us than the content of the experience of the world (p. 101)

Likewise, the content of intersubjective experience requires some kind of experiential training in order for our taken-for-granted assumptions and habits to be disrupted. For the intersubjective turn to yield insight into interpersonal suffering and conflict, awaken compassion, and arouse our creative action, we need, as Depraz, Varela, and Vermersch (2003) suggest, a few phenomenological ingredients to help us become aware. These include sustained attention to the flow of experience, apprenticeships with a teacher or teachers that lead toward our own self-mastery in examining experience, and feedback and encounters with others about what we discover (intersubjective validation). These elements are important because they help guard against becoming ensnared by our conditioned ways of perceiving.

Simply put, these three ingredients imply constructive alignment as an organizing principle in any educational experience that develops awareness and empathy, because they emphasize repeatedly and skillfully direct student attention to first- and second-person experience at every opportunity and to making space to discuss, share, reflect, and write about their inquiries. I elaborate further on these points in the closing reflection.

Closing Personal Reflections

With a few exceptions at the beginning of the course, all the students reported enjoying or finding the mindfulness and contemplative arts activities very rewarding. What is more promising, I believe, is that the mindfulness practices, group check-in, and contemplative group activities seemed to support the explicit focus in the class conversations and final course reflections on the skills required for self-awareness, empathy, and character. The skill set was broad and open enough, I think, to let students enter into and reflect upon their experiences in ways that served an intentional agenda of skill development rather than getting caught up by the forms, language, and practices we engaged in.

I think it is equally true the mindful speaking and listening practice, the check-in, and the *ensō* painting exercise (among others in the course) were offered with the kind of guidance and structure required to provide optimal opportunities to take safe-enough risks and practice the personal and interpersonal skills students were being asked to work on. For example, giving students instructions to rest as they speak and listen to teach other, check-in with the whole class using one word, share more deeply with a partner using the 1-2-4-All activity, and a debrief that connected experiences to skills provided a contained and collective exploration of subjective experience that had focus and limits.

Such guidance and containment from the educator, I believe, is critical for the use of relational contemplative practices in classrooms. Without some broader educational framework for their use, contemplative practices, classroom disclosures, and personal reflections may serve to reinforce limiting beliefs and perceptions students have of themselves and others or be perceived as some kind of therapy seeking to heal wounds or fix problems. Rather, these practices and experiences are more likely to be seen as part of one's own and others' *ongoing development* of self-awareness, empathy, and character.

Equally important, of course, is the educator's embodiment of the aforementioned values and their associated skills. I was fortunate, as part of a peer review process, to have a faculty member from the Faculty of

Student Leadership and Development review my course outline and visit my classroom for a three-hour session toward the end of the course. He wrote:

> The first thing that struck me when I read Sean's course outline was the remarkable goal of creating a truly safe space for creativity and collaboration in the class. When I visited the class, I was not disappointed to discover that there was a visible amount of that safety present. Within a challenging context, Sean has obviously encouraged students (and a fairly diverse group it appeared) to engage with the learning process in ways that involve "putting oneself out there," so to speak. It is obvious that Sean cares deeply about both the creative/learning process, and the students as whole persons. It struck me that he is really attempting to encourage and support a high degree of individual choice within the course—encouraging the connection between curriculum, personal interest and experience as well. Sean also projects obviously high expectations for engagement and presence, while respecting individual boundaries and preferences as well—a fine balance.

The preceding comments indicate an overwhelmingly positive experience for myself and the students. This class was one of the best I have ever been fortunate to be with. Under other circumstances, my best intentions to work with students in cocreating a safe learning environment; offer clearly defined rationale, assignments, and practices; and provide multiple opportunities to practice have not been sufficient containers to hold myself and students in doing the work.

Whether it is my own blind spots and failures to notice what is happening with students, the relational hungers that come up in myself and the students, a clash in values about the fundamental aims of education and the place of inner experience in the classroom, or the innumerable institutional constraints with which we live in the academy, the intersubjective space can often be dominated by resistance, anger, confusion, and apathy when our cherished views of self and world are challenged and even shattered. But all of this, too, is part of developing self-awareness, empathy, and character, and it is the manner in which such challenges, strong emotions, and discomfort are held and framed by all involved that ultimately shape the kind of meaning we make from them. As I hope I have illustrated in this chapter, expressive arts practices provide a simple yet extremely potent and spacious means of supporting compassionate and mindful conversations about being seen, not being seen, and finding our Way. And most importantly, students and educators are better able to make meaning from their experiences together if the instructor and course design provide a clear enough and big enough frame for what these conversations are for and about.

Note

1. An incomplete circle allows for the development and the "perfection of all things," whereas a closed circle represents perfect form.

References

Bai, H. (2001). Cultivating democratic citizenship: Towards intersubjectivity. In W. Hare & J. P. Portelli (Eds.), *Philosophy of education: Introductory readings* (rev. 3rd ed., pp. 307–319). Calgary, Alberta: Detselig.

Bai, H., Park, S., & Cohen, A. (2016). Classroom as Dojo: Contemplative teaching and learning as martial art. *Journal of Contemplative Inquiry*, 3(1), 113–131.

Bai, H., Cohen, A., Culham, T., Park, S., Rabi, S., Scott, C., & Tait, S. (2014). A call for wisdom in higher education: Contemplative voices from the Dao-field. In O. Gunnlaugson, H. Bai, E. Sarath, C. Scott (Eds.), *Contemplative approaches to learning and inquiry* (pp. 287–304). Albany: State University of New York Press.

Biggs, J. (1996). Enhancing teaching through constructive alignment. *Higher Education*, 32(3), 347–364.

Boal, Augusto. (1992). *Games for actors and non-actors* (Adrian Jackson, Trans.). New York: Routledge.

Cage, J. (1961). *Silence: Lectures and writings by John Cage*. Hanover: Wesleyan University Press.

Cohen, A. (2015). *Attending to the human dimension in education: Inner life, relationship, and learning*. Vancouver, British Columbia: Write Room Press.

Davey, H. E. (2007). *The Japanese way of the artist*. Berkeley: Stone Bridge.

Depraz, N., Varela, F., & Vermersch, P. (2003). *On becoming aware*. Philadelphia: John Benjamins.

Kates, I. C. (2005). The creative journey: Personal creativity as soul work. In J. Miller, S. Karsten, D. Denton, D. Orr, & I. C. Kates (Eds.), *Holistic learning and spirituality in education* (p. 19). Albany: State University of New York Press.

Kramer, G. (2007). *Insight dialogue: The interpersonal path to freedom*. Boston: Shambhala.
Lipmanowicz, H., & McCandless, H. (2013). *The surprising power of liberating structures*. Seattle: Liberating Structures Press.
Park, S., & Cohen, A. (2010). Exploring the dao-field: Practicing alchemy and philosophy in the classroom. *Transformative Dialogues*, 3(2), 1–17.
Yoshiko, A. (2007). *Ensō: Zen circles of enlightenment*. Boston: Weatherhill.

11

A Three-Tiered Monastic Approach to Intersubjective Dialogue for Application within Higher Education

MARY KEATOR

> Man becomes truly free only insofar as he belongs to the realm of destining and so becomes one who listens and hears, and not one who is simply constrained to obey.
>
> —Martin Heidegger, *The Question Concerning Technology*

The contemporary contemplative movement within higher education is hardly a new movement. The roots of this movement reach all the way back to the East to the Ancient Greeks in the fourth and third centuries BCE where the purpose of education was to transform the soul.

> Plato seeks to show that the essence of *paideia* does not consist in merely pouring knowledge into the unprepared soul as if it were a container held out empty and waiting. On the contrary, real education lays hold of the soul itself and transforms it in its entirety by first of all leading us to the place of our essential being and accustoming us to it.[1] (Heidegger, 1998, p. 167)

For the Ancient Greeks, education was rooted in the concept of *paideia*. Paideia (from the Greek *pais, paidos*) referred to the nurture, care, and education of a child, seen in the words *pedagogy* and *pediatrician*.

In *Paideia: The Ideals of Greek Culture*, Jaeger describes *paideia* as "the process of educating man into his true form, the real and genuine human nature" (Jaeger, 1965, p. xxiii).[2] Students' minds were not perceived as empty containers waiting to be filled with the teacher's wealth of information; rather, education was seen as the process of leading students out of ignorance and into wisdom, to a deeper sense of self, to what Plato calls in the preceding passage "the place of essential being." This meant that students, themselves, had to be actively engaged in the process of learning.

In the early Christian schools, including the School of Alexandria in the third century CE and the desert schools in Egypt in the fourth century CE, the formation of the whole person was the purpose of education, and the pedagogical method used by the monks was the practice of *lectio divina* (Keator, 2018). *Lectio divina* (sacred reading) is a way of listening and seeing, a way of being in and with the world. It incorporates four main movements—*lectio* (listening), *meditatio* (a type of active embodied analysis), *oratio* (response), and *contemplatio* (contemplation)—that flow in and out of each other, much like a dance, leading the practitioner to an awakening moment, *contemplatio*. In the monastic schools, students' training began with *lectio*, the act of reading via listening. Listening was the first step in monastic formation.[3] Through the act of listening, students opened their ears to encounter the words of a text. Through repeated listening, they came to know the text, even repeating the words of a text as they participated in the encounter. As they came to know the text and experience it more deeply, they came to know themselves.

Lectio divina teaches and builds sustained attention, deep reading and critical thinking. Through *lectio divina*, students learn to search deeper into the text, themselves, and one another to awaken to wisdom. The contemplative method of *lectio divina* engages the whole student—body, mind, heart, and soul—in the learning process. Applying the method of *lectio divina* to biblical stories and other classics stirred the minds and hearts of the monastic listeners and drew them beyond their accustomed mental borders. Challenged and inspired by the practice, monastic students began to break free from the limited confines of the ego, ascend to a higher moral order, and awaken to wisdom, love, and compassion. Learning was a lifelong process and the practice of *lectio divina* offered a way for students to develop their full potential in order to become contributing members of society. *Lectio divina* was a gradual process that required the dedication and commitment of both teacher and student.

In *Contemplative Practices in Higher Education: Powerful Methods to Transform Teaching and Learning*, Barbezat and Bush lay out four main objectives of contemplative practices:

1. Focus and attention building, mainly through focusing meditation and exercises that support mental stability

2. Contemplation and introspection into the content of the course, in which students discover the material in themselves and thus deepen their understanding of the material

3. Compassion, connection to others and a deepening sense of the moral and spiritual aspects of education

4. Inquiry into the nature of their minds, personal meaning, creativity and insight (2013, p. 11)

Contemplative practices as part of the humanities "provide the opportunity for students to develop insight and creativity, hone their concentration skills and deeply inquire about what means most to them" (Barbezat & Bush, 2013, p. 8). Situated on the generative branch of the tree of contemplative practices, *lectio divina* is a method of deep reading, study, and reflection, leading students to a transformative experience. By applying the contemplative pedagogical method of *lectio divina* to courses, students have the opportunity to engage in the creative process of forming and transforming themselves. *Lectio divina* is a method of listening that brings together the *vita activa* and the *vita contemplativa* in a contemporary way. In the practice of *lectio divina*, the monks learned to listen and dialogue with the texts, their deeper self, and with one another, and today, as students engage in *lectio divina*, they too, learn to dialogue with texts, their deeper self, and one another. Through these sustained periods of listening and dialogue, students come to know the text, themselves, and one another more intimately.

In this chapter, I will approach the topic of intersubjective dialogue through the lens of *lectio divina*. I maintain that this ancient monastic practice offers viable pedagogical tools that can be used in all educational settings, both sacred and secular. It is my sincere desire to share a sample of these contemplative practices in hopes that instructors can adopt and implement these ancient monastic practices in their classrooms as a way to help students come to know the text, and through that engagement, come know themselves and one another.

Intersubjective dialogue is an integral part of the *lectio divina* practice. Intersubjective (literally, *between subjects*) understands that there is an active, conscious, and communal field that people can access and cohabitate, known in intersubjective theory as the "intersubjective field." Gunnlaugson observes, "Unlike either third- or first-person methods, second-person approaches offer the benefits of rich engagement not only within, but also between participants and the intersubjective field of conversation."[4] This living, vibrant intersubjective field is infused with *logos*. Dialogue (literally, *through logos*) is the practice of listening and sharing with and through *logos*. According to Gorman, the early Geeks understood *logos* to be the dynamic principle guiding and connecting all life, including the intuitive knowledge that translates directly into action (2009, p. 10). However, critical to listening and sharing with and through *logos* is a stance of active and receptive listening. More recently, Scott has shared through his research on Buber's I-Thou relationship that "the intrinsic value of dialogue as a contemplative practice lies in its ability to create, uncover, explore and develop meaning: to manifest an *I-Thou* relationship which reveals and affirms self and other; and to serve as a way of being in the world" (Gunnlaugson, Sarath, Scott, & Bai, 2014, p. 237). Intersubjective dialogue, therefore, uncovers and awakens creative, healthy ways of being in the world. This way of being in the world, as Wilber points out, is "not only between you and me, but between the highest I and the highest Thou of this and every moment" (2007, p. 162). Intersubjective dialogue as a contemplative practice is a way of being opening to, being present with, and moving together with the dynamic principle of life (*logos*) within and between conscious beings, as we seek the highest I-Thou relationship possible in every given movement.

In my teaching, I use a three-tiered approach to intersubjective dialogue that I gained from my time studying and practicing the monastic practice of *lectio divina*. This fluid approach flows, much like a dance, as students learn how to suspend judgment, hold paradoxes, and engage in an openness of receptivity (Zajonc, 2014, pp. 21–24) as they listen to their dialogue partners. These partners include the literary text, their deeper self, and one another. Like the early monastics, students learn to lean in, bend their ears, and listen, not knowing what they will hear, where it will take them, or how it will affect them.

In the remainder of the essay, I will first explore what it means to engage in an intersubjective dialogue with a text. Then I will move to what it means to engage in an intersubjective dialogue with one self, and then after that, I will explain what it means to engage in an intersubjective dialogue with others. Along the way, I will offer readers practical examples that can be modified for use in the classroom.

Intersubjective Dialogue—Listening to the Voice within the Text

Many people think that dialogue begins with speaking, but it is actually the contrary. Dialogue begins in being. It is a conscious turning toward, "a meaningful engagement with the other, be it a person or persons, another member of the biosphere, an inanimate object, or the world itself" (Scott, 2014, p. 333). It is to offer one's full attention to listen to the intelligent flow of beingness in the other. On the first day of class, I hold up the book we are about to begin reading and share with my students that this book is more than words on a page. It contains a voice that is still speaking, and it is our task to lean in and listen, echoed beautifully by Niebuhr:

> In deep reading we do not have a text 'before' us as much as a 'presence' of voices, of living words and symbols, around us. . . . Reading of this kind is similar to living in a sprawling house, in which we climb up and down and explore adjoining rooms, halls and yard. (1985, p. 40)

It may seem strange to think that a student can enter into an intersubjective dialogue with a text, but consciousness is not time bound; therefore, the consciousness speaking within the pages of the literary text is still speaking, which means that all students have to do is open their ears, minds, and hearts and begin listening to it. Therefore, I invite my students to put aside their assumptions and prejudices, give their full attention, and listen to the voice speaking within the pages of the text.

For monastics, listening (*lectio*) was the first step in the *lectio divina* practice. *Lectio* teaches students to slow down, listen, and take in what they are hearing. They learn to read and reread. They learn to listen for the rhythm, the mood, and tone of the voice within the text. By doing so, students begin first to notice things about the texts that they may not have noticed if they had read hurriedly, but this noticing slowly leads to pondering and deeper reflection. As Heidegger noted, "it is one thing to have heard and read something, that is, merely to take notice, it is another thing to understand what we have heard and read, that is to ponder" (Heidegger, 1966, p. 52). When students bring their full attention to listen to the voice within the text, they begin to feel the presence of the other. This is often a new experience for students as they are used to reading words, but not accustomed to listening to the presence within the text. As they do, I notice they begin to open, to listen deeper to this presence within the text with a type of curiosity and a sincere desire to come to know this presence a little better. Listening affects them in palpable ways as they begin to reevaluate their own prejudices and preconceived notions. Listening leads students to reflection, reflection to conversation, and conversation to transformation.

> I value from this class . . . the lesson I got on looking at something with no prejudices. I think that is one of the best things I can take away from these readings and this class is if you look at something through an opinion you already formed, you aren't letting both sides get an equal chance to be heard. (student comment, World Literature I, 2016)

One *lectio* technique I incorporate is reading aloud together, as I have found that reading aloud helps students to listen better and deeper. As we read, we do so mindfully, slowly, and carefully, using various voices, tempos, and inflections in order to bring the story to life before us. Sometimes, I read just one word and stop, and then reread it. Other times, depending on the story, I read part of line or a verse, stop, and then reread it. I may move on to complete the verse or short passage and then stop, reread the same line a few more times, and then invite students to share what they heard. Invariably, at the beginning of the semester, someone will ask, "Are we going to read this slowly the whole time?" At, which point I once again explain the practice of listening to them, stating, "When I read slowly, it opens up space for you to listen to the words and hear what they are saying. However, in order to hear what the text is saying, you need to be actively listening." After modeling the practice of listening attentively and patiently, I read the text quickly as a way of contrasting the two modes of listening. Usually, this quick demonstration gets the point across. Then we move back to the passage and I read it again, aloud and slowly as they continue to practice listening.

Another way that we listen to the text is to engage in performative reading. One method of performative reading I use, especially when reading a dialogue, is to invite students to select a character they wish to give voice to in the literary text. Such reading is optional, but I have found that after a short while, students enjoy it and want to participate in this practice. At times, I will choose a character to give voice to that no one else has chosen. Here, preparation for slow, deliberate reading is important because students are in the habit of speedreading through a text, glossing over words, lines, and phrases that are packed with meaning. As noted by Studzinski, "The modern day reader is more like a tourist or commuter who wants to get to a destination as quickly as possible rather than a pedestrian or pilgrim who takes in everything along the way at a more leisurely pace" (1996, p. 110).

Students are in the practice of reading word after word without either pause or reflection. They generally do not stop to think about the background context, the character who is speaking to them in the text, and how the words spoken are intended to convey a particular meaning. However, when students do pause and reflect on the words and think about the character, they begin to encounter and see the character as a living person within the story who has the potential to challenge their own thinking and feelings. Characters can sometimes comfort students, but at other times, they can disturb them, triggering old memories and unearthing feelings that they have buried. Characters often bring students to think and feel things that they have not thought or felt before.

In order to read a dialogue properly, students need to pay attention not just to the words and the characters, but also to punctuation, because, by not doing so, they limit their ability to understand and interpret the text. As the monks needed to learn how to read and reread texts slowly and deliberately, students also need guidance and practice on how to read slowly and deliberately. Slow, deliberate reading conveys a different tone and message, but also different meanings and interpretations.

> Because texts inevitably have gaps, they can never tell the whole story; they invite in each reading the reader's unique creative efforts to fill in the blank spaces, to make connections. Each time a text is reread different efforts to fill in the gaps can be pursued. (Studzinski, 1996, p. 201)

When students read slowly, deliberately, and leisurely, like monks strolling through a vineyard, they can begin to listen and notice that how words are read affects how words are heard.

As students begin to recognize the connection between the way they read and meaning, they can begin to experiment with tone. For example, in *Antigone*, Haemon confronts King Creon (his father) about his decision to bury Antigone alive (ll. 695–736). If a student reads this passage as though Haemon is polite and solicitous, students will get one sense; however, if they read it as though Haemon is insolent and demanding, they will get a different sense of his character. In the story of Jesus and the Woman of Samaria, we read that Jesus, tired from his journey, stops to rest by the well where he encounters an unnamed woman. He says to the woman of Samaria, "Give me a drink" (John 4: 7). Does he command her, or ask her, or invite her?[5] We try different ways of reading the line using tone and inflection, and students notice that they begin to see Jesus and the woman in a different light depending on how they read the story. On student commented at the end of the semester,

> While reading *Jesus and the Woman of Samaria* we discussed how the tone we read in affects the meaning of a text. We read and reread, "Give me a drink" (John 4: 7) and found that Jesus could be using a demanding tone, could be saying it casually or he could be asking a question by emphasizing "drink." Depending on how we read it the story can take on an entirely different meaning. It was important for us to use these tones because how the text is interpreted affects the entire story. It is essential to think about tone because it affects the meaning and determines the character's personality as well as setting the stage for the rest of the reading. (student comment, World Literature I, 2015)

By drawing on the ancient monastic practice of slow, deliberate reading and rereading, focusing on words, tone, and punctuation, students' listening deepens and they begin to encounter, hear, feel, and experience the story on a deeper level.

As we move through this exercise, students begin to recognize that listening requires focus, effort, and patience.

> Deep listening is a way of hearing in which we are fully present with what is happening in the moment without trying to control it or judge it. We let go of the inner clamoring and our usual assumptions and listen with respect for precisely what is being said. Very few students have developed this capacity for listening. (Simmer-Brown & Grace, 2011, p. 137)

Some students are able to relax and not feel intimidated by the exercise, but others begin to worry that we will not be able to listen without distractions and are left feeling inadequate.[6] Yet, I explain to them that this takes time to learn. I try to help them realize that listening is not just a class activity, but it is also a way of life that teaches them to listen attentively with their minds and hearts to the voice within the text, their own inner voice, and the voice of others. Students note the effort it takes, but also the benefits.

> You have to apply yourself to the book to see the hidden meaning but it's there and can be a lifetime of knowledge. By reading slower, asking questions, and really listening to the text you can find that meaning and make more of a text than many can see. You can have those words live in you and be part of your life . . . (student comment, World Literature I, 2016)

Through the practice of *lectio*, students develop patience and learn to listen compassionately without judgment to each voice as it presents itself—a challenging task for most students. Yet, I have noticed that within a short amount of time, students do become more engaged in a text, and this engagement leads them within to reflect on and question what they have just heard.

Intersubjective Dialogue—Listening to the Self

As students continue to listen to the voice within the literary text, they are drawn deeper within. Listening to the voice within the literary texts moves them into their inner world, where they begin to engage in self-dialogue. While reading *Antigone*, I went around the room and asked students to repeat Antigone's statement to her sister Ismene, who is commenting on her right to bury her brother, even though it is against the orders of King Creon, "He has no right to keep me from my own" (l. 50), as a way of deepening their listening. In this short statement, Antigone is speaking with her sister Ismene about Creon's edict that there shall be no burial or mourning of her brother, Polynices. One student commented, "Once I remember a classmate used a tone while reading Antigone's voice that was soft and timid. I remember thinking Antigone would never sound like that: she was a brave, strong willed female character" (student comment, World Literature I, 2015). This student became aware of the fact that not all students heard Antigone's voice the way she did. Listening to the literary text moved this student into self-dialogue.

As the movement of dialogue deepens into students' inner world, the practice of listening can become more difficult, as it often reveals things to them that they either had pushed aside or had not even considered before. Listening to the *Katha Upanishad* led one student deeper within to face a painful truth.

> "These pleasures last until tomorrow, and they wear out the vitals of life" (*Katha Upanishad* 1.26). For me this made me think of a similar passage in Matthew 6:19–21, "Do not lay up for yourselves treasures on earth, where moth and rust destroy and where thieves break in and steal, but lay up for yourselves treasures in heaven, where neither moth nor rust destroys and where thieves do not break in and steal. For where your treasure is, there your heart is." Both of these spoke to me. They made me reevaluate my life. What was my purpose for living? I came to the conclusion that for a while I have been living for the pleasures of the flesh, these pleasures that will eventually fade . . . I could have gone snowboarding less and helped work at soup kitchens. I could have waited to buy a bike and maybe donated some money. My actions lately have been all about me. (student comment, World Literature I, Fall 2015)

Note the student's language. He comments, "both of these texts spoke to me." He is in dialogue with the *logos* still speaking both within the text and within himself. Although intersubjective dialogue with oneself is often uncomfortable as the information they just heard presses upon their assumptions, prejudices, beliefs, and worldviews, it is fruitful as demonstrated by this student.

The intersubjective dialogue within oneself is a complex process that remains hidden from view. It is an interior process, which opens the field of consciousness between the ego and the self as it engages in dialogue. However, there are times when students reveal their inner dialogue, exposing their process.

> In the *Dhammapada*, the line "they leave darkness behind and follow the light" (p. 127), when I couldn't break down the

text enough, I wrote it down on a post-it note, and put it in the bathroom on my mirror for weeks. After I broke down the text, I reflected on it and how I would want to live my life which I made it seem like the darkness is depression or anxiety, and where the light represents happiness or enjoyment out of life. By breaking the text down, I realized that I would rather live life in the light rather than living in the darkness because I rather live a happy life with enjoyment than live life with depression or anxiety being upset and not caring what is going on around me . . . "Let us live in joy, never hating those who hate us" (p. 177). This quote I have written on the wall in my room with chalk because I found that I really need to keep this in sight, because I always used to hate on the people who hated me but since it's been written on the wall I've been much happier in life. Just by living with that quote written on the wall I feel like I have learned to be happier which I wouldn't have been if it hadn't been for reading the *Dhammapada*. (student comment, World Literature I, 2016)

The aforementioned student shares the dialogue happening in her inner world. First, we hear that she struggled to listen to the voice in the text and to deepen her process, she "wrote it down" in a place where she could see it (listen to it). After continued listening to the text, she shares that she "reflected on it," demonstrating the intersubjective dialogue with herself. These first two stages of intersubjective dialogue (with the text and then with self) led her to admit a powerful truth, "I always use to hate people who hated me." However, what is so incredible is that this student does not hide her new truth; instead, she voices it, demonstrating the fluidity and flow of intersubjective dialogue as it winds its way from text, to self, and to others.

Intersubjective Dialogue—Listening to Others

Intersubjective dialogue with another is by far the most challenging of the three movements as students come to the dialogue tainted with their own limited worldviews formed by particular assumptions, prejudices, and beliefs; therefore, they need to learn the skill of suspending these assumptions, prejudice, and beliefs before engaging in dispassionate analysis. As David Bohm points out,

> The object of dialogue is not to analyze things, or to win an argument, or to exchange opinions. Rather it is to suspend your opinions and to look at the opinions—to listen to everybody's opinions, to suspend them, and to see what all that means. (1996, p. 30)

If students are not prepared, they can often shut down or, even worse, hurt another with a quick reaction. Therefore, it is important for students to engage first in intersubjective dialogue with the literary text and then with their deeper self, before moving into dialogue with another. One way I demonstrate intersubjective dialogue with another is through the biblical story of Jesus and the Woman of Samaria. While reading the story, I invite students to consider what the text has to share about living in right relationship with others. For example, Jesus, as a Jewish rabbi, took a risk, when he entered into a dialogue with a woman of Samaria, defying cultural-religious norms, as did the woman of Samaria. As students explore the dialogue further and break open the dialogue, they begin to see the way in which Jesus's dialogue with the Samaritan woman works to mend a broken relationship and give new meaning to their lives. Reflecting on the dialogue between Jesus and the woman of Samaria, one student noted,

> I don't find many people capable of this kind of dialogue with one another, including myself. It is a skill we have lost over the course of time and with the development of technology. Will we ever regain this dialogue? . . . I am afraid we never will. It is important however, that we learn how to create proper dialogue with others . . . (student comment, World Literature I, 2015)

This student expressed her fear about the impact technology is having on peoples' ability to have authentic intersubjective dialogue, which she now sees as vital to living in right relationship with others. As students explore the dialogue between Jesus and the Samaritan Woman, they begin to see the intersubjective field opening and deepening, in both Jesus and the woman of Samaria, which leads each to express a deeper truth. In my classes, I encourage students to engage in intersubjective dialogue with one another in a variety of ways, including class dialogue and thinking cafés.

Class Dialogue

As noted already, intersubjective dialogue begins with listening to the voice within the literary text, followed by listening to one's inner voice. One method I use to follow this flow is to have students keep a contemplative workbook. In the past, I have asked students to write in their notebooks, but this semester I created a contemplative workbook based on the *lectio divina* method and passed it out to each student. After reading aloud together, I ask students to select a word, phrase, or sentence that spoke to them (inspired, provoked, annoyed them, etc.). First, they write down the word or phrase and then they slowly repeat it to themselves, listening to it. Next, they bring questions to it and write these down. Finally, they reflect on what they are hearing and write down their thoughts. Afterward, I invite a class sharing. During the sharing, I listen to students and they listen to each other. I do not interject with right and wrong or add commentary; rather, we all just listen to one another. I continue to be amazed at the power of this practice as students share with one another their word/phrase, their questions, and reflection. As we continue to move through this practice, I witness the intersubjective field in the classroom opening, growing, and deepening.[7] It is though sparks of insight dance from one student to another, enlightening consciousness along the way. Students have shared that this method helps them to feel comfortable to express their thoughts without fear of being of being wrong.

> Previously, I never liked to speak out in class because I never felt comfortable but in this class. I felt as if what I said wasn't wrong and it was okay to speak what came to my mind. This helped me to grow as a student because it allowed me to explore my thoughts instead of pushing them away as if they were wrong before I even said them. . . . I have become a more confident person because of this class and that is something I am surely proud of. I was able to open up and let people see a part of me that I usually don't let many see. (student comment, World Literature I, 2016)

If we want students to share with one another, then we have to hold space for them to work through their thoughts and feelings without being judged, but also without attaching our commentary to their thoughts and feelings. When students have the opportunity to listen to one another, they begin to grow in consciousness.

> Being aware and welcoming of others' opinions is something I have realized through this course as being very crucial to being a good reader. . . . If we take into account what others are getting from a story, we can grow as readers as we too learn their view on the story. (student comment, World Literature I, 2016)

Notice that the student stated, "I have realized." Realization is a movement toward greater awareness. The field of consciousness continues to grow and expand through these moments of intersubjective dialogue.

Listening Cafés

The idea of incorporating classroom listening cafés came from my own experience with World Café developed by Brown and Isaacs (2006). The process, as noted by Margaret Wheatley in the introduction to *The World Café,* "reawakens our deep species memory of two fundamental beliefs about human life. First, we humans want to talk together about things that matter to us. . . . Second, as we talk together, we are able to access a greater wisdom that is found only in the collective" (Brown & Isaacs, 2006, p. ix). In my World Literature class, I have adapted the world café model. Three students are responsible for leading one listening café, which consists of placing students into groups of four or five, selecting three lenses in which to look at the story and three meaningful questions to help student think deeper about something within the story. Each group gets a question and reads it aloud, then one by one students take turns and answer the question as the rest of the group listens. No one responds until every student has had his or her minute to speak. At the completion of the designated time, the students get up and move to a new table to work with another question. After completing two rounds, the group in charge leads a class dialogue on the small group sharing. For example, while reading *Antigone,* one group chose the lens of Gilgamesh and presented the following question for during the listening café: "'If my grief is violent enough, perhaps he will come back to life again.' Grief is experienced many times throughout the tragedy. Perhaps the most violent grief in the story is held by Ismene and Creon. Do you agree with this?" I have to say that it was amazing to see the students decide on their own to bring two of the course texts (*Gilgamesh* and *Antigone*) into dialogue during the listening café.

As a new practice in my class, I was not sure what to expect but I am witnessing the class listening to one another, acknowledging one another's thoughts, and coming to new insights together. Students have commented that the listening café "provides an opportunity that might otherwise not occur . . . a safe space to have dialogue about thoughts/views/opinions [with] peers." Students share with me that they are learning a lot through the listening cafés. They share statements like, "I'm learning that opinions can drastically differ in a small group but some opinions can also be universal"; "I am learning to think outside the box . . . it opens the blinders that you naturally hide behind . . ."; "I am seeing that my perspective is not the only one and I have new insights."

Summary

In summary, the ancient monastic practice of *lectio divina* is a contemplative practice, which incorporates intersubjective dialogue. The whole of aim of the monastic method was to engage in dialogue with *logos*, whether within sacred texts, within themselves, or with each other with the purpose of awakening to a deeper way of knowing, being, and living in the world.

Although a time-consuming practice, I have found bringing in the intersubjective practices of *lectio divina* to be a worthwhile. Students begin to open, listen, and share with one another. They begin to reconsider previously held assumptions and make space to listen to and experience the voice behind the text, themselves, and their classmates better. As one student noted at the end of the semester,

> It may sound corny but this course has done more than just teach me about world literature, it has taught me more about myself. This is something that you don't find in every college course you take. This is something that is different, special, and rare. The readings and assignments allowed me to open up and expand my thinking further than it has ever been. I was capable of understanding and relating to characters from hundreds of years ago, which is something I would never have been able to do before this class. I was also encouraged to

form relationships with my classmates, which also made this class much more relaxed and stress free. By getting to know one another, we were comfortable to share our deep thoughts without fear of judgment, which is once again something you don't have in every classroom. (student comment, World Literature I, 2016)

I have found that as students move through the ebb and flow of contemplative intersubjective dialogue, they begin to experience the transformational power of deep listening as they sustain attention, suspend judgments, and open to deeper possibilities that are arising in the silence and spaces created. They discover that their time spent listening is not wasted, but is in fact productive, fruitful, and nourishing as they see their minds opening, their hearts softening, and their consciousness expanding.

Notes

1. Heidegger explains, "*Paideia* means the turning around of the whole human being. It means removing human beings from the region where they first encounter things and transferring and accustoming them to another realm where beings appear" (1998, p. 167).

2. The equivalent to the Greek *paideia* is the Latin word *humanitas*, from which we get the humanities.

3. Since many monks were illiterate and few texts were available, monks first practiced *lectio* with their ears, meaning they listened as their teacher read. Later, as monks began scribing texts, *lectio* incorporated both listening and reading.

4. For more on the intersubjective field, see Gunnlaugson, Sarath, Scott, and Bai (2014, p. 305).

5. The Greek word δός has a variety of meanings, including "to give, to grant, to offer, to command."

6. Listening is a challenging practice for students, mostly because they have not been trained to listen. According to the Listening Center, "We spend about 45 percent of our time listening, but we are distracted, preoccupied, or forgetful about 75 percent of that time. The average attention span for adults is about twenty-two seconds. Immediately after listening to someone talk, we usually recall only about half of what we've heard and within a few hours, only about 20 percent" (Listening Center, 2009).

7. See Bache (2008).

References

Bache, C. (2008). *The living classroom: Teaching and collective consciousness.* Albany, NY: State University of New York Press.

Barbezat, D., & Bush, M. (2013). *Contemplative practices in higher education: Powerful methods to transform teaching and learning.* San Francisco: Jossey-Bass.

Bohm, D. (1996). *On dialogue.* New York: Routledge Classics.

Brown, J., & Isaacs, D. (2006). *The world café: Shaping our future through conversations that matter.* San Francisco: Berrett-Koehler.

Gunnlaugson, O., Sarath, E. W., Scott, C., & Bai, H. (Eds.) (2014). *Contemplative learning and inquiry across disciplines.* Albany: State University of New York Press.

Heidegger, M. (1962). The memorial address. In J. Anderson & E. Freund (Trans.), *Discourse on thinking.* New York: Harper & Row.

Heidegger, M. (1998). Plato's teaching on truth. In W. McNeill (Ed.), *Pathmarks.* Cambridge: Cambridge University Press.

Jaeger, W. (1965). *Paideia: The ideals of Greek culture* (G. Highet, Trans.). Cambridge: Oxford University Press, 1965.

Listening Center. (2009). *The sacred art of listening.* http://www.sacredlistening.com/ylc_listening101.htm

Niebuhr, R. (May 1985). The strife of interpreting: The moral burden of imagination. *Parabola, 10*(2), 40.

Scott, C. (2014). Buberian dialogue as an intersubjective contemplative practice. In O. Gunnlaugson, E. W. Sarath, C. Scott, & H. Bai (Eds.), *Contemplative learning and inquiry across disciplines* (pp. 325–340). Albany: State University of New York Press.

Simmer-Brown, J., & Grace, F. (2011). *Meditation and the classroom: Contemplative pedagogy for religious studies.* Albany: State University of New York Press.

Sophocles. (2005). *Antigone.* Clayton: Prestwick House.

Studzinski, R., OSB. (2009). *Reading to live: The evolving practice of "lectio divina."* Trappist: Cistercian Publications.

Wilber, K. (2007). *Integral spirituality: Starting a new role for religion in the modern and postmodern world.* Boston: Integral Books, 2007.

Zajonc, A. (2014). Contemplative pedagogy in higher education: Toward a more reflective academy. In O. Gunnlaugson, E. W. Sarath, C. Scott, & H. Bai (Eds.), *Contemplative learning and inquiry across disciplines* (pp. 15–30). Albany: State University of New York Press.

12

No Mind in Community

Cultivating "Fields in Good Heart" in an Intellectual and Professional Praxis-Enhancing Commons

ARDEN HENLEY

Introduction

In the halls of the academy there are rumors of a new way of knowing that is an old way, a relief from the restless and competitive search for instrumental knowledge, a promise of hope, a faint smell of incense. Mindfulness. Contemplation. Intersubjectivity.

Mindfulness especially and, in current use, intersubjectivity are concepts that refer to states of mind or awareness that flow from various contemplative traditions of practice. In the absence of these traditions of practice these concepts bear little fruit; as expressions of these traditions they have tangible effects on lives and relationships (Trungpa, 1969). The purpose of this chapter is to describe and further account for the impact of these traditions of contemplative practice on the evolution of a university community.

> Sages have no mind of their own
> their mind is the mind of the people
> (from chapter 49 of *Tao Te Ching*; qtd. in Red Pine, 2009,
>   p. 98)

> Because it is empty
> the mind of a sage can receive

> Because it is still
> it can respond
> (Hui-Tsung,[1] qtd. in Red Pine, 2009, p. 98)

The ultimate goal of contemplation is "no mind," a state in which the mind is empty, clear, and unimpeded; not devoid of content, but unattached to content. This no mind is as invisible as the wind and like the wind, its presence is known by its effects. In being nowhere no mind is "in between," around, and through all that transpires. Though it nourishes all processes, it does not conjecture, manipulate, or butt in, remaining a mystery and ineluctably in service.

Within "no mind" flows the collective mind of communities like currents and eddies in the vast ocean, carrying the community's best intentions, hopes, and aspirations as sediments, as "about to happen" configurations, as tendencies in search of materializing. This collective mind we refer to as the intersubjective field.

What of materializing these best intentions, hopes, and aspirations? Contemplation brings intentions, hopes, and aspirations to the awareness of individuals and groups, and ethical conduct provides guidance for their materialization. The more caring, respectful, and attuned our relationships, the more we enact this touching, but invisible inheritance and the more a gentle sensibility of the sacred begins to pervade the environment. The more virtuous and heartfelt our demeanor and relationships, the more gently the willow bends to the breeze, the more troubles dissolve, and the more philosophy edges aside neurosis. Far from a reflection of idealism, the ennobled intersubjectivity of no mind is in its manifestation as practical as wood, tile, and brick.

Broadly defined, virtue renders more accessible the mercurial "flow through" of intersubjectivity, making energy and information available to realize the shared best intentions, hopes, and aspirations of the community. In more conventional terms, this accessibility may be read as a "blessing." The etiology of blessing, then, entails a combination of an awareness through which collective intentions become known and spoken as wishes, visions, and values; virtuous community relations; and a superintending and subtle aura of the sacred.

The traditions that instruct the contemplative arts are ancient, highly evolved, and rich in content and nuance. Though, for the most part, these traditions do not eschew the intellect, the intellect is viewed as a servant and not a master. Often brightened and sometimes surprised, the intellect is enhanced by contemplative practice, but because it traffics in language and is bounded by culture, it is not a vehicle by which the view of views can be attained. The intellect so desires, but must retire. A further indelicacy: when it comes to the contemplative arts, the cook may be more qualified to teach than the professor.[2]

What of the battered and much-maligned intellect? Perhaps, what the intellect can provide is signposts, traces, maps destined to fade, then disintegrate, but maps nonetheless. And in this respect where would I send you, dear colleague? I would send you to the Buddhist *Heart Sutra* and there your intellect will find delight and yet suddenly experience its own limitation in an unexpected and delightful moment (McCleod, 2007).

> Sitting quietly in the pre-dawn light
> quite suddenly I am overtaken
> by a raucous cry
>   a CAW
>
> before there is a listener and before there is a crow
>   there is a CAW
> self and crow an afterthought.[3]

I am left with this: the fundamental design is connection and not separation.

The Commons

Respecting connection as the fundamental design, what precedents are there for the social and institutional embodiment of an environment based on connection? I ran across some inspiration in my British heritage: in the form of the commons. This metaphor has the additional appeal of addressing the field-like quality of intersubjectivity.

The "commons" refers to lands, typically pasture lands and fields that were shared and managed according to collectively "agreed upon" principles and regulations (Menzies, 2014, p. 22), cared for by all, "owned" by no one. Commons appear in different forms worldwide, but were prevalent in the Northumbrian lands of my ancestors until they were halted by the UK Enclosure Acts (in which individual property rights to land previously held in common were established in law) beginning in the 17th century. Broadly speaking, the "commons" is a way of organizing social and economic relations based on egalitarian and collaborative principles (Rosenman, 2016) and assuming the primacy of the connection of people to one another and the natural world.

Fields in "good heart" describes a situation in which the commons achieved a level of consensus and harmony that is, in turn, reflected in the sustainability and productivity of commonly held lands (Menzies, 2014, p. 21). Likening it in some way to a commons, my intention is to speak to ways in which the intersubjective field in a postsecondary learning environment can be enhanced and informed by principles and practices that emerge from contemplative practice and to introduce the reader to the "practitioner commons" that we have evolved at City University of Seattle in Canada as a field in good heart or an intersubjective terrain based on "good-heartedness."

Let me take a minute to share with you the story of what we have created thus far. We are currently a set of graduate programs in counseling and education in four cities across Canada's two western provinces, operating under the auspices of City University of Seattle. To this we have added continuing education focused on building capacity in the nonprofit sector and on a range of topics related to counseling and education. There are approximately 600 students and 75 full- and part-time faculty involved.

The avowed aim of CityU Canada is the transformation of society through relevant and accessible postsecondary education. We feel we have a responsibility as a university to contribute to building communities and to respond to the pressing issues of the times, as well as prepare our graduates for employment and/or enhanced responsibilities in professional communities of practice. Our conscious aspiration as an "engaged university" is to create a robust intellectual- and practice-enhancing commons for the professions and shape this commons in a way that consciously serves the community. A further unique feature of this endeavor is our commitment to scholar/practitioner instruction. We bring the best of practitioners to the classroom, though these practitioners are, at the same time, persons who have written, presented, and published as their practices have evolved (Henley, 2013). The result is salty mix of theory and practice that we sometimes refer to as "conversations in the agora" because of its proximity to the real-time worlds of professional practice and community life (Henley, 2011, p. 38).

Communitas

My work as a professor and administrator of the CityU in Canada programs is informed by contemplative practice and, on a good day, the intersubjective field around me benefits from the energy and wisdom of these practices and the Masters who transmit them. The good fortune of this kind of learning is shared by a number of my colleagues, each in his or her own way and in relation to different contemplative traditions. However, rather than explicitly introduce the contemplative arts on a systematic basis that as beginning learners ourselves is beyond our current levels of practice, we have chosen instead to translate this ethos into relational terms and to focus on engendering a profound respect for one another and our students. No doubt, some of the pedagogical practices in which we engage are informed by contemplative practice and, occasionally, such practices "break through" and appear explicitly. But, such practices have not been branded or formalized in the curriculum, and to date we have made no effort to do so. We have referred to this approach as "exemplifying the alternative."

In everything that we do, from program development to instruction, recruitment to graduation we consciously factor the significance of relationship. We understand the quality of education we provide to be directly connected to the quality of the intersubjective field and the states of mind and relationships that form it. At its best, our environment is infused with a subtle and unimposing atmosphere that inspires us as we face the challenges of postsecondary education in a rapidly changing and complex world and is apprehended time and time again by visitors and guests.

Anthropologists have described this atmosphere as "communitas." From the individual's perspective, communitas is a state of mind and warmth of feeling that arises in the context of unbounded connection to others and a deep sense of belonging. From the collective point of view, it arises when the usual norms of society are usurped by unexpected events or intentionally suspended by rites of passage or ceremony (V. Turner, 1969, 1974). In our case, it is an outcome of a focus on relationship and, perhaps, on the presence flowing from the contemplative practices of a number of the staff and faculty.

We also believe that in dialogue we recognize one another, enhance our relationships, exchange ideas, and compose our collective future. There is the feeling in our commons that there is time to "have a word" and everyone can be an active part of the dialogue that emerges (Scott, 2009, 2014). We provide many different shapes and sizes of meetings and encounters and make use of an array of conversational technologies, such as Appreciative Inquiry (Bushe, 2011; Cooperrider & Srivastva, 1987; Cooperrider & Whitney, 2001; Cooperrider, Whitney, & Stavros, 2008).

Please sit down and join us for a cup of tea, or coffee, if you prefer.

The Tea Ceremony

It is 4:30 p.m. and tea and coffee are being served in an office near the reception desk in Vancouver. On this occasion two IT staff members visiting our downtown campus from the university's headquarters in Seattle are "sitting in." They are both big men and I notice how delicately and respectfully they are holding their well-earned cups of tea with their large hands. Several advisors and administrative staff cluster around a desk on which tea, coffee, and cookies are laid out. Less visible seated by an outside window, one of our faculty sips on his coffee. Everything from stories of the day's work to date-square recipes circulate in a warm and congenial atmosphere.

Hosted by the Site Manager, this is a daily ritual. When it began, I could not tell you. Who instigated it, I could not say. Attendance is no way compulsory and the composition of those in attendance varies. I do know that this ritual of inclusion lends a kind of coherence to the situation, coherence that visitors, whether they are faculty, staff, or technicians, are immediately drawn to. There is a feeling that this is what people do and it is completely natural. In this sense it is a reflection of the "self-organization" of the intersubjective field (Wheatley, 1999, p. 87). There is no need to devise ways to create, manufacture, or manipulate such rituals; they emerge of their own accord from the preexisting sentimentality and connectedness of the intersubjective field. My contribution as an administrator may be to stay out of the way. This kind of emergence corresponds to "not doing" (*wu wei*) in the Taoist cannon (see, for example, Bai, 2004; Henley, 2006; Slingerland, 2006), but it has roots in the many cultures from which we all as participants originate.

Each and Every One of Us

She is disheveled. I am the principal and as a student she feels hauled on the carpet. One of our academic advisors has noticed that she is missing classes and acting distracted. A follow-up call and email resulted in the advisor finding out she is experiencing difficulties. Based on a consultation with the advisor, we located an experienced counselor in the community and made a referral. After a couple of sessions, the counselor phoned me with the student's permission. I could tell from the counselor's voice that this very experienced counselor was concerned. There were further complications and some possible danger.

Back on the carpet, I take the position that the police must be involved. We are all getting in over our heads, I feel. We agree on a way to involve the police who, in turn, contact the family. The family agrees to engage. She provides me with her family's telephone number and I call and leave a message inviting them to join me for tea. The family demurs because of the brevity of their visit, but the process of moving this young woman out of harm's way is under way. Two weeks later she is on the way home. After several weeks at home she writes to let us know that she is putting the pieces of her life back together and hopes to resume her studies at a later point.

Our intersubjective field or commons manifested as a safety net that formed underneath this woman based on an ethic of kindness, compassion, and care (Bai, 1999; Bai, 2004; Cassidy, Bai, Beck, Hawley, & Van Poelgeest, 2009; Cohen & Bai, 2008). This ethic is fundamental to the cultivation of the intersubjective field. In some ways an ethic of care is a "gate" that opens to the intersubjective field, as well as a means to cultivate its good-heartedness. In order to engender good-heartedness, an ethic of care needs to be enacted as a priority in the midst of competing demands for time, attention, and energy.

Another term for this ethic of care from African culture is *ubuuntu*. Introducing the concept of ubuuntu in a conversation with the Dalai Lama, Desmond Tutu described it as follows:

> In our country, we speak of something called ubuuntu. When I praise you, the highest praise I can give you is to say, you have ubuuntu—this person has what it takes to be a human being. This is a person who recognizes he exists only because others exist: a person is a person through other persons. When we say you have ubuuntu, we mean you are gentle, you are compassionate, you are hospitable, you want to share, and you care about the welfare of others. This is because my humanity is caught up in your humanity. (Dalai Lama & Chan, 2004, p. 69)

Honoring the Space

The smell of sage and sweet grass fills the classroom. The swishing of an eagle feather sends ripples through the air. A First Nations medicine man and his assistant are purifying the space and then cleansing each and every participant. It is the second year of the Master of Counselling program. We are acknowledging that the land upon which our building stands is unceded First Nations' land and further acknowledging the 10,000-year history of learning that has already taken place here. The medicine man responds with a further blessing of the space and extends his best wishes for our endeavors. A sacred song follows. Before leaving, he makes a gift of a sacred object to remain in the space.

The medicine man has evoked a contemplative experience through ritual, prayers, and song. A paradox is expressed in these moments: though the context is a university, the intellect is not the primary means of apprehending the sacred qualities or properties of the intersubjective field. The intellect is limited to "pointing at the moon" or describing and reflecting on the effects of an awareness of the sacred qualities of intersubjectivity and sharing accounts of its experience. This ritual provides a more direct experience of the intersubjective field.

Reincorporation

It is the cohort's last class in its master's degree program. I want to help them mark the occasion. Prior to the class I have asked them to purchase a gift of approximately $10 in value with the intended purpose that each person will be the donor and recipient of a gift. Everyone remembers. At the outset of the class we pull back the desks and chairs, leaving a space at the front of the room in which I walk out a circle. This is the "gift circle." Each student places her or his gift in a smaller circle marked out in the middle of the larger circle. We establish a "gate" at the east side of this imagined mandala and the students line up to enter the circle one by one. The task at the gate is to voice a wish on behalf of the well-being of others and to express it in one's first language. It turns out that five or six members of the class of 15 make their wish in a language other than English. For many participants, this is the first time that they speak in and are heard in a language other than English by their classmates. One by one, the wishes are profound, ranging from an end to violence between people to the sustainability of the planet.

Having expressed a wish and entered the circle, each participant then walks to the center and selects a gift, then leaves the circle and stands at its perimeter. Deep feelings arise and move around the room like clouds in the sky. Communitas arrives. There is something very poignant about the last person entering the circle to pick up the remaining gift. Now, the room is reshaped into a feast table and a potluck dinner commences.

I was inspired in this by an encounter with van Gennep's description of rites of passage in Michael White and David Epston's book entitled *Narrative Means to Therapeutic Ends* (van Gennep, 1960; White & Epston, 1990, p. 7) in which White and Epston describe therapy as the performance of rites of passage. Perhaps, education is also a rite of passage. Rites of passage have three stages: separation, liminality, and reincorporation. In the first phase, the person(s) "separates" from his or her present identity. In the classic rites of passage embodied in many cultures through which children or adolescents become adults, such as the Jewish Bar and Bat Mitzvahs, the identity separated from is that of a child or adolescent. During a middle or "liminal" period, a learning process typically takes place by which the participant acquires the knowledge and skills to perform a new identity and assume new responsibilities and obligations and enjoy new rights and privileges: in this example, that of an adult. At the conclusion of this middle period there is often a "test" to assure that the requisite learning has taken place and, almost inevitably, a celebration through which the participant reenters society with this newly defined identity. This third phase is referred to a "reincorporation." In our graduate degree in counseling, the conclusion of the program represents a moment at which the student will then be reincorporated in the community of counseling practitioners with a new identity.

Skunkworks

Faculty and staff filter in to this weekly agenda-less meeting. Images flash on a screen at the front of the classroom. The webmistress at the front of the room, now evidently very pregnant, plies her laptop, which is somehow connected to what appears on the screen. Connecting remotely today is an internet wizard from the university's headquarters in Seattle, several senior faculty from Alberta, and local faculty. We are looking at our virtual presence in the interconnected domains of our website, Facebook, LinkedIn, and Google Plus. As the images slip by, a running commentary between the wizard and the webmistress begins—potential sources of images and ways to store images are being explored. From the classroom, a faculty member, also a photographer, adds his considerable expertise to the mix. This is our community in its virtual expression, and administrative assistants and senior academics alike express their ideas with aplomb and evident relaxation. The webmistress scribbles notes as the lively discussion continues to unfold. These notes will later be circulated to all those in attendance in the form of Notes from the Skunkworks. Next week, a neighbor from several floors above in our multistory building, an experienced media consultant, will visit on a "just for fun" basis and give us feedback about how we are communicating in this virtual arena. I know he will ask us: "What do we want to say to whom and for what purpose?" This same media expert is a presenter in our Executive Leadership—Non-profit sector continuing education program. Just as effortlessly as the meeting began, it ends. In a conversation in the hall after the meeting, several participants speculate about the possibility of playing music together or otherwise sharing our artistry. This collective and previously unexpressed dimension is somehow being evoked in these meetings.

What are the principles at play in this evocation of the whole person? I am not intellectually sure what they are altogether; however, the creation of "agenda-less" space is one and the situational collapse of hierarchy is another. A third is what I would describe as throughput created by the continual introduction of virtual and face-to-face guests. The result is another version of community self-organizing.

"Agenda-less space" reminds me of a seminal article by my colleague, Charles Scott, in which he makes the point that dialogue frequently entails "hanging out" (Scott, 2009, 2014). From this perspective, the presence of an agenda forecloses dialogue by focusing it within narrow, preconceived limits. Nothing wrong with this in certain contexts and for certain purposes; in fact, I would be the last person to suggest that all meetings proceed in the absence of agendas. The situational collapse of hierarchy is the same kind of idea. Hierarchy is useful for certain kinds of purposes, but it does not need to obtain in all organizational contexts. The throughput affected by the continual presence of guests and visitors, as well as having intrinsic value, is designed to disrupt habitual patterns of social interaction and cognition and evoke creative expression. What makes these phenomena a reflection of contemplative practice is the flexibility of discernment and tolerance of ambiguity that enable effortlessly shifting from agenda-based meetings to agenda-less meetings, from hierarchy-driven interaction to egalitarian exchanges, from the emptiness of form to the form-ness of form.

Let me pause at this point to address an important issue. All of what I am sharing here presupposes an agreement about the importance of relationships and the significance of community, in this case, in a postsecondary environment. In our environment, this is explicitly stated and even celebrated. The value proposition is that the connection and belonging of people is fundamental to our well-being, including our capacity to learn, grow, and transform, and further, that connection and belonging are preexistent and sacred (Waldegrave, Tamasese, Tuhaka, & Campbell, 2003). It does not suggest, however, that chaos should prevail and that productivity and educational outcomes should be tossed out of the window. It is simply to insist that there are different social ordering principles that can result in more satisfying relationships, community development, and learning and that these principles arise naturally in the context of contemplative practices and a focus on relationship.

Checking In

I am a guest in this particular graduate class. Along with the students and professor I sit in one of the chairs formed in a circle in the classroom, occasionally sipping on the cup of green tea that I have brought with me. As everyone is seated, a kind of quiet descends. The professor acknowledges that there is a vacant chair in the circle and notes that it will be subsequently occupied by a student who is late today. The professor then calls for five minutes of "clearing," a kind of silent mental housekeeping in which the expectation is that everyone will bring themselves further and further into the room, becoming aware of and letting go of distractions and preoccupations from other parts of their lives. Some would call this meditation, but perhaps it is not necessary to label it as such, although it certainly can be seen as a contemplative practice. This silence is followed by "checking in," during which everyone has the opportunity to share what is on his or her mind to whatever extent is comfortable. Some students speak of very personal developments and preoccupations, others of academic issues about which they are currently concerned. Not everyone speaks, nor does there appear to be a pressure to do so. Next, as an academic guest, I am invited to speak about my experience of theory and the ideas that I had found most influential. I find myself promoting further dialogue in my presentation by asking questions and inviting critical commentary on examples of theory in practice. It felt like a mutually satisfying and informative experience for all. The professor who was hosting this meeting has written extensively along with his colleagues about the philosophy of education that this approach embodies (Cohen et al., 2012).

Moved by this experience, I carried it forward to an Education Advisory Board meeting that evening from 4:30 to 6:00 p.m. The Board consists of senior educators, such as school superintendents and municipal leaders, most of whom are extremely busy, if not harried. With some sense of risk, I waited until everyone was comfortably settled. Then, I said the following, "I know that you likely have had very busy days beginning early in the morning and, perhaps, for some of you, continuing on after this meeting." A palpable feeling of relief swept across the room. I asked, "Would you like to take a moment to fill us all in about what your day has been like and what is on your mind as you enter this meeting?" I was touched as person after person caught us up on just what their days had been like, the challenges they were facing, and the reactions that those challenges were evoking in them. The initial feeling of relief was replaced by a deeply satisfying intimacy rarely in evidence in such meetings. After about 20 minutes we turned to the agenda and accomplished a number of purposes with a high degree of effectiveness.

What is at play in these accounts? I suppose it is the recognition that everyone has an active "inner life" and that inner life is a significant part of both the learning process and the evolution of community. Contemplative practices enable the awareness and externalization of these "inner workings" and the enhancement of presence, an important element in the evolution of the intersubjective field. Such internal development practices contribute to the opportunity to bring the whole person to the learning process and paradoxically are in themselves inherently intersubjective. The more the person becomes aware of her or his "inner life," the more she or he becomes aware of other(s).

Concluding Thoughts

My experience is that the intersubjective field is preexistent. There is no need to devise ways to create or manufacture it. But, there are ways of accessing it, becoming more aware of it, and enhancing the conditions that influence its properties or qualities through various communal practices that make space for its spontaneous and self-organizing emergence. Many of these practices are informed by contemplative traditions that historically, as well as in the present day, take place in group contexts and are in and of themselves inherently intersubjective.

Ironically, in our case as scholars, the intellect is not the primary means of apprehending the qualities or properties of the intersubjective field. The intellect is limited to describing the effects of the experience of intersubjectivity, sharing stories and accounts of its existence, and identifying the principles that enhance its efficacy. Accepting this limitation, our experience has been that an intersubjective field in a university environment informed or infused by contemplative practice becomes a "field of good heart." While this "field of good heart" is a product of contemplative practice, at the same time, because of its warmth, openness, and acceptance, participation in it is itself an intersubjective contemplative practice.

I hope that you will accept this as an invitation to join us in whatever way time, space, and energy permit. The kettle is on. Just around the corner you may encounter Heesoon Bai, Avraham Cohen, Charles Scott, or David Epston. You may encounter a reference in person or just enjoy a cup of tea at the end of the day.

Notes

1. Hui-tsung is the Wade-Giles romanization of Huizong, the eighth emperor of the Song dynasty, who lived from 1085 to 1135 CE. His personal name was Zhao Ji. He promoted Taoism in the Court.
2. This section is inspired by John Blofeld's 1958 translation of Huang Po.
3. This is a poem I wrote for the occasion of the Contemplative and Integral Inquiry in the Context of Eco-social Change and Holistic Education colloquium held at the Simon Fraser University Downtown Campus on March 11, 2016.

References

Bai, H. (1999). Decentering the ego-self and releasing the care-consciousness. *Paideusis*, 12(2), 5–18.

Bai, H. (2004). The three I's for ethics as an everyday activity: Integration, intrinsic valuing, and intersubjectivity. *Canadian Journal of Environmental Education*, 8, 51–64.

Blofeld, J. (1958). *The Zen teaching of Huang Po: On the transmission of mind*. New York: Grove Press.

Bushe, G. R. (2011). Appreciative inquiry: Theory and critique. In D. Boje, B. Burnes, & J. Hassard (Eds.), *The Routledge companion to organizational change* (pp. 87–103). Oxford: Routledge.

Cassidy, W., Bai, H., Beck, K., Hawley, M., & Van Poelgeest, D. (2009). *Dare to care: Transforming schools through the ethics of care*. (DVD). Vancouver, British Columbia: Life Is Short Entertainment & National Film Board of Canada.

Cohen, A., & Bai, H. (2008). Suffering loves and needs company: Buddhist and Daoist perspectives on the counsellor as companion. *Canadian Journal of Counselling, 42*(1), 45–56.

Cohen, A., Porath, M., Clarke, A., Bai, H., Leggo, C., & Meyer, K. (2012). *Speaking of teaching . . . inclinations, inspirations and innerworkings*. Rotterdam: Sense.

Cooperrider, D. L., & Srivastva, S. (1987). Appreciative inquiry in organizational life. In R. Woodman & W. Pasmore (Eds.), *Research in organizational change and development, Vol. 1* (pp. 129–169). Stamford: JAI Press.

Cooperrider, D. L., & Whitney, D. (2001). A positive revolution in change. In D. Cooperrider, P. Sorenson, D. Whitney, & T. Yeager (Eds.), *Appreciative inquiry: An emerging direction for organization development* (pp. 9–29). Champaign: Stipes.

Cooperrider, D. L., Whitney, D., & Stavros, J. M. (2008). *Appreciative inquiry handbook (2nd ed.)* Brunswick: Crown Custom.

Dalai Lama & Chan, V. (2004). *The wisdom of forgiveness: Intimate conversations and journeys*. New York: Riverhead.

Henley, A. (2006). A social and communal view of leadership. (Unpublished doctoral dissertation). Simon Fraser University. Burnaby, Canada. Retrieved June 16, 2016, from http://summit.sfu.ca/item/2358

Henley, A. (2011). *Social architecture: Notes & essays* (pp. 38–45). Vancouver, British Columbia: Write Room Press.

Henley, A. (2013). *Legitimate peripheral participation: Learning reconceived as a transformation of social identity*. In K. D. Kirstein, C. E. Schieber, K. A. Flores, & S. G. Olswang (Eds.), *Innovations in teaching adults: Proven practices in higher education* (pp. 175–183). North Charleston: CreateSpace.

Menzies, H. (2014). *Reclaiming the commons for the common good: A memoir and manifesto*. Gabriola Island, British Columbia: New Society.

McLeod, K. (2007). *An arrow to the heart: A commentary on the Heart Sutra*. Bloomington: Trafford.

Red Pine. (2009). *Lao-tzu's Taoteching: With selected commentaries from the past 2,000 years*. Port Townsend: Copper Canyon Press.

Rosenman, Ellen. "On enclosure acts and the commons." BRANCH: Britain, Representation and Nineteenth-Century History. Retrieved March 13,

2017, from http://www.branchcollective.org/?ps_articles=ellen-rosenman-on-enclosure-acts-and-the-commons

Scott, C. (2009). Hanging out: One of the high arts of dialogue. *SFU Educational Review*, 1, 3–21.

Scott, C. (2014). Buberian dialogue as an intersubjective contemplative praxis. In O. Gunnlaugson, E. W. Sarath, C. Scott, & H. Bai (Eds.), *Contemplative learning and inquiry across disciplines* (pp. 325–340). Albany: State University of New York Press.

Slingerland, E. (2006). *Effortless action: Wu-wei as conceptual metaphor and spiritual ideal in early China*. Oxford: Oxford University Press.

Suzuki, D. T. (1959). *Zen and Japanese culture*. New York: Pantheon Books.

Trungpa, C. (1969). *Meditation in action*. Boulder: Shambhala.

Turner, E. (2012). *Communitas: The anthropology of collective joy*. New York: Palgrave Macmillan.

Turner, V. (1969). *The ritual process*. Ithaca: Cornell University Press.

Turner, V. (1974). *Dramas, fields, and metaphors: Symbolic action in human society*. Ithaca: Cornell University Press.

van Gennep, A. (1960). *The rites of passage*. Chicago: University of Chicago Press.

Waldegrave, C., Tamasese, K., Tuhaka, F., & Campbell, W. (2003). *Just therapy—a journey: A collection of papers from the just therapy team*. Adelaide, Australia: Dulwich Centre.

Wheatley, M. J. (1999). *Leadership and the new science: Discovering order in a chaotic world* (Rev. ed.). San Francisco: Berrett-Koehler.

White, M., & Epston, D. (1990). *Narrative means to therapeutic ends*. New York: W. W. Norton.

Contributors

Heesoon Bai is Professor of Philosophy of Education in the Faculty of Education at Simon Fraser University (SFU) in Canada. She researches and writes in the intersections of ethics, ecological worldviews, contemplative ways, and Asian philosophies. She understands philosophy's task for today's troubled world to be, in the words of Raimon Panikkar, "to know, to love, and to heal." She brings this threefold task of philosophy into her teaching and research. She is a codeveloper of a Master's in Education program in Contemplative Inquiry and Approaches to Education at SFU. You can find Professor Bai's published works here: http://summit.sfu.ca/collection/204. Her faculty profile at SFU can be found here: http://www.sfu.ca/education/faculty-profiles/hbai.html. She is a coeditor, along with the other editors of this volume, of the two previous volumes in this series, *Contemplative Learning and Inquiry across Disciplines* and *The Intersubjective Turn in Contemplative Education: Theoretical Foundations*.

Anne Bruce is Professor at the School of Nursing, University of Victoria. Her research interests include arts-based inquiry, narratives of living with chronic fatal conditions, Buddhist perspectives of death and dying, and contemplative practices in health and nursing education.

Kathryn Byrnes directs the Baldwin Program for Academic Development in the Center for Learning and Teaching at Bowdoin College, Brunswick, Maine. She works with higher education faculty, staff, and students to integrate mindfulness practices and principles into the theory, scholarship, and practice of teaching and learning. Her research focuses on contemplative pedagogy in higher education and PreK–12 education and has been published in several journals and edited books. Kathryn has taught Education and Mindfulness courses at Lesley University, Bowdoin College, the University of Colorado at Boulder, and Colorado College.

She served as the past board president of the Mindfulness in Education Network (mindfuled.org), the education program officer at the Mind & Life Institute developing a "Call to Care" program for educators and students, as a curriculum coordinator at a contemplative K–5 elementary school, trained as a facilitator for the Cultivating Emotional Balance project, taught high school psychology, and is a certified yoga instructor (www.kathrynbyrnes.com).

Jessica S. Caron is a teacher at the Landmark School in Beverly, Massachusetts. She works with high school students with language-based learning disabilities, such as dyslexia. She teaches language arts, supervises student dormitories, and leads annual all-girls hiking trips. Additionally, she is the director of programming at the Boston branch of Young Education Professionals. She graduated from Bowdoin College in 2009 with a degree in English and a minor in Teaching and completed Professor Byrnes's Mindfulness in Education course in 2008.

Thomas Falkenberg is Professor in the Faculty of Education at the University of Manitoba, Canada. He is the editor or coeditor of a number of books, including *Sustainable Well-Being: Concepts, Issues, Perspectives, and Educational Practices* and the recently published book *Indigenous Perspectives on Education for Well-Being in Canada*. From 2011 to 2016 Thomas was the coordinator of the interdisciplinary Education for Sustainable Well-Being Research Group at the University of Manitoba (www.eswbrg.org). More details about his research and academic background can be gleaned from http://home.cc.umanitoba.ca/~falkenbe/index.html.

M. Andrew Garrison is the president and CEO of BODYFACTS Wellness Services (bodyfactswellness.com) where he delivers personal and worksite wellness as a speaker and trainer. His expertise is recognized by the American Council on Exercise, where he validates international tests for personal trainers and health coaches. He and Sally K. Severino are coauthors of the award-winning book *Wellness in Mind*. He lives with his wife and two children in Albuquerque, New Mexico.

Michael A. Gordon is in his 25th year of Aikido teaching and training (6th Dan) and is founder and director of an independent aikido organization based in British Columbia, Canada. A psychotherapist in private practice, he is also an author, teacher, and lecturer, and is a

PhD candidate in philosophy of education at Simon Fraser University. His dissertation explores illuminations from Aikido and psychotherapy toward a "praxis and pedagogy of love."

Olen Gunnlaugson is Associate Professor in Leadership and Organizational Development within the Department of Management in the Business School at Université Laval, in Quebec City, Canada. He brings an increasingly transdisciplinary approach to his current research in dynamic presencing, conversational leadership, as well as contemplative management skills and coaching. His research has been published in several books as well as numerous international academic journals and presentations at leading conferences. He is currently collaborating with colleagues on a number of books and articles. Recently, he was the chief coeditor of the management book *Perspectives on Theory U: Insights from the Field*, a 2013 anthology featuring applied research on Theory U by 30 faculty members and associates from North America and Europe. He is a coeditor, along with the other editors of this volume, of the two previous volumes in this series *Contemplative Learning and Inquiry across Disciplines* and *The Intersubjective Turn in Contemplative Education: Theoretical Foundations*.

Arden Henley is Vice President of City University of Seattle and Principal of Canadian Programs. Previously he was Director of White Rock Family Therapy Institute, Director of Clinical Services at Peach Arch Community Services, and Executive Director of the South Okanagan Children's Services Society. He has a BA from McMaster University, an MA from Duquesne University, Pittsburgh, USA, and a Doctorate in Education Leadership from Simon Fraser University. Arden is the former chair of the Board of the BC College of Traditional Chinese Medicine and Acupuncture Practitioners. Well known for his innovative leadership style and thought-provoking presentations on a range of social, educational, and organizational issues, Arden has practiced organization development and family therapy for over 40 years and consulted broadly with community and government agencies about organization development issues. *Social Architecture: Notes & Essays* summarizes Arden's experience as a therapist and organization development consultant. Arden has been involved in founding, designing, and developing several major community service and educational projects, as well as graduate programs in education and counseling at City University of Seattle in Canada.

Mary Keator is Assistant Professor in the English Department at Westfield State University, Westfield, Massachusetts. Mary's courses focus on the development and flourishing of the human being through the study of Ancient and Medieval World Literature and writing courses such as Writing about Yoga. In addition, Mary lectures in the Religious Studies Department and the Education Department at Our Lady of the Elms College, Chicopee, Massachusetts. Mary is author of *Lectio Divina as Contemplative Pedagogy* (Routledge 2018) as well as contemplative articles, including "Reclaiming the Deep Reading Brain in the Digital Age," "The Gift of the Sublime: A Contemplative Reading of Mary Shelley's *Frankenstein*," and "Interfaith Dialogue: The Art of Listening." A member of Contemplative Mind in Society, Spiritual Directors International, and RYTA (registered yoga teacher), Mary's research focuses on ways to cultivate and deepen what it means to be human in an age of advanced technology.

Karen LaRochelle is an elementary-level, French Immersion teacher in the Vancouver School District who was seconded for many years as a faculty associate and coordinator for the preservice teacher education programs at Simon Fraser University. Her work with student teachers and with children and youth in the public school system is about creating classroom communities that are open to cultural difference and linguistic diversity. She is well supported in her classroom by her dog, who provides a daily reminder for her students of animal coexistence. Karen is a yoga practitioner, horse rider, and avid kite boarder.

Michael Link is a doctoral candidate and educational developer at the University of Manitoba. He also served as an elementary school teacher for 13 years in Surrey and Abbotsford, British Columbia, as well as an instructor for seven years in the Faculty of Education at the University of Manitoba. His research focuses on contemplative practice, well-being in education, and outdoor learning. Michael can be reached at michael.link@umanitoba.ca.

Ian Macnaughton has been a teacher and practitioner of mind-body and family systems psychotherapy for 45 years and is a Bodynamic Analyst and trainer. Ian also has owned a number of businesses and advises families in business, families of wealth, and various organizations. He is on the teaching faculty for and a fellow of the Family Firm Institute, and his clients include many government ministries and corporations. Dr.

Macnaughton is an associate faculty member of City University (Vancouver site) and has taught at numerous universities and colleges, both undergraduate and graduate levels in psychology and in business. His publications include *Embodying the Mind and Minding the Body, Body, Breath, and Consciousness: A Somatics Anthology*, and "The Role of Breath in Mind-Body Psychotherapy" in *The Handbook of Mind-Body Psychotherapy and Somatic Psychology*. His other writings on family business have been published in a number of venues as well as his work in Systems Science published in *Comprehensive Systems Design: A New Educational Technology*, NATO Workshop on Systemic Educational Design.

Sean Park is a freelance scholar, coach, educator, and curriculum consultant. He completed an MA in Education at the University of Toronto focused on complex adaptive systems theory and inquiry-based learning. Sean holds a PhD from Simon Fraser University in Arts Education, where he combined his interests in embodiment, creativity, and contemplative education. He is currently pursuing creative and scholarly projects in sacred ecstatics, cybernetics, and design thinking as foundations for spiritual, interpersonal, and social transformation. He has served as a faculty member in the Interdisciplinary Expressive Arts program at Kwantlen Polytechnic University and the MED School Counselling program at City University of Seattle (Vancouver). Sean is currently the program manager for the Studio Y fellowship in Systems Leadership at MaRS Discovery District in Toronto. He is an instructor in design thinking and health at McMaster University and leads an Afro-Brazilian percussion orchestra in his hometown of Hamilton, Ontario.

Edward W. Sarath is Professor of Music, director of the Center for World Performance Studies, and director of the Program in Creativity and Consciousness Studies at the University of Michigan. He is founder and president of the International Society for Improvised Music and active worldwide as performer, composer, recording artist, author/scholar, and change visionary. In addition to his book *Improvisation, Creativity, and Consciousness* (2013), the first to apply principles of an emergent worldview called Integral Theory to music, he has published six other books as author, coauthor, and coeditor and numerous articles in journals spanning a wide spectrum of disciplines. He has performed and recorded with top names in jazz and contemporary music across the globe, and his recording *New Beginnings* features the London Jazz Orchestra performing his large ensemble compositions. He is a fellow of the American Council of Learned Societies, MacDowell Arts Colony, and National Endowment for the Arts (in both performance and composition). Recent keynote addresses include National Association of Schools of Music, Society for Consciousness Studies, University of Melbourne, and Kingswood College and Nelson Mandela University in South Africa. He is a coeditor, along with the other editors of this volume, of the two previous volumes in this series, *Contemplative Learning and Inquiry across Disciplines* and *The Intersubjective Turn in Contemplative Education: Theoretical Foundations*.

Charles Scott is Adjunct Professor in the Faculty of Education at Simon Fraser University and Associate Professor at City University of Seattle, in Vancouver. His research and teaching interests include contemplative inquiry and practices in education, and dialogue and its applications in education, particularly the applications of Martin Buber's work. His own contemplative practices are based in the Rāja Yoga tradition. He is a coeditor, along with the other editors of this volume, of the two previous volumes in this series, *Contemplative Learning and Inquiry across Disciplines* and *The Intersubjective Turn in Contemplative Education: Theoretical Foundations*.

Sally K. Severino received her MD from Columbia College of Physicians and Surgeons. She served 17 years at NewYork-Presbyterian Hospital/Westchester Division before becoming Professor and Executive Vice-Chair, Department of Psychiatry, University of New Mexico Health Sciences Center, where she is currently Professor Emeritus of Psychiatry. She is a Felician Associate of the Assumption of the Blessed Virgin Mary Convent in Rio Rancho, New Mexico, and has practiced contemplative prayer for over 20 years. She and M. Andrew Garrison are coauthors of the award-winning book *Wellness in Mind*. Her work is profiled at www.neurospirit.net.

Stephen J. Smith is Professor in the Faculty of Education and Associate Dean in the Faculty of Health Sciences at Simon Fraser University. His scholarly work pertains to curricular and instructional practices in physical education and health education, pedagogical theorizing, and the somatic aspects of teacher formation. Illustrative publications are the 1997 book *Risk and Our Pedagogical Relation to Children: On the Playground and Beyond* and various journal articles in outlets such as *Phenomenology & Practice*, *Quest*, *Qualitative Health Research*, and the *Journal of Dance and Somatic Practices*. His recent work addresses relational dynamics with horses and other companion species. This scholarship remains grounded in movement practices that include flow arts, circus arts, and the disciplines of horse riding.

Deborah Sally Thoun is Associate Professor at the University of Victoria, Victoria, British Columbia, Canada. Scholarly interests include philosophical inquiry, disciplinary study and extension of nursing as a human science, humanbecoming-guided research and practice, and contemplative practices in health and education.

Véronique Tomaszewski is a bilingual (French-English) cultural theorist and social philosopher who has been teaching at York University since 2000. Practicing yoga and meditation has inspired her to develop an experiential and intersubjective pedagogy for which she received the Principal Teaching Award 2011 in recognition for "excellence in teaching and outstanding contribution to the life of Glendon College." Professor Tomaszewski has a Master in Sociology of Culture from the Université de Montréal and a PhD in Social and Political Thought from York University. Her research interests are (visual, oral, and textual) spiritual narratives and systems of representation and scientific approaches to consciousness. Applying Nonviolent Communication and Restorative Circles skills, she models UNESCO's mandate to build a culture of peace through education.

Coby Tschanz is Assistant Teaching Professor at the School of Nursing, University of Victoria, and a staff nurse at Victoria Hospice Society. Her scholarly interests include theory-guided nursing, hospice palliative nursing, contemplative and poetic pedagogies, and humanbecoming living experiences.

Nancy Waring is the founder and director of the Lesley University Mindfulness Master's Degree Program, which launched in 2013, and the Advanced Graduate Certificate in Mindfulness Studies. She began developing and teaching mindfulness theory and practice-based courses at Lesley in 2004. A meditation teacher since 2003, Waring began practicing insight meditation in 1983 and has since regularly attended silent meditation retreats and Buddhist studies courses. She completed her advanced professional training in Mindfulness-Based Stress Reduction at UMass Medical Center in 2004 and works privately with groups and individuals living with chronic conditions. She is a frequently invited speaker and consultant on mindfulness at conferences, academic institutions, hospitals, and other venues. She is a student of well-known Buddhist scholar/teachers, focusing on Buddhist psychology and the early teachings of the Buddha. As a journalist, she has been editor of several magazines; her freelance work, much of it focused on women in conflict with the law, has been featured in numerous publications. Her writing focuses on western and integrative medicine, mindfulness, and social justice. Her most recent publication on mindfulness is the chapter "Integrating Mindfulness Theory and Practice at Lesley University," in *Contemplative Learning and Inquiry across Disciplines* (State University of New York Press 2014). She is a recipient of a City of Cambridge Peace and Justice Award for her longtime advocacy on behalf of women with HIV/AIDS. She holds a BA in English magna cum laude from Tufts University and a master's and PhD in English from Cornell University.

Index

1-2-4-All, 170–171, 174

Abram, David, 60, 66
Accelerated Experiential Dynamic Psychotherapy, 114
affective attunement/domain/involvement, 46, 50, 61, 68, 110, 149
Agazarian, Yvonne, 115
Aikido, 87ff
   as Art of Peace, 87
   definition of, 87
Antigone, xxi, 192
Appreciative Inquiry, 208
attachment, 66, 149, 175
attachment theory, 114
attunement, xix, 29, 31, 32, 33, 37, 110, 175
   interpersonal/relational, 29, 32, 37, 59, 61, 67, 111, 118
   somatic, 108
awareness, viii, xii, xv, xix, 1, 3, 13, 14, 19, 29, 33, 37, 38, 44, 46, 67, 68, 89, 90, 91, 98, 108, 110, 112, 118, 123, 198, 203, 204, 214
   embodied, 96, 119
   emotional, 16, 17, 20, 22
   in groups, 51
   intersubjective/interpersonal/relational, viii, xx, 29, 53, 128, 130, 150
   meta, 90, 95, 96
   nondual, 93
   of breath/breathing, 2
   of energy field (*ki*), 95
   pre-conceptual, 74, 82
   self-, xx, 1, 23, 28, 51, 52, 90–91, 101, 104, 133, 116, 141, 161ff, 179
   somatic, xvii, 20
   teachers', 73
Awareness Notes project, 133, 135, 139

banking education, 34
Barbezat, Daniel, vii, 137, 187
basho, 94, 103
being image, 154–156, 158
   cocreating, 156
betweenness, 89, 94, 103
Boal, Augusto, 175
bodhicitta, 93
body mind connection, 43, 51, 53, 87, 88, 94, 95–96, 99, 100, 101, 103n10, 107, 175–176
body/mind/heart, 43, 51, 186
body awareness, 32, 115, 120, 121–122, 163, 173
body image, 155
body scan, 52, 134
body to body awareness, 150
Bodynamic Analysis, 114, 124
Bohm, David, xviii, 27, 28, 31–34, 36, 38, 39, 95, 195

Index

Bowen, Murray, 114
boundaries, viii, 51, 55, 60, 66, 121, 124, 165, 182
Bowlby, John, 114
brain science. *See* neuroscience
Buber, Martin, ix–x, 39n2, 44, 53, 101, 152
Buddhism, 35, 36, 89, 90, 93, 94, 100, 101, 104, 171, 175
  meditation approaches in, xix, 29, 89–90, 93, 94–95, 99
Bush, Mirabai, 137, 187

Cage, John, 175
California Institute of Integral Studies (CIIS), 28
care/caring, 60, 63, 68, 69, 130, 131, 135, 177, 182, 185, 205, 209. *See also* ethic of care
care of the self (Hadot, Foucault), 102n1
Cartesian view of truth, 43
Case Study, xx, 3, 45, 147, 152, 158
centering, 118, 119, 120
character, 162ff
Chee, Ashley, 127
Christian contemplative practices, 185ff
Christian contemplative schools, 186
Christian students, 42, 48
City University of Seattle, 206
commons, xxi, 205–207, 209
communitas, xvii, xxi, 207, 211
community of learners, xvii, xviii, 2, 3, 10, 12, 13, 15, 21, 24
compassion, xviii, 6, 14, 21, 27, 31, 49, 51, 56, 57, 68, 90, 129, 133, 141, 162, 164, 172, 179, 180, 186, 187, 209
compassionate speech, 35
conflict resolution, 49, 91, 93, 99, 102, 118

connection(s), 8, 9–12, 18, 33, 36, 37, 39, 48, 64–69, 91, 92, 93, 94, 109, 111, 113, 114, 116–118, 129, 121, 131, 140, 162, 169, 178, 179, 187, 205–206, 207, 213
  body-mind-heart, 43, 51, 53
  coenesthetic, 60
  pedagogical, 67–69, 182, 191
contemplatio, 186
contemplation, xi, xvii, xxii, 8, 28, 29, 31, 32, 36, 47, 48, 129, 134, 178, 186, 187, 203, 204
contemplative inquiry, vii–ix, xi, xiii, xvi–xviii, xx, xxi, xxii, 1–3, 6, 7, 13, 15, 20, 24, 26
  first-person, xi, xii, xvii, 2, 11, 20, 73ff, 82–83, 89, 91, 97, 99–100, 152, 155, 188
  integral perspective of, xxi
  second-person, xi, xii, xiii, xv, xvi, xvii, xix, xx–xxii, 2, 20, 45, 48, 73–76, 78, 80, 82–84, 88, 89, 99, 100, 102, 147, 154, 157, 157, 181, 188
  third-person, xi–xiii, xxi, 1, 89
contemplative practice, viii, xiiff, 2, 47, 68, 73ff, 94, 99, 101, 109, 114, 128–130, 133ff, 147, 161, 162, 179, 188, 199, 205–207, 212–215
  checking in as a, 213–214
  importance of, viiiff
  intersubjective, xv, xvii, xix–xxi, 60, 68, 69, 75, 78, 109, 162
  objectives, 187
  relational, xx, 68, 162ff, 181
context, viii, xii, xiv, xv, xvi
Cozolino, Louis, 153
critical thinking. *See* thinking
curriculum, xiii, xiv, 24, 25, 55, 68, 161, 179, 180, 182, 207, 220
  integrated, 55, 179

Index

Dalai Lama, Fourteenth (Tenzin Gyatso), 210
De-ai, 92–93
Dhammapada, xxi, 194–195
dialogue, ix, xii, xv, xvii, xx, 2, 3, 7, 20, 27, 29, 31, 33, 37–39, 47, 54, 88, 101, 108, 117, 149, 162, 174, 198–199, 207–213
   Bohmian, 28, 30, 33–34
   Freirean, 33–35, 38
   Insight, xviii, 27ff, 173
   intersubjective, xx, 187–189, 193ff, 279, 280, 281, 287–291, 293, 294
dichotomy
   inner-outer, 91
   sacred-profane, 47
   self-other, 91, 97, 99
   student-teacher, 55
   subject-object, xix, 55, 66, 87
dualism, xix, 87, 95, 96

education, vii, viii, xiiff, 1ff, 30, 34, 45, 55, 56, 61, 63, 68, 75, 102, 108, 109, 128, 129, 130, 135, 138, 142, 147, 156, 162, 163, 166, 167, 180–182, 185, 186, 187, 206, 207, 211, 213, 214
   contemplative, 73, 75, 89, 102n4, 110, 162
   continuing, 206, 212
   higher/postseconday/university, vii, viii, xiii, xv, xvi, xx, 3, 30, 41, 56, 57n1, 75, 129, 185, 187, 206, 207, 213
   integrated, 8
   mindfulness in, xvii, xviii, 2, 7ff, 20, 57n2
   teacher, xviii, xix, 1–3, 13–15, 20, 21, 24, 27, 30, 34, 36, 42, 44, 47, 51, 55–57, 59, 60, 61ff, 68, 73–76, 80, 82–84, 92, 102, 103, 107–109, 111, 113, 114, 116, 118, 124, 129, 133, 134, 141, 142, 147, 153, 157, 162, 171
   transformative, xv, 23, 88, 101ff, 123, 161, 175, 187
Eliot, T. S., 15
empathy, ix, 37, 59, 68, 90, 148, 154, 162ff
   kinesthetic, 60
   reiterated, 100
empiricism, 53, 55, 93, 128, 129
   Goethe's gentle, 6
Emptiness/emptiness, 97, 103n8, 213
Ensō painting, 175–177
ethic of care, 209
expressions, xvi, xvii, 15, 63, 66, 67, 139, 150, 203
expressive arts, 161ff

facilitated equine-enhanced learning (FEEL), 61ff
family systems, 114, 222
field of good heart, xxi, 203ff
first-person contemplative experience/orientation/practice, xi, xii, xvii, 2, 11, 20, 73ff, 89, 91, 99, 100, 155, 188
First Nations, 210
focusing, xviii, xxi, 17, 24, 48, 51, 53, 56, 108, 114, 177, 187, 192, 212
Fosha, Diane, 108, 114
Foucault, Michel, 57, 102
freedom, situated, 137–138
Freire, Paulo, xviii, 27, 31–35, 36, 38

Gendlin, Eugene, 59, 108, 114
gentleness, 5–8
Gergin, Kenneth J., 156
gestures, 63, 65, 66, 67, 111, 112
Gilgamesh, xxi, 198, 199
Gotama, Siddhartha (the Buddha), 27
grounding, 122, 172

Hanh, Thich Nhat, 60
Hattam, Robert, 56, 57n3
Heart Sutra, 205
Heidegger, Martin, 185
Hindu tantricism, 42
Hinduism, 50
hooks, bell, 44, 56
horses, xviii, xix
being with, 59ff
human experience, 128, 130, 138
humanbecoming theory, 131
Husserl, Edmund, ix

I-You (Thou) relationship, ix–x, 46, 48, 53, 54, 57, 152, 188
illimitability, 136–137
Inner Creator, 170
Inner Critic, 170, 172
inner/outer dichotomy, 91
inner life experiences, 73, 74, 82, 83, 84
insight, 16–18
Insight Dialogue, 173
Integral perspective/studies, x, xxi
interbeing, ix, x, xv, xviii, xix, xxii, 59, 60, 66, 67, 109
interdependence, 53, 60, 88–90, 93, 101–102, 131
interdependent relationality, xix, 88
Interdisciplinary Expressive Arts Program (IDEA), 161
interhuman, x
interpersonal, xiv, xvii–xx, 27ff
 neurobiology, 37, 107–108, 124, 152
interspecies communication, 60ff
intersubjective, ix–xxii, 3, 27, 43, 46, 50–52, 55–56, 60, 68–69, 87–88, 90, 94, 95, 101, 102, 107, 111, 124, 128, 131, 147, 152, 155, 156, 157, 175, 180, 182, 188, 199, 206, 207, 214, 215
 collective methods, 3
 methodology, 50
 relationships, xvi, 43
 validation, 180
intersubjective dialogue, 187ff
intersubjective (relational) field, xii, 46, 75, 94, 116, 111ff, 119, 188, 196–197, 200n4, 204, 206–214
intersubjective theory, ix–xi, 188
intersubjective turn, ix, xvi, xviii, 43, 88, 180
intersubjectivity, 230
 fourth level of, 151
 in Aikido, 88
 neuroscience of, 147–152
 primary level of, 149, 150
 relational field of, 171ff
 secondary level of, 150
 tertiary level of, 151
intervention, 89, 116, 130, 136
intimacy, 1, 3, 7, 8–10, 172, 214
Islam, 41, 48, 50

Jewish ceremonies, 211
Jewish people, 42

Katha Upanishad, xii, 194
Kates, Isabella Colalillo, 168, 170
ki (life energy), 87, 88, 91, 93, 95–96, 98, 100
kinaesthetic/kinesthetic, 45, 67, 68
kinesthetic empathy, 60
kinetic-kinesthetic-affective dynamics, 61, 67
Kramer, Gregory, xviii, 27ff, 171–173

Laird, Ross, 161
leadership, xii, 46, 52–53, 62, 65
 nonresistant, 100
 pedagogical, 100–103
Leadership Model for Social Change, 52

Index

learning
  active, xi, x, 20, 48, 120, 178, 188, 190, 214
  as cocreative and emergent, 108, 147, 154, 155
  assessment of, 167, 179
  cognitive dimension of, 43, 55
  collaborative, xvii, xix, 13, 62, 65, 157
  community, 3ff
  contemplative, xvii
  contracts, 165ff
  creativity in, 167
  experiential, xiv, xviii, 3, 20, 40, 43–46, 50, 52, 54, 56, 78, 80, 84, 89, 91, 94
  group, 166
  holistic, 41ff, 107, 164
  multifaceted, 46ff
  online (Moodle), 47
  peer, 166–167
  reflective practice in, 46ff, 130, 139–142. See also reflection(s)/reflective practice
  relational, xvii, 108, 150, 157, 165, 186, 188, 208
  safe classroom, 51, 109, 110, 112–113, 116, 121, 123, 124, 129, 157, 164, 171, 172, 174, 180–182, 199
  second-person intersubjective, xx, 147
  Think-Pair-Share activities in, 157
Lebenswelt, ix
lectio, 186
lectio divina, viii, xx, xxi, 186–189, 197, 199
Lesley University, 27
Levinas, Emmanuel, 101
Levine, Peter, 122
Liberating Structures, 170–171

lifeworld/life-world, viii, ix, 94, 103n5. See also *Lebenswelt*
listening
  to self, 193–195
  to others, 138, 195–196
  with compassion, 193
Listening Cafés, 198–199
logos, 28, 188, 194, 199

ma-ai, 92, 93
martial arts, 95
meditatio, 186
meditation, viii, xv, xviii, xx, 2, 6, 7, 13, 14, 16–17, 20, 25, 54, 89, 90, 94, 99, 130, 134, 162, 163, 165, 166, 173, 187, 213
  breathing practices in, 47, 54
  Insight (*Vipassana*), 172
  interpersonal, 27ff
  posture, 172
  walking, 172
Merleau-Ponty, Maurice, 101
Miller, John (Jack), 56, 57n2
mind body connection. See body mind connection
mindfulness, viii, viii, xvii, xix, xx, 1ff, 28ff, 42, 43, 48, 52, 53, 56, 60, 73, 74, 75, 82, 83, 89, 90, 94, 107, 114, 124, 130, 135, 162, 172, 181, 203
  in corporations, 103n6
  inter-corporeal, xvii, xviii
  interpersonal/relational, 27ff, 171
  relational, 171–172
Mindfulness in Education (MIE), 1ff
mindset, xxii, 8, 13, 19, 21–23, 25
mirror neurons, 37, 110, 111, 149, 152
Muslim student(s), 48, 49, 52, 54
musubi, 92–93

Neo Pagan, 54

neuroception, 112–113
neuroscience, 25, 32, 109, 124, 147, 152
  of intersubjectivity, 147ff
nexus of a we, xiii
no mind (*mushin*), xxi, 103, 203ff
nondual
  awareness/consciousness, 50, 87, 88, 93, 102
  existence/being/ontology, 88, 93, 102
  relationships, xviii, 43, 50
nonduality, xviii
  embodied, 102n3
  energetic field of, 94
nursing, 127ff
  contemplative practices in, 127ff
  education, 127ff
  holistic, 135
  practice, 127ff
  theory, 128ff

Oliver, Mary, 12
ontological security, 55
ontology, ix, x, 101
  dual, 129
  nondual, 93
oratio, 186
other/Other, the, x, xi, 13, 39, 60, 68, 90, 94, 97, 98, 99, 109, 111, 118, 148, 149, 150, 151, 189, 190
otherness, 67, 69, 131

paideia, 185, 186, 200n1,n2
paradox, x, xix, 87, 103n8, 131, 136, 137, 138–139, 188, 210, 214
participation in learning, 13–15
pattern recognition, 136
pedagogy
  collaborative, 52, 147
  contemplative, 128ff
  Continental European approach, 42
  deconstruction, 50
  holistic, 51ff
  integrated, 42
  kinesthetic, 45
  of liberation, 33–35
  participatory, 43, 147
  relational, 42ff, 162
phenomenology, ix, 60, 94, 101, 137
physical fitness, xx, 147ff
Plato, xiii–xiv, 185, 186
Porges, Steven W., 112, 113
postsecondary education. *See* education, postsecondary
  contemplative practices in, viii. *See also* education, contemplative
  purpose of, 206
postures, 63, 66, 67
practice(s), contemplative viii, 56, 57n3, 59ff, 73ff, 87ff, 109, 114, 119, 124, 128ff, 147, 161ff, 186ff, 203, 206, 207, 212
  clinical, 107
  cultural, 148
  importance of, viii, xii, xiv, 93, 203, 205, 206, 213, 214
  nursing, 128ff
  theory and. *See* praxis
praxis, viii, xiii, xiv, xvii, xix, xxi, 56, 88, 90, 93, 101–102
prereflective awareness, 93, 137 150
presence, xix, xx, 12, 46, 54, 56, 79, 96, 97, 108, 109, 114, 124, 128, 129, 135, 136, 138, 162, 176, 182, 189, 190, 204, 207, 211, 212, 214
  problem-posing education, 34
  proprioception of self/thought, 33, 95
  in Bohmian dialogue, 32–33

reading(s), 20, 32, 34, 42, 50, 133, 175
  collective, xv
  contemplative, 11, 134, 186, 187, 189ff

Index

performative, 190–191
sacred, xv, xx, 44, 47, 186, 187, 199, 204, 210, 213, 223
reflection(s)/reflective practice, xiii, xiv, xvii, xix, xx, 6, 14, 19, 25, 32, 37, 38, 46, 47, 59, 64, 78, 83, 94, 98, 102, 103, 109, 128, 130, 133, 134, 140, 142, 157, 162, 166–168, 174ff, 187, 189, 191, 197, 212
  self-, 47, 59, 82
  personal, 181
  relational, ix, xiii–xx, 27, 29, 30, 35, 48, 52, 64, 68–69, 88, 89, 96, 97, 99, 101, 142, 154, 155
  attunement, 61
religion, 41ff
  as multidimensional, 45
  Women and Religion class, 54
respect, xvii, 1, 3, 4–5, 7, 11, 13, 39, 42, 44, 45, 47, 65, 66, 93, 96, 117, 154, 162, 172, 182, 192, 204, 205, 207, 208
right listening, 35
right speech, 32, 35–36, 39n4, 90

sacred and profane dichotomy, 47
Said, Edward, 48
Samaria, Woman of, xii, 192, 196
Schafer, R. Murray, 175
School of Alexandria, 186
Scholar-practitioner(s), xiii, xvii, 206, 211
second person contemplative approaches/orientations/practices, xi, xii, xiii, xv, xvi, xix, 2, 20, 73, 74ff, 89, 100, 102n4, 147ff, 181, 188
  cocreation of, 235, 238
  I-You (Thou) relationships in, ix–x, 46, 48, 53, 54, 57, 152, 188
  orientation, 45, 99

self
  actualization, 89
  awareness. *See* awareness, self-; proprioception
  bodily, 150
  contemplative, 43
  cultivation of, 101
  deconstructed, 57n3
  depersonalized, x
  dialogue, 194
  dualistic, 94
  egoless, 94
  harmonizing with all creation, 88
  image, 30
  listening to the, 193–195
  regulation, 112, 172
  reified, 57n3
  relational, 171
  sociological, 43
  transformation of, 90, 91, 123, 186
  with others, 59ff
self-care, 59, 60, 68, 69
self-other dichotomy, 10, 97, 89, 91, 99
selfother co-unity, 99, 131
Siegel, Daniel, 37, 111
Skunkworks, 211–213
social field, 1, 9, 10
sociology of religion, 41ff
somatic communication, 66
somatic, definition of, 109
Somatic Experience, xix, 109, 115
Somatic Experiencing®, 115
somatic knowing, xiv, xvii, 60
somatic learning, xix, 107, 108, 110, 115, 121
somatic practice, xiv, 61, 66, 68
student-teacher relationship, 53ff, 133
student-teacher dichotomy, 34, 55
subject-object dichotomy, xix, 55, 66, 87
suspending agendas/judgment, 173, 188, 195–196, 200

Index

synchrony, 98, 99, 148, 149
synchrony in action, 156
Systems-Centered Group Psychotherapy (SCT), 114, 115–116
Systems-Centered® Training (SCT), 107
Systems of Analyzing Verbal Interactions® (SAVI), 108
systems science, 124

Tagore, Rabindranath, 56
tea ceremony, 208
teacher
  as embodied, xviii
  as learner, 20–25, 34, 102, 141
  as mediator, 55
  as reflective, 82
  development/education/training. *See* education, teacher
teacher-student copresence, 53–55, 107, 131
teacher-student relationship, 53ff, 133
teacher ideal, 84
teaching
  as collaborative practice, 73ff
  as contemplative professional practice, 73ff, 127, 138, 147ff
  as *kinethically attuned*, 68
  coteaching, 13
  effective, 110, 179
  holistic, 41ff, 107, 164
  in nursing, 128ff
  mindfulness in, 82
  of scholar-practitioners, viii
  relationships in, xvii
  state of mind in, 79
teaching creativity, 161ff
teaching-learning, 102, 141–142
technologies of (the) self (Foucault), 57n3
text(s), 12, 13, 47, 55
  interpretation or decoding of/being open to, xvi, xxi, 31, 55, 186ff
  sacred, xv, 49

theoria, xiii–xiv
theory, intersubjective, ixff, 188
theory-empiricism dichotomy, 55, 93
theory of mind (ToM), 148, 151
theory into practice, xiii, xv, xxi, 24, 206, 213–214
thinking, 8, 18–19, 33–34, 46, 49, 80, 90, 163, 186, 199
  being lost in, 111
  challenging one's own, 191
  collective, 108, 117, 166
  creative, 117
  integrating thinking within being, 56
  reflective awareness of, 80
  sleeping mind as manifestation of, 141
  synthetic, 136
thinking cafés, 196
third-person contemplative experience/orientation/practice, xi–xiii, xxi, 1, 89
third space, 131
transformation, 2
  individual, xiv, 1, 3, 15–16, 18–25, 25–26n1, 38, 56, 90, 124, 167
  learning as, 2, 142, 190
  listening as a means of, 200
  of society, 124, 206
transpersonal, x, 90
  Aikido practice as, 90
trauma, 10, 36
Tutu, Desmond, 209

ubuuntu, 209
Ueshiba, Morihei, 88–90, 93, 94, 95, 99, 102n, 103n, 104n
university education (*see* postsecondary education), 206, 207

Verbal Defense and Influence methodologies, 153
Vipassana, 172

virtue, 204
vulnerability, xvii, 1, 3, 10–13, 25, 55, 114, 177, 180

wellness, 52, 152, 156–157
  being images of, 156
Wicca, 54
Winnicott, Donald W., 113

Woman of Samaria, xii, 192, 196
World Café, 198

yoga, viii, 2, 6, 14, 20, 21, 42–44, 94, 103, 134

Zajonc, Arthur, vii, 1, 4, 8, 13, 15, 25, 25n1

www.ingramcontent.com/pod-product-compliance
Lightning Source LLC
Chambersburg PA
CBHW020646230426
43665CB00008B/329